THE ONLY PROVEN ROAD TO INVESTMENT SUCCESS

THE ONLY PROVEN ROAD TO INVESTMENT SUCCESS

EVERYONE'S SIMPLE GUIDE TO A SAFE TRIP

CHANDAN SENGUPTA

John Wiley & Sons, Inc.

Library of Congress Cataloging-in-Publication Data:

ISBN: 0-471-44307-7

Printed in the United States of America

10 9 8 7 6 5 4 3 2 1

For Preety

CONTENTS

◆

PART III

GETTING ON THE ROAD AND HAVING A SAFE TRIP

PART IV

FOR THE MORE ADVENTUROUS TRAVELER

ACKNOWLEDGMENTS

♦

The two people I want to thank first are, Tim Koller, my long-time friend, and Pamela van Giessen, my editor at Wiley. Tim introduced me to Pamela, and Pamela decided to publish the book and provided valuable suggestions along the way to improve it considerably. This book may never have been written without their involvement.

My friend Gary Stephens of Fordham University read almost the entire manuscript of the book as I wrote it and offered numerous ideas that are reflected throughout the book. Thanks, Gary, for your time and help. Another friend, Ashvin Shah, also read parts of the book in its early stages. Ashvin was meticulous with his comments and suggestions, as he is with everything he does. I thank him for his help.

I also want to thank John C. Bogle, the founder of the Vanguard Group, Kevin Laughlin, his associate, and Professor Burton G. Malkiel of Princeton University for their help and for providing some of the data I have used in the book.

At this point most authors thank their spouses for their support, understanding, and patience. My wife, Preety, deserves thanks for much more. I want to thank her for inspiring me to write this book. Having watched her patiently write 24 highly regarded books by hand and thoroughly enjoy it all, I had to find out for myself if this could really be fun. Also, I have never been able to get her even a tiny bit interested in learning how to program a VCR or invest money. It seems true intellectuals delegate these things to others who are only good at such mundane tasks. Nonetheless, her not knowing anything about investing has always worried me. It finally occurred to me that if there is an investment book written for people just like her, and if the book is even dedicated to her, she may not be able to avoid learning about investing any longer. (For the record, I have no plan to write a book on how to program a VCR, although there may be a true need and huge demand for such a book.)

INTRODUCTION
♦

This book has a simple message and a simple objective.

The message is: Even if you know nothing about investing and have never invested a dime, in a matter of weeks you can learn everything you need to know to invest your money successfully and with confidence. There is a very good chance that you, on your own, will be able to earn higher returns on your investments than any investment advisor or professional money manager can for you because in investing the pros have no particular advantage; the odds are actually stacked against them. And managing all of your investments successfully on your own will take no more than a few hours a year.

The objective is: To provide you in one place, in simple, jargon-free language and assuming no previous knowledge of investing, all the information and tools you will need to accomplish what this book's message promises.

Although all of us have to save and invest for the future, almost none of us gets any formal training in investing. So we all approach investing with a lot of trepidation, in no small part because from what we see and hear, everything about investing seems complex. And the investment management community does its best to preserve and exaggerate that image. Out of fear, we put off investing for as long as we can and then, after we finally get started, we switch from one investment book to another, one investment method to another, and one investment advisor to another. Because we never know for sure what to expect, we are rarely comfortable with how we manage our investments or feel satisfied with our investment results. In the meantime, all this switching around ends up being frustrating, sometimes traumatic, and in almost all cases detrimental to our financial future because we can never make up for the money we miss making during the years we wasted in all the trial and error.

Fortunately, it does not have to be this way. There really is one—only one—proven road to investment success. It is a simple and safe road that anyone can easily learn to take. There is no question that over a lifetime almost anyone taking this road would end up accumulating a lot more money with a lot less emotional stress than he would following any other investment method. All an investor has to do is learn how to take that road and then stay on it through all the ups and downs of the markets ignoring all distractions. This book is your complete guide to a life-long safe and pleasant trip down that road.

You are probably skeptical about these bold claims. I would be too if I did not know that they are based on extensive scientific research in investing done by some of the most brilliant financial minds of our time over a period of more than three decades. A number of Nobel Prizes in Economics have been awarded for the theories and research work this claim is based on, and these theories have been independently verified and endorsed by hundreds of other researchers. In fact, there are few areas of finance in which there is such near-universal agreement among finance professors and researchers. There is no other investment method that has stood up to this kind of scrutiny or received this kind of acceptance from this knowledgeable and impartial group.

But this is not just a view from the ivory tower. The smartest investors— the people who are actually responsible for investing hundreds of billions of dollars for pension funds, endowments, and foundations—have been increasingly switching to the investment method I describe in this book because they have also come to recognize that this is the Only Proven Road to Investment Success.

Why then hasn't the public heard more about it? Why are millions of individual investors wasting billions of dollars every year on exorbitant fees to brokerage houses, to financial advisors and money managers, and to mutual fund companies when all of them actually waste for their clients additional billions of dollars in poor investment performance?

There is a simple explanation: No one has a vested interest in preaching the message of this book. In fact, there are a number of influential groups who have a vested interest in downplaying or even drowning out this message, because if it catches on, they will lose a big part of their income.

If you follow the message of this book, you will buy or sell stocks or mutual funds at most a few times a year. That would drastically reduce the fees your broker earns from you. You will stop buying the glossy magazines and watching the all-day financial news channels because you will realize that the latest hot stocks, mutual funds, and market predictions they breathlessly promote are not the solutions to but the causes of most people's investment problems. That would drastically reduce their ad revenues—the main source of their income. You will stop investing in the mutual funds that charge high management fees and rack up huge costs by frantically trading stocks and still deliver poor performance. That would drastically reduce the income of the mutual fund companies. And you will even reduce or defer, for a very long time, much of your tax bill.

So why would any of these people want to preach this message? They wouldn't. They don't. And without a powerful sponsor, it is essentially impossible to get this message delivered to you over the deafening noise that all these various parties to the investment management game create by their "carpet bombing" of investors with investment information and advice of dubious value.

This book is designed to help you learn the truth about investing, free yourself from your dependence on the investment management community, and become a self-reliant, successful investor.

WHO THIS BOOK IS FOR

This book is a complete guide for all investors, even those who haven't yet started earning and thinking about investing. Whether you know nothing about investing or you are an experienced investor, whether you have just a few thousand dollars to invest or you have a few million dollars to invest, whether you are just starting off in life or you are already retired, the book covers everything you need to know to manage all your investments. The book is universal and timeless because its message and the investment method it advocates are universal and timeless.

Even those who are happy with their past investment results, whether they have been investing on their own or relying on professionals, will benefit from reading this book. One of the lessons this book emphasizes is that in investing good past performance does not guarantee good future returns. Good past performance is often the result of good luck, and sooner or later everyone's luck runs out. Investing for the future, for buying a home, for children's education, for retirement, is too important to be just left to luck. So even those who have so far had good luck with their investments may be able to learn from the results of the extensive research upon which this book is based and change their investment approach before their luck runs out.

HOW YOU WILL BENEFIT FROM THIS BOOK

The most important benefit you will get from this book is peace of mind. For most of us, investing and the stock market are constant sources of anxiety because they generally remain mysteries all through our lives—we never know for sure how we should invest and what we should expect from the market. After reading this book, you will be convinced that there is only one investment method that is right for you—it is simple and it has stood up to the test of time. So once you adopt it, you will, probably for the first time in your life, feel comfortable about your investments. The stock market will keep fluctuating; nothing can stop that. But you will understand the nature of the market and you will know what you should and should not expect from it. So the ups and downs of the market will not worry you as much.

To have a secure financial future, you have to create and follow an overall investment plan. You need to know how much of your money should be invested in stocks and how you should invest the rest of your money in different stages of your life. That's called asset allocation. Experts agree that having the right investment plan and doing your asset allocation right are crucial to your investment success. In this book you will learn a powerful new approach to investment planning and asset allocation. You will then use your personal investment Guru on the compact disc to do all the number crunching for you and make sure you are doing everything right. That will be the second benefit.

A third benefit will be that in the process of doing your investment planning and asset allocation right, you will learn how to decide and take the amount of risk that is right for you and earn the highest return for that level of risk. So you will know for sure that you are not missing out on any opportunities.

Finally, once you learn and adopt the right investment method, it will take you very little time to manage your investments—probably no more than a few hours a year. So, you will have a lot more time to spend on other things that are important to you. That is a major benefit.

HOW THE BOOK IS ORGANIZED

Let me start off with some encouraging news. This book is much smaller than it looks because almost no one has to read it cover to cover right away. It is organized in layers so that you can customize it to match your background and needs. The following description of how the book is organized should help you do that and use the book efficiently.

PART I: AN OVERVIEW OF THE TRIP

Part I has two chapters. Chapter 1 is a brief discussion of how and why most conventional investment methods lead to the investment disappointments and disasters familiar to most investors. Chapter 2 is a comprehensive summary of the book and its investment method. It is actually a complete and concise investment book on its own, and covers everything you need to know to be a successful investor. The rest of the book fills out the detail. Because this book is not just a collection of information but really a guide to a life-long trip you are about to take down the Only Proven Road to Investment Success, Part I gives you the overview of your trip that you will find helpful to have in front of you to maintain your perspective. This is probably the part you will refer to again from time to time to refresh your memory on all aspects of this book's investment method.

PART II: PREPARING FOR THE TRIP

Part II covers in detail the conceptual and practical aspects of investing. I have organized this discussion around eleven Rules instead of traditional chapters on specific topics because the Rules approach will help you remember, I hope permanently, what you need to remember about successful investing. There is one chapter for each Rule, and the Rule itself is the ultimate summary of the chapter. But at the end of each chapter I have also given you a somewhat expanded summary of the chapter called "Things to Remember" that you should find handy for future reference. The Rules are numbered in a particular order to give you the necessary information in a logical sequence. For the first reading, going through the Rules in order instead of skipping around will save time and help in understanding. There is also a list of "potholes"—mistakes you must avoid—with brief discussions that you will find handy.

PART III: GETTING ON THE ROAD AND HAVING A SAFE TRIP

Part III covers the nuts and bolts of managing your money using this book's recommended method. It first summarizes the overall investment strategy for you and then takes you through the four steps of actually investing and managing your money.

Step 1: Taking your financial inventory. In this step you will create a comprehensive picture of what investments you currently have, how much you expect to be able to save annually in the future, and what future needs you want to save for.

Step 2: Creating your investment plan. Here you will prepare a plan for how much you will save annually for each type of future need, how much of your savings will go into taxable versus tax-deferred accounts, and then how much you will invest in stocks and how much in safe investments.

Step 3: Making your investments. In this step you will implement the plan you create in Step 2.

Step 4: Reviewing your progress and making adjustments. Here I will show you how you should review your plan annually or whenever there is a major change in your life and make necessary changes and adjustments.

PART IV: FOR THE MORE ADVENTUROUS TRAVELER

Part IV includes additional detail on a few topics. I have included them here instead of in the first three parts because most investors will not need to read this material right now. You can flip through the two chapters here to know what is there and read them when you need to.

GURU: YOUR PERSONAL INVESTMENT ADVISOR ON COMPACT DISC

Throughout the book I caution you against listening to most investment advisors. After you have learned this book's investment method, the only investment advisor you need to listen to is Guru, the computer program on the compact disc. Guru will do all the necessary calculations and tell you how much you need to save for your future needs such as retirement, how you should split your investments between stocks and other assets, and how you should adjust the mix over time. You will be able ask it a variety of questions, and by putting in information and assumptions specific to your own situation, you will be able to get customized answers. You will also be able to ask "what if" questions to set the right goals and make the right decisions for yourself. Guru is based on sophisticated financial theory, but it is intuitive and easy to use. It also includes extensive help and explanations at every step. You will be able to start using it almost without any effort and you should start playing around with it early on. It is a lot of fun.

APPENDIX

Here I include my specific recommendations on mutual funds and fund groups as well as other investment resources.

PART I

OVERVIEW OF THE TRIP

This part has only two chapters. Chapter 1 recounts the roller coaster ride technology stocks went through in the last few years to show how the investment methods most investors follow and the investment management community so ardently promotes invariably lead to investment disappointments and disasters. Chapter 2 then describes the Only Proven Road to Investment Success that every investor should take.

Chapter 2 is one of the most important and useful chapters in the book. It is a summary of the entire book and its investment method, and it is a concise and complete investment book by itself. If you are familiar with the basics of investing and are in a hurry, you will be able to start using this book's recommended investment method right after you finish reading Chapter 2, although you should at least skim through Part III and learn to use Guru. If you are a beginner, Chapter 2 will serve as an excellent introduction to investing. Although it is concise and covers a lot of ground, you should not have much difficulty understanding everything in this chapter. If anything is not completely clear, however, just be patient and you will find all the detailed explanations you need in the subsequent parts.

◆

CHAPTER 1

THE MANY PROVEN ROADS TO INVESTMENT DISASTERS

◆

On March 9, 2000, the Nasdaq Composite, an indicator that primarily tracks how the stocks of the large technology companies are doing, closed above 5,000 for the first time in its history (Figure 1.1 is the "one picture is worth a thousand words" version of the story I am going to tell). It kicked off major celebrations in the entire investment management community as well as in the homes of millions of investors. Anyone who had invested in those or other technology stocks in the past few years had made an incredible amount of money in an incredibly short period of time and, as usual, the investment management community had managed to make huge profits by participating in the game from all sides.

That evening, the cable business news channels that provide play-by-play coverage of the tiniest twists and turns of the stock market from early morning till evening every day, were ready with their Nasdaq 5,000 specials. These were actually more than specials. These were more like victory parades because these channels played a key role in the market's triumph. Day after day they had tirelessly trotted out the super-bullish stock market gurus who then cheered on investors to keep investing in technology stocks. When the Nasdaq first closed above 2,000 in July 1998, a number of these gurus were there to explain why the Internet and the new information technology were going to change everything and make investors untold amounts of money. They were

FIGURE 1.1

Nasdaq Composite

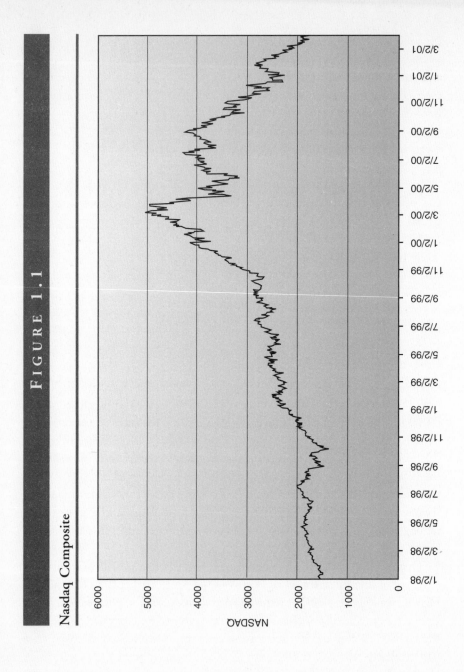

the most prescient ones. By the time the Nasdaq crossed 3,000 in early November 1999, the line of market seers willing to step in front of the camera and make more and more outrageous predictions about the stock market, especially individual technology stocks, was growing long. The market was getting into a frenzy. Anyone who was not ready to climb on the bandwagon was going to miss the opportunity of a lifetime because the technology stocks, especially the darlings of Wall Street, were never going to sell at these bargain prices again.

It took Nasdaq only 38 more trading days to cross 4,000 just before the end of 1999 to end the year on a jubilant note. The bullish gurus, some of whom had by now achieved super-guru status, were there again to routinely predict a climb to 5,000. Lest anyone think that this was all getting ridiculous, they had cogent explanations of why this growth was perfectly logical and implied that people who lacked the vision to recognize and embrace such an obvious revolution did not deserve to be listened to.

Of course, all the action was not just in the large technology stocks such as Microsoft and Cisco. Nasdaq's going from 2,000 to 4,000 meant that, on average, these stocks had gone up 100% over a period of just 18 months. At any other time this would be considered incredible performance. But in the prevailing environment these large companies could almost be called laggards. Some stocks were going up a few hundred percent a year based on the "sky is the limit" forecasts by experts. The public was being offered stock in dozens of new technology companies, and these companies were not only not making any money, but they did not have any reasonable prospect of ever making money. Yet even these stocks were scooped up even before they started trading in the market and increased in value by a few hundred percent in a matter of days, if not on the very first day, because of the hype and frenzy created by the experts.

It took the Nasdaq only 49 more trading days to climb from 4,000 to 5,000. By the evening of March 9, 2000, when the business news channels were ready to air their Nasdaq 5,000 specials, all the investment gurus were already wallowing in their own investment genius. They all stopped by to accept their kudos and make their obligatory predictions about the Nasdaq going to 6,000 soon. Some of them even mentioned that after such a dizzying climb, the market might have to catch its breath for a while and take in some oxygen. But no one predicted that it would have to come back down to the ground level to get that oxygen.

On March 10 the Nasdaq closed slightly above the previous day's level. Over the next few days it came down some, which all experts claimed was to be expected before the next climb could begin in earnest. By March 27, the

Nasdaq was back very close to 5,000 again. But that was its last hurrah because starting on March 28 it seemed like someone had pushed it off the top of a cliff and there was nothing it could hang on to. It fell precipitously down to a little above 3,000, kept going up and down for months and finally in March of 2001, less than 3 years after it had first closed above 2,000, the Nasdaq was back below 2,000. It was estimated that from the market top, over $4 trillion of wealth had been lost in less than a year.

All the way down the gurus kept professing surprise. They kept predicting that the Nasdaq would go back up again soon and kept claiming that these were golden opportunities to buy stocks of outstanding companies at bargain prices again. But as the market kept going down, it was becoming harder to find out what the super-gurus were saying anymore because the business news channels were now a little embarrassed to put them on too often. They had moved on to new gurus.

In the meantime individual investors were reeling not just from their huge losses but from margin calls, because although the Nasdaq was down only (!) 60%, along the way some individual technology stocks—including some of the darlings of Wall Street—had gone down 90% or more and many had even filed for bankruptcy. After all, even after a stock goes up 1,000%, it only takes a 100% drop to lose all of one's original investment as well as any interim gains. If this were a golden opportunity to buy, investors had no money left to buy with. And, in any case, many of those who had followed the advice of the experts and bought in at Nasdaq levels of 4,000 or 5,000 had by now sworn off the stock market, for a very long time if not forever.

A LOOK AT WHAT HAPPENED TO THE STOCKS OF SOME TECHNOLOGY COMPANIES

To you and many other investors, the Nasdaq may be just an abstract concept because very few people invest in the Nasdaq. So let me give you some examples of what did happen to the stocks of some well-known technology companies to bring it all closer to home. I hope you never got to know any of these companies well enough to invest money in them (although your favorite mutual funds might have done so).

Table 1.1 shows the highs that some technology stocks reached during the euphoria, the lows they fell to during the subsequent debacle, and the losses from the highs to the lows in percentage terms. Almost all the stocks reached their highs in late 1999 or early 2000. So those losses took place over a period of a year or less.

TABLE 1.1

High and Low Prices for Some Representative Technology Stocks

	High Price	*Low Price*	*Loss*
Cisco	$80.06	$13.19	83.5%
Intel	$75.81	$22.25	70.7%
Sun Micro	$64.66	$12.85	80.1%
Oracle	$46.47	$13.00	72.0%
Lucent	$84.19	$5.50	93.5%
Dell	$59.69	$16.25	72.8%
Compaq	$34.88	$14.30	59.0%
Gateway	$84.00	$14.18	83.1%
AMD	$48.50	$13.56	72.0%
Amazon	$113.00	$8.10	92.8%
Yahoo!	$250.06	$11.37	95.5%
CMGI	$163.50	$1.75	98.9%
Priceline	$165.00	$1.06	99.4%
eToys	$86.00	$0.01	100.0%
Webvan	$31.38	$0.06	99.8%
AskJeeves	$190.50	$0.75	99.6%
Inktomi	$241.50	$2.40	99.0%
DrKoop	$45.75	$0.09	99.8%
Teligent	$100.00	$0.25	99.8%

It is likely that you are familiar with many of the companies in the first group of companies listed in Table 1.1 because they have been and are the leaders of the information revolution. In the past year their revenues and earnings have not grown as fast as expected because many of them misjudged their markets and overexpanded. Also, the economy slowed down, creating additional problems. But there is nothing new about any of this. It happens all the time. What has been new is that the investment management community had hyped up the futures of these companies and the prices of their stocks so much that when the inevitable slowdown hit, the prices of these stocks collapsed. Many of these companies will continue to be the leaders of their industries in the future. Their stock prices will most likely recover a lot from these lows, but they probably will not attain their previous highs any time soon.

The stories and futures of most of the stocks in the second group shown in Table 1.1 are different. Many of them have already gone out of business, and some of the others may not survive either. But what is more important to note is that the stocks of most of these companies probably should never have been sold to the public, at least at the time they were, because they had almost no prospect of making any money and becoming established profitable companies. Their stocks were hyped up and sold to the public for only one reason: to make money for the investment management community, venture capitalists, entrepreneurs, and others with no regard for the well-being of the clients. Unless you are familiar with what goes on in the financial world, it will be impossible for you to appreciate how far out of hand things got.

The numbers themselves tell the story better than anyone can in words. So I will skip any further commentary except for reminding you that all the way through their rise to the highs and, in most cases, even all the way down their fall to the lows, these companies were the darlings of the investment management community. The experts almost unanimously recommended them to their clients, bought them for portfolios they managed, and scoffed at anyone who tried to raise any doubts.

WHY MOST INVESTMENT METHODS ARE PROVEN ROADS TO INVESTMENT DISASTERS

Although what happened to the Nasdaq and technology stocks over the past 3 years has been disastrous for millions of investors, this was not unique. Similar disasters have occurred many times before, and investment disasters of smaller proportions (investment disappointments) happen every other day. Over the years the investment management community has claimed to have discovered numerous proven roads to investment success and led investors down those roads. They all have turned out to be proven roads to investment disappointments and disasters. And yet nothing seems to change.

The business news channels are still going on from morning till night, trotting out a new group of investment gurus and trying to create excitement out of every twist and turn of the market. The financial magazines are continuing to recommend new groups of stocks and mutual funds with unflagging zeal, even as those who followed their advice in the past are reeling from their enormous losses. The brokerage houses are still putting out their lists of recommended stocks and pounding the table about their favorite stocks of the week. The fund companies are still advertising the funds that have done well recently, although there is not much reason to believe they will continue to do well. And even the gurus who were so spectacularly wrong so recently are still out there confidently predicting what the market will do next and promoting stocks that they are now sure will be the winners of tomorrow.

No one has come forward to apologize to investors for having misled and failed them and caused them so much pain and suffering. No expert has explained why, after the astounding failures of recent years, anyone should listen to him again. Instead everyone in the investment management community is ready to lead investors down the same old well-trod roads to investment disasters once again with the implicit promise that this time it is going to be different because they have figured out what went wrong.

But it won't be any different in the future, just as it has not been different after similar disasters in the past. It won't be different because neither the investment management community nor the investors are willing to face up to the most important reality about investing in stocks:

> **No expert and no investment method can predict reliably and consistently what any individual stock or the market is going to do in the future. No one can consistently pick tomorrow's winning stocks today.**

This has been demonstrated to be true beyond any reasonable doubt, not just by numerous events like those of the recent past but by numerous independent and reliable scientific studies by hundreds of finance professors and researchers. Any investment method that relies on predicting the future is doomed to fail. And because all investment methods used and recommended by the investment management community do rely on such predictions, they are all doomed to fail.

It is not difficult to understand why everyone in the investment management community keeps promoting trips down these proven roads to investment disasters: they make a great living doing so—at the cost of the investors. But why do investors keep falling into the same old traps again and again? In part because they are rarely told the truth and in part because they do not want to believe the truth. They see that there are experts in every field, they are told and made to believe that investing is complex, so they want to find and follow the experts in investing who can lead them through the maze of the world of investing to great success.

Alas, investing has no Michael Jordan or Tiger Woods you can imitate or

rely on to consistently earn much better than average returns on your investments. But there is one—only one—proven road to investment success that
you can take on your own. It may not be exciting, but it has proven to work
consistently over time. The sooner you face up to the truth about investing,
abandon your search for the ultimate investment guru or investment method,
and decide to take the Only Proven Road to Investment Success, the better
off you will be.

♦

CHAPTER 2

THE ONLY PROVEN ROAD TO INVESTMENT SUCCESS—IN A NUTSHELL

♦

In spite of the risks, historically stocks have provided significantly higher returns than all other investments. There are good reasons to believe that this will continue in the future. So, to provide for our long-term needs such as retirement, we can greatly benefit from the opportunities the stock market offers us provided we learn how to invest in stocks the right way by following the Only Proven Road to Investment Success. Learning how to be a successful investor involves learning how to invest in stocks, how to decide how much of our money we should invest in stocks, where we should invest the rest of our savings, and how we should adjust this mix of our investments over the years to fit our individual needs and circumstances. It sounds like a lot, but it's not. In this chapter I will concisely cover everything you need to learn about investing and then expand on them in the rest of the book.

WHAT IS INVESTING?

Surprisingly, investors rarely think about or ask, "What is investing?" And yet, if you clearly understand what investing is, you will not only be a much better investor, you will also be able to avoid most of the proven roads to investment disasters.

A useful definition of investing is committing money or capital, that is, making a financial commitment, with a reasonable expectation of earning a reasonable return over a reasonable period of time. By this definition, buying a stock or a mutual fund expecting a 50% or 100% return over a year, as people were doing during the recent technology stock frenzy, is not investing; jumping around from one stock to another or from one mutual fund to another is not investing; and buying into get-rich-quick schemes is not investing. People generally call these speculating or gambling because in all these cases the financial commitment is based on an unreasonable expectation of making an unreasonably high return over an unreasonably short period of time with a high probability of ruin. Investing requires having a long-term perspective and reasonable expectations.

> **Investing is making a financial commitment with a reasonable expectation of earning a reasonable return over a reasonable period of time.**

WHAT IS INVESTMENT SUCCESS?

Most people think of investment success as earning 20%, 30%, or even higher annual returns on their investments. But historically the stock market has earned an average return of about 10% per year. So even though there have been years when the market earned returns of 20% or 30%, that is hardly the norm. If you set unrealistic targets, you probably will take imprudent risks and end up losing a lot of money instead of being a successful investor.

There are two aspects to investment success. One is learning to take only the risks you can afford to take. The other is to invest in such a way that over the long run you can expect to earn the maximum return commensurate with your chosen level of risk. The market puts a limit on what return you can earn for the level of risk you are willing to take. To be a successful investor you have to recognize and respect that limit.

> **Investment success is taking only the risks you can afford to take and investing in such a way that over the long run you can expect to earn the maximum return commensurate with those risks.**

HOW THE ONLY PROVEN ROAD TO INVESTMENT SUCCESS WAS DISCOVERED

Although people have been investing for a long time, extensive and systematic scientific research into investing started only a little over 3 decades ago, after high-speed computers became widely available to do the necessarily enormous amount of number crunching. Since then, investing has been one of the hottest areas of research, in part because it is an interesting subject and in part because anyone who can come up with a better investment method stands to make a lot of money. Over the years this research in investing has attracted thousands of the brightest professors, researchers, and students at our best universities and research centers. This research work has been of such importance and high quality that a number of Nobel Prizes in Economics have been awarded for various aspects of it.

What questions did the researchers ask and what did they find? They asked simple questions like, "How well do the traditional investment methods work?", "Which investment methods can best pick the stocks that will do better than the others in the future?", and "What investments have performed the best over long periods of time?"

Many of the answers they found are not just surprising but startling and contrary to what investors have been led to believe for a long time. But this research work has been so thorough and extensive and the results have been verified independently by so many researchers that no investor can afford to ignore them.

The Only Proven Road to Investment Success is a combination of the key results of this scientific research into investing. It has been endorsed by the most knowledgeable group of finance people and has stood up to the kind of impartial testing and scrutiny that no other investment method has. As a matter of fact, there are few areas of finance in which there is such near-universal agreement among finance professors and researchers.

One group that has been steadily turning away from Wall Street's traditional investment methods and taking the Only Proven Road to Investment Success is the institutional investors—those responsible for managing the giant pension funds, foundations, endowments, and so forth. This is probably the best-informed group of investors with hundreds of billions of dollars to invest and practically unlimited resources to check out all available investment methods. The fact that they are now choosing to take the Only Proven Road to Investment Success is one of the strongest endorsements of this approach to investing.

THE ELEVEN RULES OF THE ROAD

The Only Proven Road to Investment Success is a comprehensive investment method defined by eleven rules of the road. I have put the method in the form of rules to make it easy for you to focus on the key aspects of investing and remember them:

1 Keep everything simple and then simplify some more.

2 Allow the Magic of Compounding to work its magic.

3 Invest only in assets that will keep you ahead of inflation.

4 Invest in stocks by buying a little bit of everything and hold on through all ups and downs.

5 Invest in stocks the most you can prudently afford.

6 Save every penny of investment costs you can.

7 Use every opportunity to reduce and delay Uncle Sam's take.

8 Have realistic expectations.

9 Invest with conviction, invest with discipline, invest with patience.

10 Choose the right companions for your trip.

11 Resist the lure of the siren songs.

Let's now learn this investment method by discussing each of these.

RULE #1: KEEP EVERYTHING SIMPLE AND THEN SIMPLIFY SOME MORE

In almost all aspects of life, the simpler you keep things, the better it works out. Investing is no exception. As we will see, the Only Proven Road to Investment Success is just about the simplest investment approach you can imagine, and following it will take no more than a few hours of your time per year. In investing, keeping things simple means holding only a few instead of dozens of funds, making changes to your investments rarely instead of every few weeks or months, and taking similar other steps. If an investment method is complex and takes a lot of work and time, there is almost no chance that you will keep up with it for very long. Remember that to be a successful investor in the long run you have to pick the right investment method and stay with it for not just a few years but a few decades. You will be able to do that only if you keep everything as simple as possible and make sure that you do not let layers of complexity build up over time.

Unless you follow a very simple investment method, you will not keep up with it long enough to succeed.

RULE #2: ALLOW THE MAGIC OF COMPOUNDING TO WORK ITS MAGIC

Compounding means earning return on return—reinvesting any return we earn on our investments to earn more return instead of taking it out and spending it. It seems obvious that if we let our returns compound, over the years we will accumulate more money. But it is impossible to imagine how big a difference compounding makes over the years unless we look at some numbers. So, let's look at two examples:

- If you invest $10,000 today at a low 5% annual interest rate, in 40 years that will grow to $70,400 with compounding versus only $30,000 without compounding, that is, if you do not reinvest the interest over the years to earn additional interest. That's an additional $30,400 contribution from compounding.

- If you are 25 today, can save about $650 per month earning an interest of just 5% per year and let all your interest compound, by the time you retire at 65 you will have $1 million. Of that, only about $300,000 will be money you save and contribute and the remaining $700,000 will come from interest earned with compounding. If you can earn 10% annual return on the investments, you will have to save and invest just $160 per month.

As you can see, over long periods of time the effect of compounding snowballs to an extent that almost looks magical. That is why it is called the Magic of Compounding.

Taking full advantage of compounding will be one of your most powerful weapons in achieving investment success. The ways to do so are:

- Start investing early in life.
- Make frequent additional investments of even small amounts.
- Reinvest all dividends and interest you receive.
- Let your investments grow for as long as possible.
- Fight for even small increases in return.

The Magic of Compounding is the most valuable investment freebie you will find. Take full advantage of it.

RULE #3: INVEST ONLY IN ASSETS THAT WILL KEEP YOU AHEAD OF INFLATION

Over time even moderate inflation will significantly reduce the buying power of our money and increase the cost of retirement and other needs. So, we must invest only in assets that will increase our buying power, that is, keep us ahead of inflation, no matter what inflation turns out to be. That is called providing inflation protection.

If we earn 5% return on our investments at a time when the inflation rate is 3% then our buying power increases by only 2% (5% – 3% = 2%), not 5%. That 5% return is called the nominal return and the 2% inflation-adjusted return is called the real return. Only investments that earn positive real returns provide us with inflation protection and grow our buying power. So for our long-term needs we have to find and invest only in assets that are expected to earn positive real returns—the higher, the better.

It turns out that there are only two types of assets that meet this criterion: stocks and a group of assets we call safe assets because they are essentially risk free. This is fortunate because it drastically simplifies all aspects of investing.

You need to invest in only two types of assets: stocks and a group of safe investments. Over time, stocks are expected to earn attractive real (inflation-adjusted) returns and the safe investments are expected to provide small but secure positive real returns.

Make Stocks the Cornerstone of Your Portfolio, Especially in Your Early Years

After the way stocks have performed in the past few years, why should you invest in stocks at all? For the obvious answer, look at Figure 2.1. It shows how you would have done in the past 50 years (through the end of 2000) if you had invested $1 in stocks and $1 in bonds at the end of 1950. The investment in stocks would have grown to a little over $51 and the investment in bonds to less than $3. In terms of annual returns, you would have earned an 8.2% return on stocks versus 2.0% on bonds. These are inflation-adjusted or real returns that show the increases in actual buying power.

This is impressive long-term performance, especially when you remind yourself that you are talking about a 51-fold increase in real buying power. But why am I comparing stocks with bonds? Because historically bonds have provided the second best (a very distant second best) real returns. Even then you should not invest in medium- or long-term bonds because they may not always provide the inflation protection you want.

FIGURE 2.1

Total Real Return on $1 Initial Investment (1950–2000)

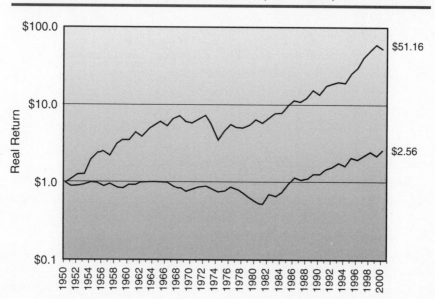

Clearly, if you want to build wealth, you have to make stocks the corner-stone of your portfolio, especially in your early years. Of course, investing in stocks is risky. But we will see that if you invest in stocks following the Only Proven Road to Investment Success, you will drastically reduce those risks. You also should remember that if you decide not to invest enough in stocks for fear of risk, over the years you will probably earn much smaller returns. So you will have to save a lot more for your future needs, leaving yourself a lot less money for your current needs.

Invest the Rest of Your Money in Safe Investments

The second type of assets that meet our investment criterion is safe invest-ments. The part of your money you are going to put at risk goes into stocks, the rest goes into safe investments. We have five choices in safe investments and they are safe in two ways: they provide essentially full protection against inflation, and your chances of losing any of your principal (i.e., your original investment) are small. Here are the five choices:

Money market funds. These are the best choice for money you want to keep readily accessible and may need within the next 6 months. The return will be the lowest in the group, but your investment will be protected against infla-tion. Also, your principal will not fluctuate; that is, if you put in $100, you will almost certainly get back the $100, along with the interest. (If you are in a high tax bracket, you should also consider tax-exempt money market funds as an alternative.)

Bank certificates of deposit (CDs) of less than 2 years' maturity. Some-times they offer returns higher than money market funds and even higher than short-term corporate bond funds. They are a good choice if you can find at-tractive returns for the duration you can afford to tie up your money. If you stay within the FDIC (Federal Deposit Insurance Corporation) limit, your principal will be totally protected. (Do not go beyond a 2-year maturity be-cause they will increase inflation and interest rates risks too much.)

Short-term corporate bond funds. These will generally provide somewhat higher returns than money market funds, but your principal will fluctuate a little bit from day to day. If inflation suddenly picks up, you will lose some money but not much. The higher return justifies taking that additional risk. (If you are in a high tax bracket, you should also consider short-term tax-exempt bond funds as an alternative.)

Treasury Inflation-Protected Securities (TIPS) funds. TIPS guarantee you a certain fixed return over and above inflation. The fixed return (say 3.5%) is established at the time you make your investment. The total return you will earn is that fixed return plus the recent rate of inflation (e.g., if inflation in a year happens to be 3%, you will earn a return of 6.5%). So you will get complete inflation protection, but your principal may fluctuate to some extent. This is a very good choice for money you want to invest safely for the long term. (Read about the tax quirks of TIPS under Rule #3 before investing.)

Series I Savings Bonds. These are your best choice for safely investing long-term taxable money. Like TIPS, these also provide you a fixed return over and above inflation. But with these your principal will not fluctuate. Another attractive feature is that you can defer all the taxes on the returns and have the returns automatically reinvested for up to 30 years because you do not have to pay taxes on the interest until you cash in your bond. One limitation is that you can buy only $30,000 of these bonds per year (under each Social Security number).

How should you distribute your money among the five? Invest in money market funds the money you need to have readily accessible or may need within the next 6 months. Put the safe money you want to invest for the long term in one of the other four choices, preferably in a TIPS fund or Series I Savings Bonds, the latter particularly to take advantage of their attractive tax deferral opportunity.

RULE #4: INVEST IN STOCKS BY BUYING A LITTLE BIT OF EVERYTHING AND HOLD ON THROUGH ALL UPS AND DOWNS

To stay ahead of inflation and build wealth, we have to invest in stocks. But with around 8,000 stocks to choose from, how do we decide which stocks to buy and how do we manage the risks of investing in stocks? Those are the questions we will now answer.

Ignore the Advice of All Experts and Be a Passive Investor

There are two major approaches to investing in stocks: active investing and passive investing.

Active investing involves either picking out and investing in stocks that are likely to be the winners in the future (called stock picking) or getting into and out of the market based on forecasts of what the market will do in the future (called market timing). Most investors use a combination of stock picking and market timing. To most people, investing is synonymous with active investing, and this is what almost all investment experts preach and practice.

Passive investing involves buying and holding onto (preferably forever) a little bit of a large number of stocks or "the market" (meaning all stocks) without trying to select stock winners or decide when the market will go up or down.

The most startling and important finding of the extensive scientific research into investing I mentioned is that investors should invest their money in stocks passively because active investing does not work. In addition, passive investing is much less work and over the years it will save huge amounts of money in investment costs (relative to active investing.)

There is overwhelming evidence that no expert and no investment method can predict with any reliability and consistency what any individual stock or the market is going to do in the future. No one can pick out tomorrow's winning stocks today.

As you can imagine, this has been the most controversial finding of the research work and is a very important issue for you because unless you convince yourself that this is true and invest accordingly, you will waste a lot of money over the years. Because many investors by now are willing to accept this as demonstrated truth, I have included a full discussion of this in Chapter 19, "The Most Dangerous Myth About Investing," instead of going into it here.

How well does passive investing work? The historical returns on stocks we looked at in Figure 2.1 are effectively the results of passive investing. They assume that the money was spread out over all stocks without trying to pick winners and losers and that the stocks were held onto ignoring all ups and downs of the market.

Invest in stocks by buying a little bit of a large number of stocks or all stocks (the market) instead of trying to pick potential winners and losers.

Reducing the Risks of Investing in Stocks

Passive investing also automatically reduces the risks of investing in stocks to the maximum extent possible. It does so in two ways.

First, the researchers found that if you spread out your investments over a large number of dissimilar stocks, you significantly reduce the risks of investing in stocks. Why? Because at times when some of your stocks do poorly, some others will probably do well, and over time you will end up with a nice average return. This is called diversifying, and it is the same as following the wise admonition, "Do not put all your eggs in one basket."

> You can significantly reduce the risks of investing in stocks by diversifying, that is, spreading out your investment over a large number of dissimilar stocks.

Second, the researchers also found that investing in stocks for the short term is very risky, but you can significantly reduce the risks by holding onto your portfolio of stocks for the long term. What this means is that the longer you hold onto your investment in a large number of stocks, the more you reduce your chances of losing any money and increase your chances of making a good return. Why does this happen? In the long run the economy keeps growing, and because the fate of the stock market is tied to the economy, the prices of stocks also go up. But in the short term the economy goes through lots of ups and downs and the stock market goes through even more ups and downs because of many random factors, including the frenzy that the investment management community whips up from time to time.

> Short-term investment in stocks is very risky. But you can reduce the risks significantly by holding onto stocks for the long term—the longer, the better.

How to Invest in a Little Bit of a Large Number of Stocks

The best way to invest in a little bit of a large number of stocks is to put your money in a particular type of mutual fund, called index funds. Index funds literally buy a little bit of a lot of stocks and passively hold them forever. Index funds also have the advantage of having very low investment costs, and if you just hold onto your fund, you won't have to pay most of the taxes on the return you earn on the fund until you sell it.

Most big fund companies offer index funds, and one stock index fund differs from another in only two major ways: the specific stocks they own and their investment costs. Because the cost issue is readily handled, let me just say that for an index fund, you should be looking for annual costs of close to 0.2% and never pay more than 0.5%.

Here are your three primary choices in stock index funds:

The Standard & Poor's (S&P) 500 Index Fund. This is the most common type of stock index fund. It owns a little bit of the stocks of essentially the 500 largest U.S. companies. An important point to note is that an S&P 500 Index Fund does not buy equal dollar amounts of each of the 500 stocks. Instead, it buys each stock in a dollar amount proportional to the company's market value. In other words, if Company A has twice the market value of Company B, then the fund will buy $2 worth of Company A's stock for every $1 of Company B's stock. This is called market-value weighting. So if an index fund is market-value weighted, then the bigger the market value of a stock it owns, the more money the fund invests in it and the performance of the bigger companies will have a lot more influence on how well the fund does. (The following two funds are also market-value weighted.)

The Total Market Index Fund. This fund owns a little bit of every stock that is traded in the United States (around 8,000 stocks). So it owns the 500 stocks that an S&P 500 Index Fund owns and then another 7,500 smaller stocks. Because it also invests more money in bigger companies, it ends up investing about 70% of its money in the 500 large stocks held by an S&P 500 Index Fund and the other 30% in the smaller stocks.

Russell 1,000 Index Fund. This fund is similar to the other two except that it distributes its investments over the largest 1,000 stocks. So it is also dominated by the large companies.

Because a Total Market Index Fund spreads out its money over the largest number of companies, it is slightly preferable to the other two. But if you invest in any one of these three or similar other index funds, you will do fine over the years. (There are two other ways to invest in a little bit of a large number of stocks, which I will discuss under Rule #4. But the index fund approach is far superior to them.)

> **Use a low-cost, broad-based index fund to passively invest in a little bit of a large number of stocks.**

The Only Proven Road to Investment Success—in a Nutshell ◆ 23

This is pretty much all there is to investing in stocks. When you think about the endless hours people spend on researching and deciding which stocks or funds to buy and then spend additional hundreds of hours agonizing over what to do when something goes wrong, you will appreciate how much easier it is to travel on the Only Proven Road to Investment Success. On top of that, you are virtually guaranteed to do better than or at least as well as almost anyone else. Remember that any money you do not invest in stocks should be invested in safe assets.

The only major question we are now left with is, "How do you decide how much of your money goes into stocks and how much into safe assets?"

RULE #5: INVEST IN STOCKS THE MOST YOU CAN PRUDENTLY AFFORD

Deciding how to distribute your investments over different types of assets— in our case just two types—and adjusting the mix over the years is called making your asset allocation. Most experts think, and I agree, that your asset allocation will have a bigger impact on how much money you accumulate over time than will any stock picking and market timing skills. Yet most investment methods do not include a good asset allocation approach. Under the Only Proven Road to Investment Success we use a simple but powerful asset allocation approach and the computer program, Guru, included with this book to do all the necessary number crunching.

The recommended asset allocation method is based on two basic principles that tell you how much money you can afford to invest in stocks and when you should sell those investments (the balance automatically goes into safe investments):

1. You should invest in stocks any money you can keep invested for the long run, meaning at least 10 years, preferably longer.
2. You should start selling stocks opportunistically well before (5 to 10 years) you will need the money for expenses. Another way to put it is to say that you should never allow yourself to get into a situation where you may be forced to sell stocks in a depressed market because you need the money right away.

Now let us see why these principles make sense and how you use them in practice. We already know that the risks of investing in stocks go down as you hold them for longer periods of time. If you plan to hold your stocks for 10 years or longer, the risks get down to reasonable levels. If you can hold stocks for that long, you will most likely earn a good return on your investment. To be more conservative, especially as you get close to retirement or are in retirement, you may want to invest in stocks only money you can keep invested for even longer (e.g., 13 or 15 years). So this is your first tool to control the risks you take. Remember that you should try to put as much of your money in stocks as you can prudently afford (complying with this principle) because this will likely significantly increase the amount of money you accumulate over the years.

We also know that holding stocks for the short term is risky. As you get closer to the time you need some of the money you have invested in stocks, the length of time you will continue to hold the stocks gets shorter, and therefore the investments get riskier. You can reduce that risk by starting to take action 5 to 10 years ahead of when you will need the money. Then if the market is doing well, you can sell the stocks and put the money in safe investments until you need it. On the other hand, if the market is depressed you will have the flexibility to sell over a period of time to make the best of the situation. This is called opportunistic selling. The key here is to not let yourself get into a time squeeze. You can control your risk by deciding how far in advance of your needs you will start to sell and put the proceeds in safe investments.

Reduce your risks and maximize your returns by investing in stocks all of the money you will be able to keep invested for 10 years or longer. Start selling stocks opportunistically 5 to 10 years before you will need the money so that you are never forced to sell in a depressed market.

You will use these two principles of asset allocation to decide how much you need to save and invest for retirement, for other special needs such as children's education, and for your general needs. Guru will do all the calculations for you and will also tell you when you should change the asset mix, that is, sell some stocks and put the money in safe investments.

Saving and Investing for Retirement

Let me give you an example of how the asset allocation principles we discussed provide you with a strategy for saving and investing for your retirement. Suppose like many people your plan is to reach retirement age with all your savings invested in stocks and then sell enough stocks every year to cover your needs. If during the early years of your retirement the stock market happens to be depressed, you will be forced to sell some stocks at the depressed prices because you will need some money to live on. In that case you may run out of money much earlier than you had anticipated even if the stock market recovers dramatically in the later years because at that time you will have less money invested in stocks to earn the higher returns and make up for the earlier losses.

How do you avoid this problem? According to our asset allocation principles, you will start to opportunistically sell a certain amount of stocks 10 years or so before retirement and put the money in safe investment. How much stock investments should you sell? Generally enough to cover your needs for at least the first 10 years of your retirement. This way by the time you retire, you will have in safe investments enough money to cover your needs for at least 10 years. Now if the market is unusually depressed during the first few years of your retirement, you will be able to draw money from the safe investments and sell more stocks only when the market recovers. On the other hand, whenever the stock market is in the normal range, you will sell enough stocks to cover your annual needs and to keep your safe investments replenished with enough money to cover your needs for 10 years or so.

When explained just in words, it can sound a little complicated. But once you start using Guru to do some investment planning and ask all kinds of "what if" questions, you will see much more clearly how these principles work in practice.

RULE #6: SAVE EVERY PENNY OF INVESTMENT COSTS YOU CAN

Investment costs are what you pay directly or indirectly to brokerage houses, mutual funds, and others for their services. It is hard to imagine how much money you will waste over the years if you do not do everything you can to minimize your investment costs. Let's get an idea by looking at an example.

Let's assume you have $100,000 to invest and you have a choice of investing it in a low-cost index fund with an annual cost of 0.2% or a typical mutual fund with an annual cost of 2%. Let's also assume that both funds earn the same 10% annual return before their costs over the next 40 years and you reinvest all returns. At the end of the 40 years, you will have $4.2 million if you invest in the low-cost index fund versus just $2.1 million if you choose the typical mutual fund. So you will waste $2.1 million or about 50% of your returns in the higher cost fund.

I hope that shocks you and drives home the need to keep your costs as low as possible. Investment costs add up to huge amounts over the years, but most investors do not pay attention to them because the costs look small, are paid in dribs and drabs, and the investment management community makes every effort to make them hard to notice or find.

The easiest way to trim down your investment costs to the bone is to invest only in no-load, low-cost mutual funds. Load is a one-time sales commission that many mutual funds charge, and this can be up to 6% of the money you invest—a huge amount. Because there are perfectly good no-load mutual funds in every category, there is never any reason to invest in a load fund. Of the other costs of investing in a mutual fund, the only one you can find easily is called the fund's expense ratio. You can find good funds in almost every category with expense ratios in the range of 0.2% to 0.5% per year. You should try to invest only in those funds. If you pay much more, you will be wasting a lot of money.

Both the load and expense ratio of a fund are shown on the fund's prospectus, and you can also find out how much they are by asking the fund company. There are a number of other costs that mutual funds charge, but it is difficult to find out or estimate how much they are for a fund. These costs mostly depend on how often a fund buys and sells stocks and bonds. Generally these costs tend to be low for funds that have low expense ratios, and they are lowest for index funds. So you should focus on low-expense-ratio funds and if you invest only in low-cost, broad-based index funds, you will automatically save all the money you can on costs. (What I have said applies to all types of mutual funds, not just stock mutual funds.)

> Over the years the investment costs charged annually as a percentage of your assets, like those charged by mutual funds, can drain away a big part of your investment returns. Drastically reduce this waste and significantly improve your returns by keeping your investment costs below 0.5% per year.

Do not buy the story that the managers of high-cost funds will make up for those costs by earning superior returns. It is not likely to happen. Just avoid high-cost funds.

Another way to cut back on investment costs is not to have a brokerage account at all. You do not need one because you should only invest in mutual funds and you can do so directly through the fund company without paying any commissions. If you decide to have a brokerage account, make sure you do not buy a bundle of services—called a wrap account or something similar—at a fixed percentage annual fee (generally 1% or more of the total value of your account). Because such annual costs can add up to huge amounts over the years, this type of account is a big waste of money.

RULE # 7: USE EVERY OPPORTUNITY TO REDUCE OR DELAY UNCLE SAM'S TAKE

Unless you are very careful, over the years you may end up paying a lot of money in taxes, probably a lot more than you will in expenses. But there are two steps you can take that will drastically reduce your tax bills.

The first step is to contribute the maximum to retirement accounts such as 401(k) programs, individual retirement accounts (IRAs), and others where taxes won't have to be paid until you retire. These are called tax-deferred or tax-advantaged accounts. The extra returns you will earn in the intervening years on the taxes you defer will add significantly to the money you accumulate over time. Many employers even match part or all of an employee's contribution to a 401(k) account. Also, some of these accounts, such as 401(k)s, let you make contributions from your pretax income, which allows you to hold back and earn returns on even more of Uncle Sam's money for years. You should contribute to this type of account before any of the others, but try to take full advantage of all of these tax deferral opportunities.

The second step is to drastically cut down the taxes that you may have to pay every year if you keep switching stocks, funds, or assets in taxable accounts, that is, accounts that do not get any special tax treatment. All you have to do is invest in index funds or Series I Savings Bonds (I Bonds), keep adding to them even small amounts of money regularly, and hold onto them. You will pay almost all of the taxes on the returns on these investments only when you sell your stocks or cash in your I Bonds to cover expenses. In the mean time you will earn additional returns on Uncle Sam's money. This really is deferring taxes on any amount of money you want—your own unrestricted, unlimited tax-deferred account.

Save on taxes by taking full advantage of retirement accounts such as 401(k) accounts and holding onto investments in stock index funds and Series I Savings Bonds in taxable accounts.

Every time you switch assets in a taxable account and you have a profit on the transaction, you have to pay taxes on the profit that year. So if you do not take the actions I just recommended, you can easily end up paying taxes of 2% or more per year on your total savings. We have already seen how big the effect of an annual drain of even that size can be on the money you accumulate over the years.

Here are two more things you can do to reduce or defer taxes on your investments:

• To the extent possible, put in taxable accounts investments that will earn most of their returns in the form of capital gains (e.g., stocks or stock mutual funds) and put in tax-deferred accounts investments that will generate interest income or significant dividend income. This will allow you to defer taxes on more of your investment returns.

• If you have to sell in a taxable account any investment that has capital gains, try to hold it for at least 1 year to qualify for the lower long-term capital gains tax rates. Also, if you are selling investments with capital gains, consider offsetting the gains by selling some other investments that have capital losses.

RULE #8: HAVE REALISTIC EXPECTATIONS

Unless you have realistic expectations you will be constantly disappointed and become a restless investor. You will keep switching stocks, funds, and investment methods, end up taking too much or too little risk, and earn much lower returns than you could have. So you must have realistic expectations. Make sure that you base your expectations on objective analysis of long-term history and data because our general tendency is to base them mostly on recent experience.

The most unrealistic expectation investors have about investing in the stock market is that they can improve their returns by working hard or smart. If you are investing poorly by making basic investment mistakes, you can improve your returns by correcting them. But beyond that you will earn what the market gives you. This is the flip side of all the research results that show that no one can beat a simple index fund with any consistency. The simple index fund is the market, and that is the return the market gives us.

It is safest not to have any specific expectations about the stock market because the market will continue to fluctuate widely and will invariably disappoint you for long stretches of time. Still, you will need to make some assumptions to make plans for the future. Make your assumptions relative to inflation, that is, in terms of real returns because no one can predict future inflation rates. You may assume that your stock investments will earn a real return of around 7% in the long run, but in view of the long bull market we have enjoyed since the early 1980s, the real return for the next decade or so may be much lower. So use Guru to check how your investment plan will work out for a few lower rates of return as well. You should assume that the safe investments will provide real returns in the range of 2% to 3%.

Unless you have realistic expectations, you won't have peace of mind and you won't be able to stay with your investment plan for the long run.

RULE #9: INVEST WITH CONVICTION, INVEST WITH DISCIPLINE, INVEST WITH PATIENCE

Investing the right way is simple. Yet most people earn on their investments only a fraction of the return they could because they do not realize that investment success depends at least as much on psychological factors and their own behavior as it does on technical knowledge of the markets and investing. You cannot let your own behavior get in the way of your investment success.

Investing with Conviction

To succeed as an investor you have to first choose the right investment method and then follow it for decades with a true, unshakable conviction. If you let the market's ups and downs or your own fear or greed shake you out of your conviction, you will make a lot less money in the long run.

Investing with Discipline

Discipline means doing the right thing at the right time, all the time. To succeed you have to steadfastly follow your investment plan: reinvest the interest and dividend to take full advantage of the Magic of Compounding, regularly save and invest what you have planned to, and sell stocks when your plan calls for it, not out of panic or based on any market forecast.

Investing with Patience

All investment methods take a long time to work and may perform poorly for long stretches of time. In addition, the market itself may go down or move sideways for years. Unless you hold onto your investments through all such periods with patience, you will miss out on making money when the market turns around or your investment method shines. Being impatient is one of the main reasons most investors fail.

Over time the market will sorely test your conviction, discipline, and patience. To survive these tests, recruit someone close to you as your investment partner and have a written investment plan that you will follow together. Also, instead of obsessing over the market over which you have no control, focus on other things in life over which you do have some control. If you are traveling on the Only Proven Road to Investment Success, your investments will mostly take care of themselves.

Recognize that investing with conviction, discipline, and patience are going to be as crucial to your investment success as will the right investment method and luck.

RULE #10: CHOOSE THE RIGHT COMPANIONS FOR YOUR TRIP

On your trip down the Only Proven Road to Investment Success you need to take along at most three companions from the investment management community: (1) One or two mutual fund companies that have good, stable management and offer low-cost, well-managed funds in the categories you are interested in, (2) a fee-only financial planner to help you create and periodically update a comprehensive financial plan for your family, and (3) a tax advisor who will help you take advantage of tax saving opportunities and stay on the right side of the Internal Revenue Service.

Many other people from the investment management community will try to come along for the ride. But you have to be a very discriminating consumer. Keep in mind that investment management is a business like any other business. Everyone is in this business to make money for themselves, and no one is primarily concerned about your well-being. You will do well to keep your distance from everyone in this community because almost any encounter with them will directly or indirectly cost you money. Specifically, do not even open a brokerage account unless you absolutely need it, and do not listen to the investment advice from anyone in this community. As the research results have abundantly shown, no one in this community has valuable investment advice to offer.

> **Take along on your trip only the few companions you need to have a successful trip. Any unnecessary companion may cost you a lot of money.**

RULE #11: RESIST THE LURE OF THE SIREN SONGS

As you travel down the Only Proven Road to Investment Success, everyone in the investment management community will be singing their siren songs to lure you into trying one of their newfangled or recycled investment schemes, red-hot mutual fund or can't-lose stock. As the research results have shown, none of these is going to make you any more money than you can make on your own staying on the Only Proven Road. So try your best to turn a deaf ear to all these songs and stay on the path you have chosen. A few super-hit siren songs you should definitely resist are: momentum investing, investing in sector funds, investing in red-hot new funds, trading options, buying stocks on margin, short selling, and day trading.

> **Do not let anyone distract you from your chosen path.**

WHY IS THIS THE ONLY PROVEN ROAD TO INVESTMENT SUCCESS?

Now that you have learned what the Only Proven Road to Investment Success is all about, the question that may come to your mind naturally is, "With dozens of investment methods and thousands of investment experts claiming that they can produce superior investment results, why is this the Only Proven

Road to Investment Success?" The answer is, none of them can "prove" their claims beyond a reasonable doubt. For many reasons we do not need to go into here, checking out such claims is one of the most complex and challenging tasks in finance. But all of us can intuitively appreciate that, at the very least, any method or expert has to have a long enough verifiable track record before it or he can even become a candidate for our consideration. Almost no method or expert has such a track record.

The Only Proven Road recommends investing in the market, that is, buying a little bit of all stocks or a large number of randomly selected stocks. Because doing so does not require making any judgments along the way, it is easy to check out exactly how traveling along the Only Proven Road would have worked out over any period of time during the past 75 years. The data are easily available. Over any long period of time during that stretch you would have earned what the market has earned, an inflation-adjusted return of about 7% per year.

On the other hand, the performance of most investment methods or experts you may want to consider can be checked out for maybe only a 5- or 10-year period of time, probably much less. For example, if you are thinking of investing in a fund run by a star money manager, chances are the fund has only a 5- or 10-year track record under that manager, if that long. That is not long enough to make any reliable judgment. It is also likely that the manager has "adjusted" his investment method many times along the way. So even when you look at this 5- or 10-year record, you are probably looking at a much shorter track record of his latest investment approach.

There have been hundreds of money managers in Wall Street history who did spectacularly well for 2, 3, or even 5 years, came to be hailed as geniuses, and became celebrities only to end up performing miserably for the next 5 or 10 years and then disappear into oblivion. We can never claim that there has never been or there will never be a money manager or investment method that can do better than a low-cost, broadly-based index fund. But your chances of being able to find such an expert or method are so small and the potential cost of your being wrong is so high that you should not even try. Also, remember that during the recent market debacle, practically every expert was spectacularly wrong. If you had followed their advice, you would have sorely regretted that. So it may be possible to have a theoretical argument about whether this book's recommended method is the only proven road or not; but for all practical purposes, it is. Do not take a big chance with your future and financial security by betting on the wrong horse. (You can read more on this topic in Chapter 19, "The Most Dangerous Myth About Investing.")

WHAT TO DO WHEN MARKETS GET
IRRATIONALLY EXUBERANT OR DEPRESSED

The market is a manic-depressive. Over the years it will get to heights that make no sense and then it will get to lows that make no sense either. But most of the time even these extremes do not make sense only in retrospect. At the time they seem reasonable and no one has come up with a reliable method to judge if the market is too high or too low. So your best bet is to keep investing regularly in a broadly diversified index fund ignoring whether you or others think the market is too high or too low and holding onto your investments through both good and bad times.

Let's see how that would have worked out over the past few years. First, remember that the Nasdaq was at 2,000 in July 1998, went up a lot in 1999 and 2000, and fell back below 2000 again in March 2001, a period of less than 3 years. So if you were investing a small amount of money every month over a very long period of time, you would have invested only a small amount of new money at those exorbitant prices. You would have lost none of the money you already had in the market before July of 1998. If you are in the market for the long run, no great harm would have been done. If you were unfortunate enough to start investing for the first time during this period, you probably have suffered some or a lot of loss. But instead of letting that discourage you, you should take the lessons to heart, spread out your investments over time, and invest only in low-cost, broad-based index funds instead of chasing red-hot stocks.

Second, if you were on the Only Proven Road and invested in a broadly diversified portfolio, only 25% to 30% of your money would have been in technology stocks, which have suffered the catastrophic loss. Other stocks have gone down too, but by nowhere near the 60% to 90% losses suffered by technology stocks. So you would have benefited a lot from diversification.

Third, suppose you had been investing since 1980 in monthly installments in a broad-based index fund. Between the beginning of 1980 and the end of 2000, a $1 investment in such a fund grew to over $9 after adjusting for inflation. If you invested over the years, you would not have done that well, because you would have invested some of your money at fairly high prices as the market climbed over the years, and much of your money would have been invested for only part of the period. But there is no question that you would have done very well.

The problem is that we always have a very short-term perspective and focus more attention on the past 1 or 2 years than on the past 10 or 20 years.

In investing, doing so can lead to very misleading conclusions. Those who suffered most during the technology stock debacle suffered because they listened to experts, got caught in the market frenzy, and poured a lot of money into the technology stocks near the top of the market. But that's not how you are supposed to invest. People who confuse speculating with investing, who let themselves be buffeted by greed and fear, and who are willing to bet thousands of dollars of their hard-earned money on the advice of someone they see on TV for a few minutes, unfortunately, have to pay a price.

If you have the guts, buy a little more when the market is very depressed and buy a little less when you think the market is getting irrationally exuberant. But other than that, keep investing steadily and stay on the Only Proven Road to Investment Success. Even irrationally exuberant or irrationally depressed markets won't hurt you in the long run.

THE NEXT STEPS AND ACTUALLY INVESTING YOUR MONEY

Now that we have covered the basics and you see how simple this is, we will go into more detail in Part II. I recommend that you read the chapters in Part II in order so that you can benefit from the logical sequence of the Rules. You can, of course, move quickly through material you are already familiar with and spend more time on things that are new.

Then in Part III you will go through the steps of actually investing your money. If you are new to investing, do not rush. Take your time to become comfortable with all the new things you are learning before you actually invest your money. For a long-term investor, nothing can happen in the next month or two that you will regret missing out on. But do not be like people who read one investment book after another but never take any systematic action. You have to motivate yourself to take action because no book can do it for you. Take the actions you need to take.

Part IV has two chapters. Chapter 19, "The Most Dangerous Myth About Investing," is a detailed discussion of why active investing does not work, and includes some supporting evidence. To achieve investment success, you need to be absolutely convinced that you should not chase any active investment method. If there is any doubt in your mind in this respect, you should read Chapter 19 right now or, preferably, after you finish Part III. But if you are already convinced, then you may read it at your leisure. Chapter 20 discusses a few additional investment options that are popular, but I do not think they are appropriate for most investors. I have provided this information on them in case you get curious. You do not need to read it now.

You should start experimenting with the program Guru early on. It should be easy and a lot of fun to use, and the better you understand the different kinds of questions Guru can answer for you and all the things Guru can do for you, the better you will be able to utilize its power. Investing according to the Only Proven Road to Investment Success is so simple that Guru may be the only tool you will need to use in the future. But with so many people constantly trying to lure you off the Road, come back to this summary chapter from time to time to remind yourself of the Rules you should be following.

PART II

PREPARING FOR THE TRIP

This part covers in detail the conceptual and practical aspects of investing—everything you need to know to become a successful investor. I have organized this discussion around Eleven Rules instead of traditional chapters on specific topics because the Rules approach will help you remember, I hope forever, what you really need to remember about successful investing. There is one chapter for each Rule, and the Rule itself is the ultimate summary of the chapter. But at the end of each chapter I have also provided a somewhat expanded summary of the chapter called "Things to Remember" that you should find handy for future reference. The Rules are numbered and presented in a specific order to cover everything about investing in a logical sequence. In a way it is the story of investing, and you will do best to follow the story line in your first reading. After the Rules, there is a list of "potholes"—mistakes you must avoid—with brief discussions that you will find handy. This part ends with a chapter on a key decision you have to make before starting to actually invest your money.

THE ELEVEN RULES OF THE ROAD

1. Keep everything simple and then simplify some more.

2. Allow the Magic of Compounding to work its magic.

3. Invest only in assets that will keep you ahead of inflation.

4. Invest in stocks by buying a little bit of every-thing and hold on through all ups and downs.

5. Invest in stocks the most you can prudently afford.

6. Save every penny of investment costs you can.

7. Use every opportunity to reduce and delay Uncle Sam's take.

8. Have realistic expectations.

9. Invest with conviction, invest with discipline, invest with patience.

10. Choose the right companions for your trip.

11. Resist the lure of the siren songs.

◆

CHAPTER 3

TAKE THE EASIEST ROUTE

◆

RULE #1: KEEP EVERYTHING SIMPLE AND THEN SIMPLIFY SOME MORE

If you are going on a trip, especially a long trip, your best bet is to take the easiest route. It will get you there faster, everyone will enjoy the trip a lot more, and you will get to your destination relaxed and on time. It is the same with your trip to investment success. Your best bet is to take the easiest road by keeping everything simple.

Most of us have been led to believe that investing is complex, takes a lot of special knowledge, and requires a lot of work. This Rule asserts that this is not true, and that keeping things simple is essential to successful investing. We will discuss why in a few minutes, but let us start by looking at how most investors behave.

A TALE OF TWO INVESTORS

It is late Sunday evening. Our friend Busy, the diligent investor, is still hard at work on his investments. Actually he has been at it almost all weekend and had hoped to be completely caught up by this evening. But it doesn't look like that is going to happen.

Busy has already reviewed the research reports and looked at the charts for all the 53 stocks he owns. He has losses on more than half of his stocks, some pretty large, and neither the research reports nor the charts look good for many of them. He had bought them based on the "Ten Top Tech Stocks to Buy Now," "The Stocks to Buy and Put Away for Your Retirement" type of articles in the financial magazines he subscribes to. Almost 35 of the stocks he owns are technology stocks, which have been going through a really rough patch lately.

Busy also owns 17 mutual funds, a medley of aggressive growth and growth funds, some value funds, some foreign stock funds, and even some sector funds. These haven't been doing too well either. He still has to study the latest Morningstar reports on them and probably switch some funds. There were a few other things he wanted to do. He wants to read the latest technical analysis book he bought. But that will have to wait.

Actually Busy is getting a little tired and discouraged with his investments. He has been at it quite seriously for about a year now, since his second son, David, was born. He has chalked out a plan to save and invest enough for the education of his two sons, as well as for retirement. He has been devoting big parts of his weekends and any other time he can find to learn about investing and building and managing his portfolio. All this work wouldn't bother him if he was getting results and making money, which he isn't.

The market has been in the doldrums for almost 10 months now, and the technology stocks, which did spectacularly well during the preceding 3 years, have gone down sharply, starting almost right after he bought most of them. His overall portfolio is actually down quite a bit for the year, a far cry from his assumption that he will be able to earn an average annual return of about 18% in the long run. He thought that was a fairly reasonable assumption considering the kind of returns the market, especially the technology stocks, had earned in the past few years.

Busy is pretty sure he needs to change his investment strategy and figure out a better way to pick stocks and mutual funds. He thinks maybe he should get out of the market for a while because things don't look too good for the next few months. He will jump back in when the market starts moving up again. But first he has to decide what to do with his current portfolio. He even called up some of the experts on a few TV and radio shows asking for advice on some of the stocks he owns. That did not help much because he got contradictory advice from the different experts. He has to make a lot of decisions, and he is not comfortable with the situation he is in.

In the meantime our other friend Easy, the laid-back investor, is unwinding from a hectic and trying weekend family trip by watching his favorite TV show. He wants to relax, sleep well, and start the week on the right foot. He doesn't even realize that the big annual package with information on the latest medical insurance plans, investment choices, and so forth will arrive on his desk tomorrow morning and he will have to make a number of major decisions in the next few weeks. He will have to decide how much money he wants to put into his 401(k) and the other savings plans next year, how much of his expected bonus he wants to defer, which investment choices he wants all of this money to go into, and so forth. His company's plans are still inflexible, and making changes to any of these choices during the year will be difficult.

At the time Easy went through this ritual last year making choices almost arbitrarily, he had decided to start paying more attention to his investments. He wanted to come up with an overall plan and figure out how he would make these decisions more rationally in the future. He remembered this during the year and even got started a number of times. But something or other kept coming up and he is really in no position to make any better decisions this year. So he will probably do what he did last year. He will have a casual discussion with his wife, talk to some of the colleagues at work, look at how the various investment options did last year, and probably spread out his investments over all of the available choices more or less evenly as he has been doing. But the market has not been doing well at all lately, and he has a feeling that the next year is going to be a bad year for the economy and the market. So he will probably put less money in stocks this year and put more into bonds.

WHAT IS WRONG WITH THIS PICTURE?

I am sure many of you can recognize and even sympathize with both Easy and Busy. And many of you are even smiling knowingly, recognizing some of the typical investment mistakes you may have made. As we study the Rules of the Only Proven Road and start applying them, we will identify these mistakes, explain why they are mistakes, and show what Easy and Busy should be doing instead.

But the biggest problem I see here is that both Easy and Busy are violating Rule #1, "Keep everything simple, and then simplify some more." They are grossly violating the rule, and until they fix that problem, there is almost no chance they will succeed as investors and achieve their investment goals. In fact, as I look at both Easy and Busy through the lens of this rule, I have to believe that if they continue down the paths they are on, over the years Easy will probably end up with somewhat better investment results than Busy, just because his is the simpler of the two approaches. It is not guaranteed, and it is not even fair given how much work Busy has been putting in. But working hard is not the whole answer. Working smart is equally important. And keeping things simple is a big part of working smart.

As we go though the Rules, we will find again and again that they all direct us to do simple things rather than complex things. At every fork they direct us to take the simpler road. But why? Why should simple work so much better when we are dealing with investing and the financial markets, which are so complex and sophisticated?

In the spirit of keeping things simple, I will give you just two simple answers. First, nature has a strong bias toward simplicity. Second, only simple is what we can stay with in the long run. Let me explain what I mean by each.

NATURE HAS A STRONG BIAS TOWARD SIMPLICITY

That probably sounds as unscientific and inane an answer as anyone could invent. But believe it or not, some of our greatest scientists and thinkers believed it and believe it wholeheartedly. In the scientific community, one of the tests almost everyone applies to any new answer to a problem is, "Is it simple enough?" Of two or more proposed solutions to a problem, absent any proof to the contrary, a scientist would trust and pick the simpler one.

Look around yourself at the things you admire. The superstars in any sport play the simplest, most effortless games. The literature and the music, even the food and clothing, that have gone on to become classics, that is, have stood the test of time, are the simple ones. It is hard to deny nature's strong bias toward simplicity.

You probably are not disagreeing with me, but I do not think you are quite convinced, either. So let me give you another practical answer that will reinforce what I have been saying. As we go through the Rules and talk about what years of research in investing have shown, we will see that the investment method that works the best in the long run is actually just about the simplest anyone could think of. It was not picked because of its simplicity. It was picked because extensive studies supported it. But the fact that it turned out to be so simple gave the researchers a lot of comfort. It gives me a lot of comfort and a lot more confidence in expecting that this method will continue to be the best for the future and is not just another fad.

SIMPLE IS ONLY WHAT WE CAN STICK TO IN THE LONG RUN

It is not difficult to come up with a complex investment method and investment program. In fact, most of them—like Busy's—are complex and time consuming. But almost no one ever sticks with them for very long.

Even if you have never invested, I am sure you can relate to what I am saying based on your experience in other areas of life. People make a big New Year's resolution to really become good at something. They make up an elaborate plan, go out and get five books and lots of gadgets, make up a precise schedule, and get started with a big bang. In about 2 months the books and gadgets end up in the corner of the closet, the schedule gets thrown in the trash, and life goes back to the way it was before—especially if the results have not been encouraging.

Busy is acting almost exactly the way most investors act. He started with a big complex plan without a good reason to believe that his approach would work. He worked hard at it for a while, and now he is getting discouraged. If the market keeps behaving the way it has been during the time Busy has been in the market, and the market may do just that, Busy will not keep up with his complex routine. He will give up.

The problem is, if you give up on your New Year's resolution to improve your tennis game, it won't matter all that much. But if you give up on becoming a better investor, it will matter a lot. You cannot afford to do that. In investing you have to think in terms of decades, not years. You cannot afford to get started with a complex, time-consuming program that you can only keep up with for at most a year or two. Too much is at stake here. Combine that with the fact that almost all evidence shows that none of the complex investment methods work, and you have as strong a case for simplicity as anyone could want.

SIMPLIFYING THINGS TAKES KNOWLEDGE

I do not want to leave you with the impression that to succeed in anything, all you have to do is pick the simplest approach that comes to mind first and you will succeed. On the contrary, finding the simplest way to do things and doing them in the simplest way possible takes a lot of work and knowledge. It takes a lot of work and knowledge to develop a perfect golf stroke that is so simple that it looks almost effortless. It takes a lot of work and knowledge to prepare a simple grilled fish that is done so right that it tastes heavenly with just a slice of lemon. No, simple is not just doing the first thing that comes to mind. It takes knowledge and work. This is where Easy is going wrong. He is keeping things simple, but he is acting without knowledge or a well-conceived plan.

In investing, learning what is the simplest and right thing to do and how to do it is not going to take that much time or work. Others have already done most of it for you. But going on doing the simple thing decade after decade, through good and bad times and without getting distracted, will be your biggest challenge.

SIMPLICITY HELPS YOU MAKE THE BEST USE OF YOUR TIME

One side benefit of keeping things simple that you should keep in mind and take full advantage of is that it allows you to make the best use of your time. In investing, a lot of people spend most of their time first on a complex search for the right stocks and funds to buy and sell at the right time. Then they spend more time worrying when things do not go right. After all of that, they hardly have any time left to focus attention on some of the other important aspects of investing and financial planning, not to mention things outside of investing that they really want to do.

So they hurt themselves in two ways. First, as we will see throughout this book, all this frantic effort to get into and out of the right stocks and funds at the right time almost always hurts rather than helps investment performance. At the same time, by not paying attention to the other things, investors pass up sure opportunities to earn or save significant amounts of money by reducing investment costs and taxes and so forth. Keeping everything simple will free up the time you need to focus on everything that deserves your attention and may even free up additional time to do many of the other things you really want to do in life, such as spending more time with your family. After all, you should not be living for your investments; your investments are there to help you live better.

KEEPING THINGS SIMPLE HAS TO BE AN ONGOING EFFORT

The rule says ". . . and then simplify some more." The reason it says so is that no matter how simple we make things, we almost never make them simple enough. Time is a special enemy here. We often start off by making things really simple, but slowly we start adding layers of complexity. We start with just three mutual funds. Then we hear about this fund that has been doing spectacularly well and think, "I will be a fool not to put at least a little money into it." Then comes along another "must invest in" trend. And before we know, we are juggling 11 funds again and studying fund reports over the weekends.

Keeping things simple is not a one-time thing. It is an ongoing effort. Every few months we have to stop and consciously ask ourselves, "Am I keeping things simple enough?" "Do I really need five funds?" "What changes should I make to make things simpler?" That effort to keep things simple will pay off in spades.

♦ THINGS TO REMEMBER ♦

- ♦ Simplicity is a virtue in itself, and in almost all areas of life the simpler approaches work much better than the complex ones.

- ♦ There is overwhelming evidence that the simplest possible investment method works much better than all the other more complex ones.

- ♦ You should not even get started with a complex investment method that takes a lot of ongoing time and effort because you will not keep up with it, especially at times when you are not making any money or losing money.

- ♦ Remember that simplifying things takes knowledge and work. Simple does not mean doing the first thing that comes to mind.

- ♦ Make keeping things simple an ongoing goal and do not let layers of complexity build up over the years.

♦

CHAPTER 4

Pick Up the Freebies

♦

Rule #2: Allow the Magic of Compounding to Work Its Magic

If you are on a trip and come across some freebies, of course you would want to pick them up. First you may want to make sure that they are really freebies and that there are no strings attached. But after that, the more freebies you can pick up, the better. On your road to investment success, no freebie will be as valuable as the Magic of Compounding. It has no strings attached, you can pick up as much of it as you want, and its long-term benefits are simply unbelievable.

It is easiest to understand how compounding works by looking at some examples. To keep our discussions simple, in all of the examples I will use the simplest possible investment—a bank savings account. Compounding, of course, works essentially the same way for all other investments. (Note that throughout this section whenever I say 5% interest or use similar other abbreviations, I mean an annual interest rate of 5%.)

UNDERSTANDING COMPOUNDING

Compounding is earning interest on interest or return on return. Here is how it works:

Suppose you deposit $100 in a savings account. The interest rate is 5% and the interest is to be paid annually. At the end of the first year you will get $5 of interest. If you want to compound your interest income, instead of taking out the $5 in cash and spending it, you will reinvest it, that is, leave it in the savings account. Then at the end of the first year the new balance in your account will be $105. At the end of the second year you will get $5.25 (5% of $105) of interest consisting of $5 of interest on your original investment of $100 and $0.25 of interest on the $5 of first-year's interest that you will have reinvested. That $0.25 represents the interest on interest or the effect of compounding for the second year. If you keep reinvesting the interest you get at the end of each year, at the end of 10 years the total balance in your account will be about $163.

If instead of leaving the annual interest in the savings account you take it out at the end of each year and put it in a checking account where it will earn no interest, at the end of 10 years you will have a total of $150—$100 in your savings account and $50 in the checking account from the ten deposits of the $5 of annual interest.

Finally, if instead of leaving the annual interest of $5 in the savings account or putting it in a checking account you decide to take it out and spend it, at the end of the 10 years you will have just the original $100.

All of this probably sounds trivial. But clearly understanding the importance of what is going on here will be crucial to your investment success. So let us take another look at it.

- If you take out and spend all the annual interest, at the end of 10 years you will have just the original $100.
- If you do not spend the interest, but instead of reinvesting it you take it out and set it aside, earning no additional interest, at the end of the 10 years you will have $150.
- If you reinvest all the interest, that is, allow the interest to compound, at the end of 10 years you will have $163.

You increase your wealth from $100 to $150, a big jump, by holding onto and not spending the interest you earn. You increase your wealth by another $13—all because of compounding—by reinvesting all the interest you get over the years. The additional $13 is an additional 13% return on your original investment of $100.

THE MAGIC THAT IS NOT AN ILLUSION

So far the power of compounding does not seem that impressive because we only looked at a relatively short investment period (or holding period) with a low initial investment and a low interest rate. (Yes, in the realm of investing, 10 years is a relatively short period of time.) But once we hold an investment for longer periods and allow compounding to work, its effect starts to snowball and its power seems awesome, almost magical. That is why it is called the "Magic of Compounding."

To see what I mean, look at Table 4.1. This table assumes that you start with $10,000 and invest it at 5% interest, paid annually. At the end of 10 years, compounding increases the final value of your investment by, or contributes, $1,289 (compared with holding onto but not reinvesting the interest). In 20 years, compounding contributes $6,533. In 30 years $18,219. And, in 50 years $79,674.

In 50 years, if you do not reinvest your interest, you will have only $35,000, but if you do reinvest your interest, you will have $114,674. And all that starting with just a one-time investment of $10,000! Also, remember that if you spend all the interest as it is earned, all you will have at the end of any period is just the original $10,000.

That has to convince you that you must reinvest all the interest as you earn it instead of taking it out and spending it.

You can and must take advantage of compounding in a number of other ways. Again, it is easiest to appreciate the power of these alternatives by looking at a few more examples.

EVEN A LITTLE HIGHER INTEREST RATE WILL HELP A LOT

How does the effect of compounding change with variations in the interest rate you earn? Look at Figure 4.1, which shows how much money you will

TABLE 4.1

The Final Values that $10,000 Will Grow to at a 5% Interest Rate After Different Numbers of Years

Number of Years	Without Compounding	With Compounding	Contribution of Compounding
5	$12,500	$12,763	$263
10	$15,000	$16,289	$1,289
20	$20,000	$26,533	$6,533
30	$25,000	$43,219	$18,219
40	$30,000	$70,400	$40,400
50	$35,000	$114,674	$79,674

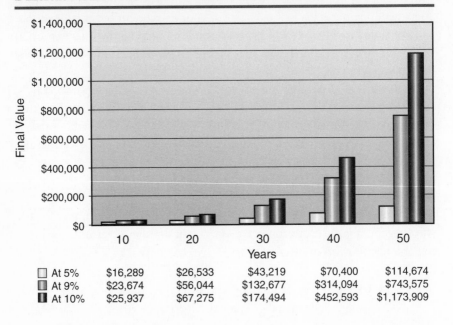

FIGURE 4.1

The Final Values an Initial Investment of $10,000 Will Grow to After Different Numbers of Years at Different Interest Rates

	10	20	30	40	50
☐ At 5%	$16,289	$26,533	$43,219	$70,400	$114,674
▨ At 9%	$23,674	$56,044	$132,677	$314,094	$743,575
▮ At 10%	$25,937	$67,275	$174,494	$452,593	$1,173,909

accumulate at the end of different numbers of years at three interest rates: 5%, 9%, and 10%. The last set of columns in the figure shows that at the end of 50 years, with compounding you will accumulate $1,173,909 at an interest rate of 10% instead of just $114,674 at an interest rate of 5%—a difference of more than $1 million! Of course, higher returns always help, but they help a lot more in the long run and with compounding.

The last set of columns also shows that if the interest rate is lower by just 1% (9% instead of 10%), you will have $743,575 instead of the $1,173,909. A big difference for just a 1% difference in interest rates. The lesson here is that for long holding periods, even a small difference in the interest rate makes a big difference.

STARTING TO INVEST EARLY WILL HELP A LOT

There is another way of looking at how the effect of compounding depends on the length of the holding period. Suppose you want to retire at the age of

65 with $1 million on hand. As you will expect, the earlier you can save and invest the necessary amount of money and the higher the interest rate you can earn, the smaller the amount of money you will have to save and invest. The numbers are shown in Table 4.2. If you can save and invest just $22,095 at the age of 25 and earn 10% interest, that's all you will have to do to have your $1 million when you get to the age of 65. If you think you will be able to earn only 5% interest, you will have to save and invest $142,046 at the age of 25. I am sure you expected that you will have to invest a lot more if you earned only 5% instead of 10% interest, but did you expect that you will have to save and invest more than six times as much? Again, it is the effect of compounding.

But now also notice how much of a difference delaying your investment makes. At the same 10% interest rate, if you delay investing until you are 45, you will have to save and invest $148,644 instead of the $22,095 you could have gotten away with if you did your investing at the age of 25. The lesson is: *Start investing as early as you can.*

INVESTING STEADILY WILL ALSO HELP A LOT

Clearly, you do not have to save and invest everything at one time. What if you can save and invest a small amount of money every month? Unless you happen to win the lottery or inherit some money, this is probably the only way

TABLE 4.2

Initial Investments Needed at Different Ages to Accumulate $1 Million by Age 65

Age	At 5% Return	At 10% Return
25	$142,046	$22,095
30	$181,290	$35,584
35	$231,377	$57,309
40	$295,303	$92,296
45	$376,889	$148,644
50	$481,017	$239,392
55	$613,913	$385,543
60	$783,526	$620,921

you will be able to save and invest. It is a wonderful habit to form, and making your investments in installments over a period of time has the additional advantage that if you are investing in stocks or some other assets whose price fluctuates, you will be investing at an average price over the period as opposed to a particularly high or low price at one point in time. Compounding, again, will help a lot here, and as you would suspect, the earlier you start saving, the more beneficial the effects of compounding will be.

Let us look at some examples. Assume you want to retire at age 65 with $1 million in cash and you want to get there by saving and investing the same amount of money every month. The amounts of money you will have to save and invest every month, depending on your age when you start investing and the rate of interest you expect to earn, are shown in Table 4.3. If you start at the age of 25 and expect to earn 5% interest, you will have to put away $653 per month. But if you think you will be able to earn 10% interest, you will have to save and invest only $157 per month. If you wait till the age of 45 to start saving and investing, the required monthly savings rates will be $2,423 and $1,306 respectively. Look at the numbers closely. At 10% interest, only $157 per month if you start at the age of 25 versus $1,306 per month if you wait until you are 45!

The last four columns of Table 4.3 are also quite revealing. They show how much money, in total, you will have to save and invest over the years and how much your interest income will contribute toward your $1 million goal. Notice that if you start your savings plan at age 25 and can earn 10% interest, you will have to save only a total of $75,273, and the remaining $924,727 will come from your interest income.

IS 50 YEARS TOO LONG A HOLDING PERIOD TO THINK ABOUT?

In some of the examples I mentioned holding periods of 40 or even 50 years. Isn't that way too long? Not really. If you are still young, those are very realistic holding periods. If you are 25 now, you may not even retire at 65. But let us assume you will retire at 65. That's a 40 year holding period right there. And it is not likely that you will pull out all your money as soon as you turn 65. You will probably take out the money from your savings over a period of 15 or 20 years or even more, and a big part of your money will have the opportunity to earn interest even after you retire. So a holding period of 50 years is very realistic.

TABLE 4.3

The Effect of Interest Rate and Starting Age on Monthly Investment Needed to Accumulate $1 Million by Age 65

	Required Monthly Savings Rate		Total Amount Saved and Invested Over the Years		Total Return Earned Over the Years	
	At 5% Return	*At 10% Return*	*At 5% Return*	*At 10% Return*	*At 5% Return*	*At 10% Return*
25	$653	$157	$313,239	$75,273	$686,761	$924,727
30	$877	$261	$368,154	$109,710	$631,846	$890,290
35	$1,197	$439	$430,763	$157,941	$569,237	$842,059
40	$1,672	$747	$501,680	$224,234	$498,320	$775,766
45	$2,423	$1,306	$581,471	$313,440	$418,529	$686,560
50	$3,726	$2,393	$670,634	$430,700	$329,366	$569,300
55	$6,413	$4,841	$769,580	$580,967	$230,420	$419,033
60	$14,644	$12,807	$878,613	$768,419	$121,387	$231,581

WHAT IF THE INTEREST RATE CHANGES
IN THE FUTURE?

In all our examples we have assumed that the interest rate will remain the same for the entire holding period—even if it is 50 years. We know that is not realistic; we can't know what interest rates will be in the future. If interest rates change, we will earn the different rates on both the money accumulated by then and on any interest income we reinvest afterward. So the amount of money we accumulate over the years is likely to be different from our original projection, and if we want to accumulate a specific sum by a certain date, we will have to make mid-course corrections. This is a type of problem we will face no matter what we invest in, and planning for and handling such changes is one of the major challenges of investing.

But none of this distracts from the Magic of Compounding. You may accumulate different amounts of money at different interest rates, but compounding will work as long as you reinvest all your interest income, and the longer you let compounding work, the faster your money will grow.

REINVESTING DIVIDENDS AND
INTEREST INCOME

By now you know that to get the benefit of compounding, you have to reinvest all the intermediate cash returns you get from your investments. But what do we mean by reinvesting if we are invested in stocks, bonds, or mutual funds instead of a savings account? In a strict sense reinvesting means that you immediately buy more of the same asset using the dividend or interest income. But you do not really have to buy exactly the same asset, nor do you have to reinvest exactly on the same day. What is important is that you invest the money as soon as possible and not withdraw and spend it. You should look at the dividend or interest income as new money you have for investing and invest it in exactly the same assets you would invest any new money at that point based on your overall portfolio considerations.

There is one special situation you should keep in mind. Almost all mutual funds provide a dividend or interest reinvestment option. If you choose this option, which you can do at any time, the fund will automatically use your dividend or interest income to buy more fund shares on the same day these are received. You do not have to do anything. I highly recommend that you choose this option right at the time of making your first investment in a fund.

♦ **THINGS TO REMEMBER** ♦

♦ To take full advantage of the Magic of Compounding, you must:

- Reinvest all dividends and interest you earn.
- Start investing early in life.
- Make frequent additional investments of even small amounts.
- Let your investments grow for as long as possible.
- Fight for even small increases in returns because over time that will make a big difference.
- Choose automatic dividend and interest reinvestment for all your mutual funds.

CHAPTER 5

♦

BE PREPARED FOR
BAD WEATHER

♦

RULE #3: INVEST ONLY IN ASSETS THAT
WILL KEEP YOU AHEAD OF INFLATION

If you are going on a long trip, you would want to be prepared for bad weather, especially because it can be so unpredictable. If you get caught in bad weather, your trip may get delayed or even ruined because you may have an accident or other serious problems. Investing is a very long trip, and one type of bad weather you have to watch out for on that trip is inflation because it is unpredictable and dangerous. If you are not well prepared for it and inflation jumps up unexpectedly, you may have a serious financial setback.

This Rule provides an important criterion for choosing the assets you are going to invest in. We will discuss why inflation is a serious threat to investors, and following the criterion provided by this Rule, we will find that we need to consider investing in only two types of assets: stocks and a group of assets that are essentially risk free. This will be an important step forward and will drastically simplify our investment program.

INFLATION: THE RELENTLESS ROBBER

Inflation is the increase in the average price of all the things we spend money on, such as food, clothing, airline tickets, and college tuition. When we say "Money just does not go as far any more," we are talking about inflation. Prices of things going up and the buying power of money going down are two sides of the same inflation coin.

Inflation is generally measured in percentage change in the average price of things over a 1-year period. The Consumer Price Index (CPI) inflation rate that the government calculates and reports every month is the most common measure of inflation. It is based on the "average basket of goods and services" that the "average" consumer buys. Because you are not the "average" consumer—no one is—the rate of inflation for you may be quite different from what the CPI inflation rate tells you. But it's a good starting point to use in making assumptions for your own financial plans.

Since 1926, the annual rate of inflation has averaged about 3%, but that average hides many ups and downs. For example, in the postwar era, the annual rate of inflation averaged 2.9% for 1946 to 1968, 7.8% for 1969-1981, and 3.3% for 1982 to 2000. Even this breakdown hides some important fluctuations. In 1979 and 1980 the inflation rate actually surged to double digit territory and things looked so bleak that everyone was predicting that the inflation rate would stay at this high level far into the future. As you can see in Figure 5.1, which shows the annual inflation rates for the postwar era, the history of inflation for this period can be summed up as: It fluctuated. Figure 5.2 shows the average rate of inflation by decades from the 1920s through the end of the twentieth century.

Incidentally, a decrease in the average price of things is called deflation. From our experience we know that inflation is much more common than deflation. On the surface it may seem that deflation would be preferable to inflation because then we would get more for our money. But this isn't necessarily true. Deflation is often accompanied by high unemployment and other problems, which makes deflation at least as undesirable as inflation.

Economists think that a moderate rate of inflation in the range of 0% to 2% per year probably represents the best of all worlds. Fortunately or unfortunately, you and I are not going to be able to do anything to influence inflation and deflation. We simply need to understand what they are and figure them into our plans for the future.

WHAT MAKES INFLATION SO DANGEROUS

It is almost impossible to overemphasize the importance of properly incorporating the effects of inflation in our financial plans and investment decisions. We can say, without any exaggeration, that the threat of higher inflation poses one of the most serious challenges for investors as well as the economy.

FIGURE 5.1

The Annual Rate of CPI Inflation (1946–2000)

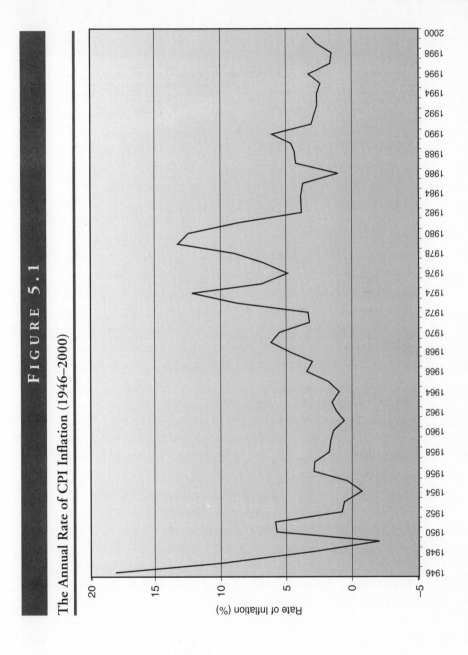

Figure 5.2

Average Annual Rate of CPI Inflation by Decade

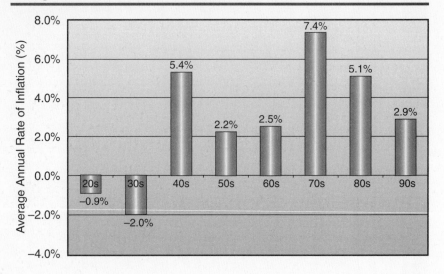

Two things contribute to the importance of inflation: the effect of compounding and the unpredictability of future inflation rates.

The Effect of Compounding

When we invest money, the Magic of Compounding, earning "interest on interest," works in our favor. But when prices of things keep going up because of inflation, the "price increase on increase" works against us and makes the overall increase over time much larger than it would be otherwise. Look at Figure 5.3 to appreciate how inflation and compounding work together to destroy the buying power of people's savings over time. Even at a modest 3% annual rate of inflation, the average for the past 75 years, your savings of $10,000 today will be worth $7,374 in 10 years, $5,438 in 20 years, and $4,010 in 30 years. If the annual rate of inflation rises to 5%, not an impossibility as history has shown, the $10,000 will be worth $5,987 in 10 years, $3,585 in 20 years, and only $2,146 in 30 years.

Let's look at it in another way. Suppose you think that if you were to retire today, you will need $3,000 per month from your savings to live on. If you are 20 years away from retirement and inflation averages 3% per year over this period, then you will need about $5,400 per month when you retire to have

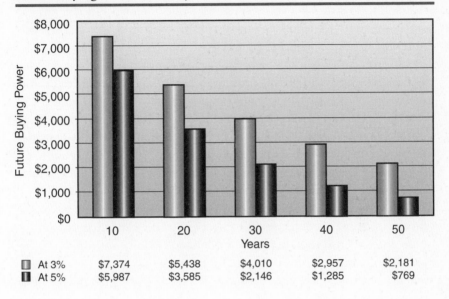

FIGURE 5.3

Future Buying Power of Today's $10,000 at Different Inflation Rates

	10	20	30	40	50
At 3%	$7,374	$5,438	$4,010	$2,957	$2,181
At 5%	$5,987	$3,585	$2,146	$1,285	$769

the same buying power as $3,000 has today. If inflation rate averages 5% per year, you will need almost $8,000 per month. And that's just for the first year of retirement. The year after that you will need 3% or 5% more money per month and so forth.

Shocking as all of this is, if the future rates of inflation were predictable, that is, if everyone knew for sure what the rates of inflation would be for the next 50 or 100 years, inflation would be a more or less manageable problem. In that case the financial markets would adjust to those future inflation rates and it would be reasonably easy to find investments that would preserve the buying power of your savings and provide some additional return on top of that.

The Unpredictability of Future Inflation Rates

The real threat of inflation derives from its unpredictability—unexpected inflation is the real threat. Never allow yourself to forget that.

Suppose you and everyone else predict that the annual rate of inflation will be 3% for a very long time and, accordingly, you make a long-term investment in a bond that will return a fixed 7% return per year for the next 20 years.

That may be a reasonably attractive investment if the rate of inflation remains at 3% as predicted. But what if the prediction is wrong and the inflation rate goes up to 8%? You will now be stuck in a situation where your investment is earning a 7% return per year whereas the value of money is declining at an annual rate of 8%. The buying power of your investment will keep deteriorating and that will significantly affect your future standard of living.

This problem would arise entirely from making an investment decision based on a wrong prediction of future inflation rate. Unfortunately, even experts cannot forecast inflation rates with any useful accuracy. In times when the rate of inflation is low, everything, at least in the inflation front, seems so quiet that everyone gets lulled into assuming that the inflation rate will remain low forever. In that kind of an environment, even those who should know better sometimes get tempted to invest in assets that offer attractive returns at the moment even though those returns are not protected against inflation. The rationalization generally is that inflation will surely remain tame or if it starts picking up, it will be possible to get out in time and change strategy.

Do not get lulled into that kind of thinking. Nobody has ever seen inflation coming until it is too late to run for cover. Actually, *nobody* is not quite accurate. There are some experts who are always predicting that higher inflation is just around the corner, and every so often they turn out to be right. But you do not need to listen to an expert for such predictions. You can make them yourself, and sooner or later you would be right too.

Because we cannot predict future inflation rates, the only sound strategy is to invest in assets that provide reasonable protections against unpredictable changes in inflation rates, that is, assets that will provide higher returns if the inflation rate goes up.

NOMINAL AND REAL RATES OF RETURN

When we earn a 10% return on an investment over a year, that 10% is called the nominal rate of return. But if during the year the rate of inflation was 4%, then our actual buying power increased by 6% (10% - 4% = 6%), not 10%. That 6% actual increase in our buying power is called the real (or inflation-adjusted) rate of return. Because the goal of investing is to increase our real buying power, it is the real return that really matters. Do not get fooled by high nominal returns if they are also accompanied by high inflation rates.

THE RELATIONSHIP BETWEEN INFLATION AND INTEREST RATES

The interest rate is the return we pay or earn when we borrow or lend money. As you know from your personal experience, there are always many different interest rates. You pay a different interest rate on your mortgage than you do on your credit card, and both of those are much higher than what you get when you put money in a savings account, effectively lending money to the bank. But what do all these interest rates depend on? The three most important factors are (a) the length of time that the money is being borrowed or lent for, (b) the borrower's creditworthiness, and (c) the expected rate of inflation for the period of the loan.

Why does it depend on the expected inflation rate? Suppose you are going to lend money to someone at a fixed interest rate for 5 years and you expect the inflation rate for the period to be 5% per year. In that case you would definitely want an interest rate of 5% plus something. Why? Because if you lend the money at less than 5% and the rate of inflation actually averages 5%, your money will lose buying power over the years. How much more you will require will depend on the creditworthiness of the borrower and a few other things. But the important thing I want to impress on you here is that the interest rate depends on the expected inflation rate and goes up and down with it.

YOUR PRIMARY INVESTMENT CHOICES

Now that we know we should be judging our various investment alternatives on the basis of their inflation-adjusted or real returns, it is time to learn what our primary investment choices are. Here we will talk about three asset classes: stocks, safe investments (money market funds, short-term bank CDs, short-term bonds, TIPS, and Series I Savings Bonds), and medium- and long-term bonds.

In discussing the investment choices, I implicitly assume that most of the investments are made through mutual funds. We will discuss mutual funds in detail under Rule #4. At the moment you can look at investing in any kind of asset through a mutual fund as essentially the same as investing in the asset directly, except that someone else does the investing for you for a fee.

ASSET CLASSES

In investing, the words *investment* and *asset* mean the same thing: something you invest in. An asset class is a group of assets with some common characteristics. Anyone can define an asset class based on some common characteristic that is relevant to him. Some commonly used asset classes are: domestic stocks, foreign stocks, corporate bonds, Treasury bonds, and money market instruments.

Most investors consider fixed income and equity to be the two most important asset classes. Investments that amount to lending money (e.g., putting money in a savings account) are called fixed income investments, although some of them may pay a variable rather than fixed interest. By contrast, when you invest in the ownership of a business (e.g., buy stock), it is called an equity investment. Because you are now a part owner, the return you will earn is not fixed any more; it will depend on how well the business does.

Fixed income investments generally provide lower but safer returns; equity investments tend to be more risky but they also provide higher return potential.

STOCKS

By now almost everyone knows that they should invest a big part of their savings in stocks, although they may not be sure why. Because stocks should be the cornerstone of your investment portfolio, it is important that you clearly understand what a stock is. You may be surprised to find that I do not talk about many of the things people think they need to understand about stocks and to know about specific stocks they may buy (e.g., price-earnings ratio). It turns out that you really do not need to know those things to successfully invest in stocks. And that's a huge blessing because not having to learn all that will save you a lot of time now, and a lot more time over the years.

What a Stock Is

A stock represents the ownership of a small slice of a company—often a tiny slice of a very large company—and when you buy a company's stock, you become a part owner or shareholder of the company. As a part owner you also become entitled to your share of the company's profits, although, as we will see, you cannot get it in cash anytime you want.

How Big a Slice Each Stock Is

A company has full freedom to subdivide itself into any number of shares that it chooses; there is no law or convention about it. However, a company almost always slices itself into pieces of equal size. To determine the portion of a company that one share represents, we have to know into how many parts (shares) the company has divided itself. This is called the number of shares outstanding. If a company decides to slice itself into 1 million shares, it will have 1 million shares outstanding, and if you own one share, then you own one-millionth of the company. Most companies have millions or even hundreds of millions of shares outstanding. So even if you own a few thousand shares of such a company, you really own only a tiny piece of it.

Because a company can almost arbitrarily slice itself into as many pieces as it wants, the price of a stock by itself tells us nothing about the company. For example, if the stocks of two companies are selling at $100 and $20, from that we cannot tell which is a bigger company or a more attractive stock or whether the stocks are over- or undervalued.

The Market Value of a Company

The size of a company is generally measured by its total market value. If the price of one share of a company is, say, $20 and it has 50 million shares outstanding, then the total market value of the company is $1 billion ($20 × 50,000,000 = $1 billion). This is the measure we use most often to compare the sizes of companies. When people talk about large companies, small companies, and so forth, this is the measure of size they are using. Because the price of a company's stock fluctuates, its market value fluctuates as well.

How the Price of a Company's Stock Is Determined

When you want to buy or sell the stock of a company, the company does not get involved at all. You have to buy the shares from someone who already owns and wants to sell them, and when you want to sell your shares, you have to sell your shares to someone who wants to buy them. Your broker finds you prospective buyers or sellers through the stock exchange. The price you pay or get is determined by supply and demand. It is important to understand that neither the company nor anyone else sets the price, nor does anyone guarantee any price. You will pay or get what the market bears. The price fluctuates all the time. In the long run the price of a company's stock reflects how profitable the company is, but in the short run the price can fluctuate with almost no relationship to the profitability of the company.

Who Manages the Company

The company is managed on behalf of all its owners, that is, shareholders, by the Board of Directors the shareholders elect. Although the shareholders are the ultimate owners and elect the Board of Managers, as a practical matter, the shareholders have very limited influence on how the Board of Directors runs the company. If you do not like the way a company is being run, your only practical recourse is to sell the stocks and move on.

Dividends

From time to time the Board of Directors can decide to pay you in cash a part of your share of the company's profits. This is called a dividend. Although as a shareholder you own your share of the company's profits, you can get in cash only the portion the Board decides to pay you as a dividend. The rest is reinvested in the business, and if the money is invested well, it will increase the value of your shares in the long run. Not all companies pay dividends—some of the best companies don't. If a company pays dividends, it generally pays them once a quarter, tries to pay them regularly, and tries to increase the amount from time to time. But neither the payment of any dividend nor the size of it is ever guaranteed. The board has the sole decision-making power in this respect. Even if a company has been paying dividends for years, if it gets into financial difficulties, it may decide to reduce the dividends or not pay them at all.

Why People Invest in Stocks

Stocks give people the opportunity to invest even small amounts of money in companies that have enormous resources, professional management, access to markets, and so forth. And once you have invested your money in a company's stock, you do not have to do much more, you cannot be held responsible for anything that the company does, and you cannot be asked for any more money. Later in this chapter we will examine the past performance of stocks in general as an investment.

How Risky Is Investing in Stocks

Investing in stocks can be very risky, but there are ways in which you can reduce the risk a lot. We will discuss all the risk related issues at great length later.

MEASURES USED TO EVALUATE STOCKS

Investors use a number of measures to judge if a stock is over- or under-priced. None of these measures work too well; otherwise, most investors would be rich. You won't need to use or even know any of these; but you may want to learn just enough to satisfy your curiosity or sound knowledgeable. I am including only a few of the most popular measures.

Earnings per Share (EPS). EPS is the net income or profit of a company over a period of time (generally a quarter or a year) divided by its number of shares outstanding. It measures the income of the company that "belongs" to each share even though a shareholder cannot take it out in cash. Despite all the brouhaha Wall Street creates over the quarterly EPS announcements of companies, it tells us very little about the long-term prospects of a company or its stock.

Book Value per Share. The book value of a company is the value of everything it owns, called its assets, minus everything it owes, called its liabilities. So the book value is supposed to be a measure of the net value of a company. Book value per share is the book value divided by the number of shares outstanding and is used as a measure of the value of each stock. However, because the values of the assets and liabilities of a company are recorded on its books at historical costs without any adjustments for inflation and other changes over time, and many assets and liabilities aren't even recorded on the books, book value and book value per share can be somewhat meaningful to totally meaningless numbers.

Price to Earnings (P/E) Ratio. It is the ratio of the price of a stock and its annual EPS. So it measures how many dollars an investor has to pay for each dollar of earning. It is by far the most popular measure. The higher a stock's P/E ratio, the more expensive it is, but that does not necessarily mean that the stock is overpriced. The P/E ratio of a stock depends on a number of factors, most importantly its expected growth rate. P/E ratios of companies can vary from single digits to triple digits, although most investors would probably consider 10 to 30 to be the normal range. Judging whether a stock is well priced by looking at its P/E ratio is about as easy or meaningful as judging how intelligent someone is by looking at his height.

Price Earnings to Growth (PEG) Ratio. The PEG ratio is considered to be a highly sophisticated measure. A stock's PEG ratio is its P/E ratio divided by the expected growth rate of its EPS. The rule of thumb many investors use is that a PEG ratio of 1 indicates a fairly priced stock. Therefore, stocks with PEG ratios below 1 are supposed to be underpriced, and those above 1 are supposed to be overpriced. The key phrase here is "supposed to be." Unfortunately, life isn't this simple.

Price to Book Value (P/B) Ratio. This ratio is calculated as the price of a stock divided by its book value per share. If a stock's book value per share really measured what a stock is worth, then a P/B ratio of 1 would mean the stock is correctly priced, a P/B ratio of more than 1 would mean it is overpriced, and a P/B ratio of less than 1 would mean it is underpriced. As we have discussed, however, the book value per share is not a good indicator of what a stock is worth. Therefore, we cannot draw any definitive conclusions from the P/B ratio.

Dividend Yield. The dividend yield of a stock is its latest dividend annualized and expressed as a percentage of its current price. For example, if the last quarterly dividend a stock paid was of $1 per share, then its annualized dividend rate is $4 per share because it is expected to pay four quarterly dividends over a year. If the current stock price is $100, then the dividend yield is 4%. Remember that dividend yield is always quoted as a percentage of the stock's current price, not the price at which you bought the stock. Because both the stock's price and the dividend may have changed since you bought the stock, its current dividend yield may not be the same as it was when you bought it or what you may be effectively earning on your original investment.

MONEY MARKET FUNDS

Investing in money market funds is one of the best options for any money you want to keep absolutely safe and readily accessible while earning a reasonable return that is protected against inflation. You can even write checks on most money market fund accounts.

Money market funds are mutual funds that lend their money to banks, large corporations, governments, and government agencies for the short term (a few days to a few months). So when you put your money in a money market fund, you are effectively lending your money to these institutions. When you invest in a money market fund, unlike an investment in stocks, the amount of money you invest, that is, your principal, remains fixed and safe. The interest you earn, however, varies every day and you will never know ahead of time exactly what interest you will earn on your money market fund over a month or a year. That may sound like a problem, but that actually is a key advantage of a money market fund. The interest you earn is generally 2% or so higher than the rate of inflation. If the rate of inflation goes up unexpectedly, so will the interest rate you earn, and vice versa. So you are protected against unexpected increases in the rate of inflation. Unfortunately, that 2% real or inflation-adjusted return is not much of a return. But that is the price we have to pay for safety. As we all know intuitively, the safer an investment, the lower the return we can expect on it.

Money market funds and the other safe investments I am going to mention do not get all the respect they deserve. People consider them to be temporary parking places for money while they look for better investment opportunities. People ask me all the time, "I have this money sitting around in money market funds, what can I invest it in?" Those who ask such questions fail to appreciate the safety and inflation protection offered by money market funds and these other safe investments. Some of the other safe investment choices provide you with a somewhat higher return over the long run with a little more risk than money market funds. But you should always keep in money market funds any money you may need within the next 6 months to 1 year.

Two other points to keep in mind. First, if you are in a high tax bracket, you should also consider tax-exempt money market funds or state-specific tax-exempt money market funds for your taxable accounts as alternatives to the regular money market funds. (For more on these, see the box on tax-exempt bonds later.) Second, banks offer something similar, called money market deposits. They generally pay lower interest than do money market funds. You can consider them as an alternative, but if the interest rate is lower, there is no reason to prefer them over money market funds. These deposits at banks are insured by the Federal Deposit Insurance Corporation, or FDIC (like your other money at a bank), whereas regular money market funds are not insured by anyone. So technically money market funds are slightly less safe, but you really do not need to worry about the safety of a good money market fund. Although money market funds are mutual funds, they are perfectly safe, and no investor has ever lost any money he invested in a money market fund.

BANK CERTIFICATES OF DEPOSIT

Just as you do when you put money in a savings account at a bank, when you buy a bank certificate of deposit (CD), you lend money to the bank. But in this case you lend it for a specific time period at a specific interest rate and if you want to withdraw your money earlier, you will have to pay a penalty. From time to time you will find short-term CDs that yield quite a bit more than money market funds and even the other safe choices, and in this situation you should consider investing in CDs any money you will not need to access during the life of the CD. As long as you keep the maturity at no more than 2 years or so, you will be reasonably well protected against unexpected higher inflation.

It is important to understand why you should keep the maturity of a CD at a maximum of around 2 years and what I mean by "reasonably well protected against unexpected higher inflation." When you invest in a CD, let us say for 1 year, you will agree to a specific interest rate for the 1-year period, and this interest rate will depend on the expected inflation rate for that 1 year. If the expected inflation rate is 3%, you may be able to buy the CD with an interest rate of 5%. Now suppose the day after you buy the CD war breaks out in the middle east, oil prices go through the roof, and over that 1-year period actual inflation ends up being 8%. Over the year at your 5% interest rate, your investment in the CD will lose 3% buying power. You really were not very well protected against inflation, were you?

But once the CD matures and you get your money back, you can reinvest it at a new interest rate. If the expected inflation rate for the next year is 8%, you may be able to get a new 1-year CD paying 10% interest. And if the rate of inflation actually turns out to be 8% for the next year, you will end up with a 2% real return. You lost buying power only in the first year. Now contrast that with what would have happened if you had bought a 5-year CD at 5.5% interest. You would be stuck with it for 5 years, and if the rate of inflation rose and stayed at 8% for all of the 5 years, you would have lost 2.5% buying power for each of those 5 years.

I am sure you now understand why I advise you to buy only short-term CDs. If things go against you and the rate of inflation goes up unexpectedly, you will lose some buying power, but for just a year or two. If you commit yourself for a longer period and the rate of inflation rises unexpectedly and stays high for a few years, you will lose buying power every year. A short-maturity CD or any short maturity fixed income investment gives you the option to reinvest your money after a short period of time—that's not full protection against inflation, but at least it's reasonable protection.

Because the rates on money market funds adjust every day, they may keep up with increases in inflation rates a little better. But if you can find a short-term CD yielding 1% or so higher than money market fund rates—and they are available more often than you may think—it will be worth taking the slightly higher inflation risk. Generally the less well-known banks offer the best CD rates. You should not hesitate to buy those CDs as long as you do not exceed the FDIC insurance limits ($100,000 if it is in just one name, $200,000 in a joint account with your spouse).

SHORT-TERM BONDS

When you buy a bond, you effectively lend money to the issuer of the bond for a certain number of years (called the bond's maturity) in exchange for a fixed rate of interest you will get semi-annually. The issuer or borrower may be a corporation, a government agency, or some other entity.

Short-term bonds issued by corporations, called corporate bonds, generally pay somewhat higher interest than what you can get on money market funds or short-term CDs. From the perspective of protection against unexpected inflation, bonds work pretty much the same way as CDs. If you keep the maturity short, you will not take all that much inflation risk, but as the maturity gets longer, the inflation risk goes up. So if you decide to invest in bonds, you would want to keep the maturity short, definitely less than 5 years, probably in the 3-year range. It is difficult to set down any hard and fast rule about how much more return you have to get to switch from money market funds to short-term bonds. You have to make a judgment based on the circumstances. But no matter which way you go, it probably won't make that much of a difference.

If you decide to invest in short-term bonds, you should definitely do so through a low-cost bond fund with an average maturity of around 3 years. Invest only in a high-quality corporate bond fund, that is, a fund that invests in bonds of safer corporations rather than just the U.S. Government, because you will get a higher return. But if you are in a high tax bracket, you should also consider tax-exempt short-term bond funds or state-specific tax-exempt short-term bond funds for your taxable accounts as alternatives. (For more on these, see the box on tax-exempt bonds later.)

One difference between bonds and CDs is that you can sell your bond or bond fund at almost any time. But if you sell it before maturity, you will have to sell it to a willing buyer at his price (not to the issuer), which can be somewhat less than what you paid for it. So, if you invest in a short-term bond fund, the value of your investment will fluctuate somewhat over time, which does not happen with money market funds or CDs.

BOND BASICS

The U.S. Treasury, corporations, municipalities, and others (called the issuer) borrow money by selling their bonds to investors. Bonds generally pay interest at a fixed rate (the coupon rate) for a specified number of years (the bond's life), and then repay the principal (the par or face value) at maturity, that is, at the end of the bond's life. Most bonds have face values of $1,000 and pay their interest semi-annually. You can buy bonds with remaining lives of a few months to 30 years or even longer.

An issuer originally sells its bonds to investors at or near face value and then redeems them at face value at maturity. In between you can buy or sell the same bond only in the market (i.e., from or to other investors) at the market price, which most often will be different from the bond's face value. The higher the current interest rates relative to a bond's coupon rate, the lower will be its price relative to its face value, and vice versa. So bond prices vary inversely with interest rate, and the longer the maturity of a bond, the more its price will change with interest rate changes. This is called a bond's interest rate risk.

All bonds other than those of the U.S. Treasury also have credit risk, meaning if after you buy a bond its issuer gets into financial trouble you may lose some or all of your remaining interest and principal. At the time you buy a bond you have to make a judgment about the credit risk of the issuer for the lifetime of the bond. Fortunately, there are a number of companies, called rating agencies, who assign credit ratings to bonds, which you can look up before buying a bond. The two major bond rating agencies are Standard and Poor's (S&P) and Moody's. Their ratings go from AAA or Aaa for the most creditworthy bonds all the way down to C or D for bonds in default. Bonds rated BBB or higher by S&P and Baa or higher by Moody's are considered investment grade bonds, meaning they are fairly safe. You should never buy any bond below this grade, nor should you invest in any bond fund that invests in bonds below this grade. (Lower quality bonds are called junk bonds, and even though at times they may offer attractive current yields, you should always stay away from them.)

Although bonds are generally less risky than stocks, they are complex, and at times medium- and long-term bonds can be quite risky. And they do not provide adequate inflation protection. That's why I recommend you do not invest in bonds (other than TIPS and I Bonds) of more than a 3-year maturity. And unless you learn a lot more about them, invest in bonds only through a low-cost mutual fund.

TREASURY INFLATION-PROTECTED SECURITIES

Treasury inflation-protected securities (TIPS) are a special category of U.S. Government bonds that have been around for only a few years. The pedigree is impeccable, as is the concept. TIPS are very attractive for money you want to invest safely for the long term (say, over 2 years).

When you buy TIPS—officially called inflation-indexed bonds—you are guaranteed to earn interest at a rate that is a certain number of percentage points higher than the inflation rate. How much higher will depend on the price at which you buy your TIPS. For example, currently you can buy TIPS that will guarantee you a return of 3.5% above inflation for the life of the TIPS. So if in a particular year the rate of inflation is 2%, you will earn a return of 5.5%, but if the inflation rate rises to 8%, you will earn a return of 11.5%. Effectively, you are guaranteed a specific real rate of return—3.5% in our example. Maybe that 3.5% real rate of return is not as high as you would like it to be, but remember, it is completely safe and it is fully protected against inflation.

Interest Payment and Tax Peculiarities

If you own TIPS directly, you will get in cash, every 6 months, the fixed rate part of your return—the 3.5% in our example. The inflation adjustment will get tacked onto the face amount and you won't get it until you sell the TIPS or they mature. However, if you are holding TIPS in a taxable account, you will have to pay taxes every year on both the fixed rate portion and the inflation adjustment portion. So most of the cash interest you get every year may go into paying the taxes, leaving you with no cash income. Because of all these complications, you should invest in TIPS only through a good mutual fund that specifically invests in TIPS. One such fund is the Vanguard Inflation-Protected Securities Fund. These funds generally sell enough TIPS every year to pay out to you an annual cash distribution equal to both the fixed rate interest and the inflation compensation parts of your return.

Price Stability of TIPS

Although TIPS have 10- to 30-year maturities, if interest rates go up, TIPS prices will not go down anywhere near as much as the prices of regular bonds of equivalent maturity. Most of the time long-term interest rates go up because the actual or expected inflation rate goes up. In such a case, unlike the holder of a regular bond who will be stuck earning a lower interest rate than the market, the holder of TIPS will earn a return that will go up more or less in step with the market. So any time you want to sell your investment in the fund (or in TIPS themselves if you bought them directly) you may get a little more or less than your original investment; but this would be a small amount. Given the other advantages, you should not hesitate investing in the fund as long as you are going to keep the money there for at least a year.

Buying and Selling TIPS

Like all other Treasury bonds, you can buy TIPS directly from the Treasury at its auctions. It is a fairly simple process and you can find all the necessary information at www.publicdebt.treas.gov. However, if you want to buy a specific maturity, you may have to buy it in the market through your broker, and you may not get very good pricing for small-quantity purchases. You will have the same problem if you want to sell them before maturity. So your best bet is to invest in TIPS through a fund, as I already recommended.

THE MECHANICS OF INFLATION ADJUSTMENT FOR TIPS

You do not have to know exactly how the inflation adjustment works for TIPS, especially if you invest in them through a fund. But in case you are curious, here's an example that explains the mechanics.

The inflation adjustment is based on the consumer price index for urban consumers (CPI-U). Assume that you buy a TIPS for $1,000 with a coupon of 3.5% at a time when the CPI-U is 100. Let's also assume that 6 months later, when your semi-annual interest is due, the CPI-U goes up by 2% to 102. For the TIPS you will receive $17.50 (0.5 × $1,000 × 3.5% = $17.50) of fixed-rate interest in cash, and the principal will be increased by the 2% increase in the CPI-U. So the face value of the bond will now become $1,020. Your fixed-rate interest 6 months later will be calculated at the 3.5% rate on the new $1,020 face value of the bond, and then the face value will be adjusted again depending on how the CPI-U changes during the 6 months.

TAX-EXEMPT BONDS

Debts of state and local governments and certain other governmental authorities (e.g., port authorities) are called tax-exempt securities or bonds because you don't have to pay federal income tax on your interest income from them. (These debts are also called municipal securities or bonds.) In addition, you do not have to pay state and local income taxes on the interest income on debts of issuers from the state you live in.

Because of these tax advantages, these debts pay lower interest than corporate debt of equivalent maturity and quality. However, if you are in a high tax bracket and want to invest in debt securities in taxable accounts, you may be able to earn a higher after-tax interest income by investing in tax-exempt debt instead of taxable corporate debt.

Let me give you an example of how you decide which is the better investment for you. Let's assume that you are in the 28% tax bracket and have the option of investing either in corporate bonds offering 5% interest or in tax-exempt bonds of equivalent quality and maturity offering 4% interest. If you invest in the corporate bond in a taxable account, you will earn (and keep) an after-tax return of 3.6% because you will have to pay 1.4% (28% of 5% = 1.4%) of the interest income in taxes. Because you will pay no taxes on the tax-exempt bond, both your before-tax and after-tax income from it will be 4%. So in this case you will earn a higher return on the tax-exempt bond. Clearly, the higher the tax bracket you are in, the more likely it is that you will be better off investing in tax-exempt debt. To find out for sure, you have to compare them on an after-tax basis as above.

Tax-exempt bonds come in a wide range of maturities and are also rated by rating agencies. Some of them are insured or guaranteed by other entities, but that will already be reflected in their credit ratings. As with corporate bonds, you should invest only in investment grade tax-exempt bonds. You can buy tax-exempt bonds, including bonds of issuers from your state, through a broker. Generally you do not have to pay a brokerage commission. But that does not mean that there is no investment cost; it is just not visible. The hidden investment cost, called bid asked spread, is often very high. There are numerous mutual funds that invest exclusively in tax-exempt bonds of specific quality and maturity, and unless you have a substantial sum of money to invest, you will probably be better off investing in tax-exempt bonds through low-cost tax-exempt bond funds.

Here are a few things to remember about investing in tax-exempt bonds. (a) You should never invest in tax-exempt bonds in tax-deferred or tax-advantaged accounts such as IRAs. (b) If you live in a large state like New York or California, you may be able to find funds that invest exclusively in debts of issuers from your state and meet your other requirements. Because you will avoid federal as well as state income tax on the interest income from these funds, under certain circumstances these may be your best choice. To check it out, do your calculation using your combined federal and state income tax bracket. (c) Tax-exempt funds come in all the maturities you would be interested in, from money market to long-term. So, if you are in a high tax bracket, you should always consider them as alternatives to regular money market or bond funds.

One final point. Interest income on debt and savings bonds for the federal government, that is, the U.S. Treasury, are also exempt from state and local income taxes although they are not considered tax-exempt securities. For some people who are in very high tax brackets and live in high income tax states, this tax advantage may make treasury securities more attractive than corporate securities. But for the average investor, this tax advantage is not large enough to make a difference.

SERIES I U.S. SAVINGS BONDS

Most of us have never thought much of savings bonds. But here is a winner that everyone should seriously consider. It is your best choice for any money you want to invest for the long term in a safe, inflation-protected investment in a taxable account.

The Series I Savings Bonds (I Bonds) work essentially the same way as the TIPS, except that they are much simpler to buy. The interest you get will be a fixed rate (that you will know at the time you buy the bond) plus the rate of inflation. So, just as with TIPS, if the rate of inflation rises, so will the return you earn. You are totally protected against inflation and guaranteed a fixed real rate of return.

There is even more good news. The interest is automatically reinvested as long as you hold the bond, and you do not have to pay taxes until you redeem your bonds and collect your interest (which is free from state and local income taxes). As we will see under Rule #7, the great advantage of this is that during the time you hold the bonds, you will be earning additional interest on what otherwise would have been Uncle Sam's take. This will significantly increase the return you effectively earn on these compared with, say, other short-term bonds and even TIPS, because the full force of the Magic of Compounding will work in your favor. You can hold these bonds for up to 30 years, but you can also cash them in for the full accrued value without any penalty at any time after you have held them for 5 years. (If you use the interest to pay for qualified education expenses, you may be able to exclude from your federal income taxes all or a portion of a bond's interest.)

Restrictions

There are few restrictions you should keep in mind. First, you are not going to get any of the interest from your I Bonds until you sell them. So you cannot buy them to live on the interest income. Second, you cannot cash in your I Bonds within the first 6 months, and if you do so before 5 years, you will pay a penalty equal to 3 months' interest. Third, each individual can buy only a maximum $30,000 of I Bonds per year, an annual maximum of $60,000 for you and your spouse if you are married. So if you have a substantial amount of money already saved up and want to switch it to I Bonds, you will have to do so over a number of years.

Buying I Bonds

You buy I Bonds the same way you buy other savings bonds. You can buy them through banks, credit unions, and other financial institutions whenever you want and through bond-a-month programs that many financial institutions offer. You can also buy them directly from the U.S. Treasury at your convenience or through an EasySaver plan, which will automatically deduct a specific amount of money from your bank account at specified intervals based on your instructions and issue the bonds for you. You can even buy them through payroll savings plans (if your employer offers such a plan).

You can buy I Bonds in denominations of $50, $75, $100, $200, $500, $1,000, $5,000, and $10,000. Buy them in small enough denominations so that if you unexpectedly need some money, you won't have to cash in more money than you need.

Detailed information on I Bonds, including more information on the different ways to buy them, is available at www.publicdebt.treas.gov/sav/sbiinvst.

MEDIUM- AND LONG-TERM BONDS

Although you may want to invest in short-term corporate or tax-exempt bonds for the somewhat higher interest rate they offer, I do not think individual investors should invest in medium- or long-term bonds (that is bonds of over 5-year maturity), except in some rare situations. The problem is the lack of protection against unexpected higher inflation. As I explained, the longer the maturity of a CD or a bond, the less inflation protection it provides. Beyond 5 years, you will be vulnerable to unexpected increases in inflation for no good reason because medium- or long-term bonds do not provide much more return than short-term bonds. The prices of longer maturity bonds fluctuate a lot more, and if you hold them (or hold a bond fund that holds them) and want to sell at an inopportune time, you may lose quite a bit of your money.

THE WINNER IN STAYING AHEAD OF INFLATION IS: STOCKS

We now know why this Rule says that we should invest only in assets that will keep us ahead of inflation, and we also know what our primary investment choices are. It is finally time to answer one of the most important questions in investing: Which asset or assets are likely to keep us ahead of inflation and by how much? The answer to this question will also determine which asset classes we should invest in. To answer this question, let us look at some historical data and also use our understanding of how each class of asset is likely to behave in the future. The historical data are shown in Table 5.1. I have

TABLE 5.1

Compound Annual Real Return for Major Asset Classes

	Stocks	Long-term Government Bonds	Short-term Government Bonds	CPI Inflation
1946–2000	7.7	1.3	0.6	4.2
1946–1968	9.5	−1.8	−0.6	2.9
1969–1981	−1.8	−3.8	−0.4	7.8
1982–2000	12.3	8.9	2.9	3.3

shown only inflation-adjusted or real returns because, as we have discussed, that is what matters. Let's look at each asset class.

STOCKS

Over the past two centuries, over the past 75 years, and since the end of World War II (that is, since 1946), stocks have amazingly provided the same real return of around 7% per year—the best among all the major asset classes. But on the question of the ability of stocks to provide protection against inflation, let us clearly understand that, at least historically, stocks have provided such protection only in the long run. They may fail and have failed miserably in the short term. For example, in the 1969 to 1981 period, when the annual rate of inflation averaged 7.8%, the annual real return on stocks was -1.8%— a very disappointing performance. In addition, there have been many individual years when the inflation-adjusted returns for stocks were significantly negative. Of course, there have been good periods as well. During the great bull market of 1982 to 2000, the real return on stocks soared to 12.3%.

MEDIUM- AND LONG-TERM BONDS

Over the years long-term government bonds have provided real returns of about 2% with significantly negative real returns (-3.8%) in the high inflation era of 1969 to 1981. Medium- and long-term bonds provided high (8.9%) real returns from 1982 to 2000, but that reflected a special situation that is not likely to be repeated. Even that long-term 2% real return does not seem that dependable. Remember, you will earn that real return or maybe even a little more if the rate of inflation stays at the level expected at the time you invest in bonds. But if the rate of inflation rises, you may easily end up with negative real returns or even losses. That is taking a lot of risk for the very small real return, especially knowing we can get the same real return or more on our short-term bonds or other safe investments such as TIPS and I Bonds with almost no risk.

SAFE INVESTMENTS

Table 5.1 shows no data on the safe investments (money market funds, short-term bank CDs, short-term bonds, TIPS, and I Bonds) we have discussed because they have not been around for the long periods that the table covers. Nonetheless, the returns on money market funds, short-term bank CDs, and short-term corporate bonds should be similar to or a little better than those for the short-term government bonds shown in Table 5.1. For various reasons, it is unlikely that any of these will have real returns below 2% for any long period of time. The actual real returns may be even a little higher. As for TIPS and I Bonds, if you buy them at a price guaranteed to provide a real return of around 3.5%, then that is what you will earn. When you consider that all of these investments provide almost guaranteed protection against any unexpected increase in the rate of inflation and your original investment is essentially safe, all of them come out way ahead of bonds. They are really safe investments.

THE ONLY TWO ASSETS YOU NEED TO INVEST IN: STOCKS AND SAFE ASSETS

Based on all the information and data we have looked at, we can now draw a major conclusion. We need to invest in only two classes of assets: stocks and safe assets because those are the only two types of assets that are reasonably certain to keep us ahead of inflation over the long run. Of the two, stocks are expected to provide much higher returns over the years. But as we know, investing in stocks can be risky and we can afford to invest only part of our money in stocks. The rest has to go into one of the safe investment choices. We also call these safe investments risk-free investments because they are essentially risk free in two ways: they are well protected against any unexpected rise in inflation, and there is little chance that we will lose any of the principal we invested in any of these assets.

DECIDING WHICH SAFE ASSET TO INVEST IN

In safe assets we have five choices: money market funds, bank CDs, short-term bond funds, TIPS funds, and I Bonds. It is a little difficult to put down hard and fast rules about how you choose from among these. But once you understand them well, making your choice should be easy. Here are some broad guidelines:

- Money you want to keep readily accessible and may need within the next 6 months: money market funds
- Money you can invest for 6 months to 2 years: bank CDs, short-term bond funds, or TIPS funds, depending on which one offers a higher return
- Money you can invest for 2 years to 5 years: bank CDs, short-term bond funds or TIPS funds, with higher preference to TIPS funds
- Money you want to invest for longer than 5 years: I Bonds and TIPS funds, with a preference for I Bonds for taxable accounts

For related information and specific fund recommendations, see Appendices A and B.

THE POTENTIAL REWARD OF INVESTING IN STOCKS

We intuitively know that investing in stocks is risky, and even the numbers show that there were long periods of time when stocks actually had negative returns. We will look into the risk issue more under Rule #4 and discuss what steps we can take to make the risk tolerable. But for the moment, let us get a better understanding of the potential rewards by putting them in dollar terms.

Let us say you will have average luck and you will earn the historical average real rate of return of 7% on your investment in stocks. Start with $10,000 and here's what you will have after different holding periods: in 10 years, $19,672; in 20 years, $38,697; and in 30 years, $76,123. If you don't find that

very exciting, let me remind you that those numbers are adjusted for inflation. In 30 years you will have over 7.5 times your original investment after
allowing for inflation. Anyone should jump at that.

To put it in the nominal terms you are used to seeing, let us say that the
rate of inflation in the future will also equal the long-term historical average
of 3%. This means you will have a nominal return of 10% (7% + 3% = 10%)
per year. In 30 years your $10,000 will grow to $174,494, or a multiple of
over 17 times. This sure looks more exciting, even though it is the same result. As you can see, inflation can dramatically distort nominal numbers for
long holding periods, and you are better off looking at inflation-adjusted
numbers.

WHY STOCKS SHOULD BE THE CORNERSTONE
OF YOUR PORTFOLIO

The numbers we just discussed make the historical case for investing in stocks
so well that I do not think any further discussions of the historical data are
necessary. But history is history. What assurance is there that the historical
trends will continue and stocks will provide comparable returns in the future?

We cannot get a money back guarantee, of course, but we can ask the
question, "What are we investing in when we invest in stocks?" The answer
is, when we buy stocks of good companies, we are becoming part owners of
these companies that are leaders in their businesses in the world and have access
to enormous resources, latest technology, outstanding talents, and worldwide
markets. Not all of them will do well all the time. But collectively they are the
backbone of our economy and our country. No one can say how well the stock
market is going to do in the future, but by all indications and logic, it is as
good a bet as we can make.

INVESTING IN OTHER ASSET CLASSES

There are, of course, other investment options besides the ones we have discussed. Lots of investors invest in them, and I am sure you will hear about
many of them over the years. In some years they will do better than U.S. stocks
and the safe investments and in other years they will do worse. But I believe
that over the long run investing some of your money in any of them will not
significantly increase your overall return; it will just add complications and
more worries to your life. So in the spirit of keeping things simple, I recom-

mend that you stay away from all of these alternatives. Nonetheless, here are a few observations on two of these investments, and I have addressed three more in some detail in Chapter 20.

REAL ESTATE

Almost all of us make a fairly large real estate investment in our homes. For most of us, it turns out to be the best investment we ever make. I think you should buy and live in the best house you can afford to. Because you can never measure the pleasure of that in dollars and cents, it is meaningless to try to evaluate your home as an investment. Just enjoy it and if you make money, that's all for the good. But beyond your home, be very careful about other real estate investments. It takes knowledge and often a lot of work to do well with them. You can invest in a diversified portfolio of real estate through Real Estate Investment Trusts (REITs), which trade like stocks. For a discussion on them, refer to Chapter 20.

Let me offer two cautionary notes. Many people, particularly older or retired people, buy time shares or get talked into buying them. Although in a few cases this may be a good money-saving strategy for vacations, no one should consider time shares to be real estate investments. They are not, even by a long shot. And do not get your real estate investment lessons from one of the hucksters of real estate courses on late-night TV. They are so misleading and the information they provide is so useless, and sometimes dangerous, that it is surprising no one can find a way to get them off the air.

GOLD AND OTHER PRECIOUS METALS, COLLECTIBLES, ETC.

Investors often believe or are told that they should invest in gold as a protection against inflation. But, at best, gold has a spotty record of past performance. Historically, gold provided excellent real returns during the high-inflation period of 1969 to 1981. But there were special circumstances involved, and we cannot conclude with any confidence that gold will be a good investment if high inflation returns. Gold has done poorly in all other periods. Based on historical data and the fact that gold is not used as a reserve against paper money any more, it is difficult to argue that gold will provide much of a protection against inflation in the future.

Other than for gold, it is difficult to find reliable long-term history on other precious metals and collectibles. Based on what information is available, none

of these have been good investments over the long run, especially on an inflation-adjusted basis. Many people do end up making good money on collectibles, but I think you should buy collectibles only out of passion for them
and not as investments. If you really like some kind of collectibles, chances
are you will learn enough to choose wisely and will even end up making money.
But somewhat like a home, if you are doing it for the pleasure of it, how can
you really calculate an actual or expected return, and why should you even
bother to do that? Just enjoy them.

♦ **THINGS TO REMEMBER** ♦

- ♦ Over the years even moderate inflation will significantly reduce the value
  of your savings and increase your retirement and other needs.

- ♦ Unexpected increases in inflation are one of the most serious threats you
  face as an investor.

- ♦ Do not base investment decisions on anyone's forecast of inflation rates.
  No one can reliably forecast them.

- ♦ Invest only in assets that will provide returns well protected against the
  threats of both expected and unexpected inflation.

- ♦ Invest the risky portion of your portfolio in stocks because historically
  stocks have provided the best real (inflation-adjusted) returns, and this
  benefit is likely to continue in the future.

- ♦ Invest the safe portion of your portfolio in one of the following essentially
  risk-free assets:
  - Money market funds
  - Bank CDs of less than 2 years maturity
  - Short-term bond funds of around 3 years average maturity
  - TIPS funds
  - Series I Savings Bonds

♦

CHAPTER 6

Buy the Reliable Average Car and Drive It Forever

♦

Rule #4: Invest in Stocks by Buying a Little Bit of Everything and Hold on Through All Ups and Downs

We always feel tempted to buy the exotic, great-looking car. There is nothing wrong with being tempted, but most of us have to resist the temptation because they are poor investments. Our best bet is to buy the reliable average car that will cost less to buy and run, last a long time, hold its value, and be easy to get repaired even if it breaks down in an out of the way small town. We will get much better return on such an investment.

On our drive to investment success, our best bet is also to drive the "reliable average car" that will give us the best value over time. And to realize its full value, we have to keep driving it for a very long time even if there are some problems along the way. As with cars, buying the latest red-hot stocks or funds and switching them frequently as trends change is expensive and wasteful. We will see that buying a little bit of everything, as this rule advises, is the investment equivalent of buying the reliable average car—it is not very exciting or glamorous, but it certainly is a great value.

Under Rule #3 we saw that stocks must be the cornerstone of your portfolio because they are the only investment that is likely to keep you significantly ahead of inflation over the years, and as an investor, that is one of your major goals.

We now have to answer two follow-up questions that logically come to mind: What is the best way to invest in stocks and what about the risks of investing in stocks. This Rule addresses those questions.

To answer the question of what is the best way to invest in stocks, you will have to make one of the most important decisions in your life: What kind of an investor do you want to be? That may sound a little mysterious right now, but as we will see, you have two distinct choices and the choice you make will have a huge impact on your financial future.

Unfortunately, at least on the surface, the wrong choice seems to make so much sense that most people make that choice first, waste a lot of money, and even suffer a lot before seeing the light and making the right choice. They learn by making their own mistakes and not from other people's mistakes. This, of course, makes them stronger believers in the right choice. But if you are willing to learn from other people's mistakes, as I will explain them to you, you will be able to bypass some trying experiences and make a lot more money.

Once you are convinced and make the right choice about what kind of an investor you want to be, we will discuss the risks of investing in stocks and how, by taking two small steps, you can significantly reduce those risks. And then we will discuss exactly how you should invest in stocks. Just to encourage you to keep moving ahead with enthusiasm, let me reveal right now that the investment approach we will arrive at is so simple that it will definitely make you feel good and comfortable; you will have no difficulty understanding why it is the right way to go, nor will you have any problem following it in practice. With that assurance, let's get started.

DECIDING WHAT KIND OF INVESTOR YOU ARE GOING TO BE AND WHY

There are two major approaches to investing: active investing and passive investing, and you have to decide whether you want to be an active or a passive investor. That's the big decision I mentioned. Here's what you need to know to make your decision.

ACTIVE AND PASSIVE INVESTING

Active investing is what most people envision when they think of investing. Active investors make investment decisions based on what they think is going to happen to particular stocks or to the market. They collect and analyze lots of data on companies, industries, the economy, past stock prices, and anything else they think may be relevant. And because things change or their minds change, active investors buy and sell stocks or get into or out of the market often.

Passive investing is just what it sounds like: not doing much. Passive investors believe that what individual stocks and the market will do in the future, either in the short term or in the long term, are not predictable. So they buy a large number of stocks at random and hold onto them for a very long time, essentially ignoring whatever happens to the companies or the stocks in the meantime. They believe that some stocks will do well this year, others will do well next year, and so forth, and things will average out for the good in the long run.

One of the passive investors' favorite things is to buy a little bit of all the stocks that are available. That is called buying the market because all those stocks together constitute "the market." As we will see a little later, this is actually quite easy to do through a special kind of mutual fund. Therefore, even though it is not strictly true, *passive investing* and *the market* are almost always used as interchangeable terms, and the long-term investment results of both tend to be the same.

There really aren't too many variations within passive investing. If you buy stocks of companies in the same industry and just hold onto them, that will be passive investing, too. But for reasons that will become obvious soon, passive investors do not do that. Also, passive investing does not have to apply to just stocks. If you buy any class of assets (e.g., bonds) and just hold onto them, that will be passive investing as well and many passive investors do that. The key to passive investing is that you take a hands-off attitude—you do not try to pick and choose based on any criterion, and you do not make changes every day, every month, or even every year.

There are lots of different active investing methods, which generally fall into one of two categories: stock picking and market timing.

The practitioners of stock picking believe that one should carefully pick and invest in the right stocks. They claim that the potential winners can be separated from the potential losers or also-rans through careful analysis of the companies' operations, markets, management, and so forth. And that's how they make their investment decisions. They invest in selected stocks and groups of stocks, and they keep changing their minds and buying and selling stocks either because things changed or often simply because they changed their minds.

The practitioners of market timing believe that the market is the big wave that determines whether all those little boats (stocks) will go up or down. So they devise methods to try to get into the market just before it starts a major up move and get out of the market before it is about to go down. Some investors combine stock picking with market timing; others are purists.

For reasons that will become clear in the next section, we do not need to go into any of the specific methods of stock picking or market timing. But just for your information, there are enough of them to satisfy any taste, belief, or fantasy.

(From here on, I will use mutual funds as examples in all our discussions because there are passively and actively managed mutual funds of every variety you can imagine. They are professionally managed, so it is reasonable to assume that their performance in each category should be as good as or even better than those of individual investors. Also, most people now invest through mutual funds, and data on mutual funds are most readily available.)

CLASSIFICATIONS OF STOCKS

Investors often classify stocks in various ways and then pick stocks from their favorite class to invest in. Most stock mutual funds invest in a particular class of stocks and are labeled by that class name. The two most popular stock classifications are small capitalization (cap for short) versus large cap stocks and value versus growth stocks. Investing in the different classes of stocks reflects different investment philosophies or beliefs.

Small Cap Versus Large Cap Stocks. This is the simplest and most objective classification and is made by size, that is, the market value (same as capitalization) of stocks or companies. Stocks are classified by size because companies of different sizes are believed to have different risk return characteristics. Smaller stocks are considered to be more risky with higher profit potential, whereas larger stocks are considered to be more stable and less risky with lower profit potential. Investors try to take advantage of those characteristics by investing in stocks of different sizes.

Investors generally classify stocks into large cap (over $5 billion), medium cap ($1 billion to $5 billion), small cap ($250 million to $1 billion), and micro-cap (under $250 million). Not everyone uses the same boundaries, and investors often change the boundaries depending on the market level. Otherwise too many companies will shift from one size class to another just because we moved from a bull market to a bear market. One way investors get around this problem is by calling the largest 5% of stocks large cap, the next 15% medium cap, and the rest small cap or using similar other methods instead of using specific dollar cut-offs.

Growth Stocks Versus Value Stocks. There is no objective broadly agreed upon method of classifying stocks into the value and growth categories. Companies whose earnings (or sometimes revenues) are expected to grow rapidly—generally 15% per year or higher—are considered to be growth companies. These stocks generally pay little or no dividends because they reinvest all of their earnings in new projects to generate future growth. These companies tend to have high price to earnings (P/E) and price to book (P/B) ratios. The most difficult aspects of growth stock investing is figuring out what the growth pattern of a company will be in the future and what price one should pay for that.

Value stocks are stocks that sell at low prices relative to their intrinsic or "true" values. Many value investors look at the selling price or liquidation price of a business to estimate its intrinsic value. Value stocks tend to have low P/E and P/B ratios. Some also have high dividend yields, primarily as a result of a sharp drop in the stocks' prices. Some other value stocks may pay no dividends at all because they had to eliminate them to cope with financial difficulties. A value investor's challenge is to estimate the right intrinsic value of a stock and how long it will be before other investors recognize that the company is undervalued and bid up its price.

Growth and value investors hold their beliefs with almost religious fervor. Over time neither seems to do better than the other. If you invest in a broad-based index fund or a large number of randomly selected stocks, you will be holding a mix of small cap, large cap, growth, value, and all other kinds of stocks and won't have to take sides.

THE BAD NEWS AND THE GOOD NEWS: ACTIVE INVESTING DOES NOT WORK

The bad news is that active investing does not work. What I mean is that there is no evidence that any active investor or any active investment method—whether of the stock picking or the market timing variety—can reliably outperform passive investing over the long run. To understand clearly, that means that despite all the time and effort that hundreds of thousands of professionals and millions of others put into it, no one can really pick winners and losers in the stock market with consistency. It also means that no one can reliably predict whether the market is going to go up or down.

There is overwhelming evidence and reason to believe that over the long run passively managed mutual funds are likely to beat actively managed mutual funds by at least 1% or 2% per year or even more because the investment costs of actively managed mutual funds are about 2% per year more than those for the passive mutual funds. In addition, all that buying and selling can rack up huge tax bills for you. And, finally, if no one can pick stock winners and losers, every time a fund buys or sells stocks, it may be buying losers rather than winners and selling winners rather than losers, both of which can cost a lot of money over the long run. As we have already seen, given the Magic of Compounding, if active investing earns even a few percentage points worse than passive investing per year, that will add up to an enormous difference in the final value of one's investment in the long run.

Why is comparing with passive investing the right way to decide if a particular active investment method works or not? Because passive investing is so little work and so inexpensive that unless an active investment method can outperform it convincingly and after accounting for costs, why should we bother with that active investment method? The evidence shows that no active investment method has been able to provide higher returns with any reliability over the years.

So what is the good news? The good news is, we do not have to spend time and effort pursuing any of the active investment methods. We do not have to read research reports on stocks. We do not have to follow stock recommendations by analysts. We do not have to analyze investment methods and past records of different mutual funds. And we do not have to figure out when to get into and out of the market. We can just put and keep putting our savings in passively managed mutual funds and relax for the next 20 or 30 years. What could be easier or better?

These are bold claims. But they are based on extensive scientific research in investing done by some of the most brilliant financial minds of our time over a period of more than 3 decades. A number of Nobel Prizes in Economics have been awarded for the theories and research work these claims are based on, and these theories have been independently verified and endorsed by hundreds of other researchers.

But this is not just a view from the ivory towers. The smartest investors—the people who are actually responsible for investing hundreds of billions of dollars for pensions funds, endowments, and foundations—have been increasingly switching to the investment methods I describe in this book because they have also come to recognize that this is the Only Proven Road to Investment Success.

Convincing yourself that active investing does not work and you should follow in the footsteps of the smartest investor I just mentioned is going to be crucial to your investment success. In view of their personal experiences as well as the technology stock debacle we have been through recently, many investors will have no problem accepting that active investing does not work and the so-called investment experts really have no special expertise. So, I am not going to discuss this issue here any more. However, if you are curious or need further convincing, please refer to Chapter 19, where I discuss in detail why active investing does not work and present some damaging evidence against it.

WHY YOU SHOULD NOT EVEN GIVE ACTIVE INVESTING A TRY

Despite what I have said, all of which many people know, they feel tempted to give active investing a try. I believe this is not a good idea at all—let me list some of the ways you will lose if you decide to give it a try:

- You will almost definitely make much less money in the long run compared with just going with passive investing right from the beginning.
- You will find yourself switching funds and investment methods frequently because you will keep getting disappointed. In taxable accounts, this may cost you a lot in taxes over the years. And a year with poor performance is a year lost that you can never get back.
- You will probably spend a lot more in transaction costs, which will make a big difference in the long run.
- You will waste a lot of time researching and chasing hot funds or stocks and ultimately you will pay a big psychological price because there is almost no chance that you will succeed (except maybe for a year or two here and there by chance).
- Chances are you will get totally discouraged in a few years, just give up, and end up with no systematic investment program for your retirement and other long-term needs.
- You will end up with a complex hodgepodge of dozens of funds and stocks that you won't be able to monitor or manage. You will be completely violating Rule #1: Keep things as simple as possible and then simplify some more.

Investing for the long run is hard enough. Do not make it harder for yourself by trying things that we know have not worked in the past and there is no reason to believe will work in the future.

THE RISK OF INVESTING IN STOCKS AND
HOW YOU CAN REDUCE IT

We have made a lot of progress. I hope you are now convinced that you must put a lot of your money in stocks and that you have to do so by being a passive investor from the very beginning because active investing is going to get you nowhere. But perhaps you are still worrying about the risk of investing in stocks. Even if you have tried to ignore anything that has to do with the stock market all your life, you probably have done so because you have heard again and again that investing in stocks is highly risky. And if you have paid any attention to the stock market, you have noticed yourself how the market keeps fluctuating wildly and can sometimes go down year after year. There is no question that the stock market is risky. Let's look at how risky it is and learn how you can reduce the risk in two simple ways.

But before we can even talk about risk, don't we have to define what risk is? There are few areas in finance where things get more controversial and discussions get more heated than in the area of defining and measuring risk. The discussions pretty quickly get down to the level of "How many Angels can dance on the head of a pin?" Fortunately, we can bypass all of that and you will do perfectly well thinking about the risk of investing just the way you have always intuitively thought about it: How much money could I lose? For our purposes, we can define the risk of investing in stocks—or any asset—as the possibility that we may lose some of our investment in it.

The two ways in which we can significantly reduce the risk of investing in stocks are by diversifying and by holding stocks for the long run. Let's now look into these.

REDUCING THE RISK OF INVESTING IN STOCKS
BY DIVERSIFYING

In investing, what matters to us is what happens to all of our assets together, that is, to our entire portfolio of assets; not what happens to the individual assets in it. Even if one of our assets does spectacularly well, if all the rest lose money, we are not going to be too happy.

As it turns out—and this is one of the most important insights of modern financial theory—we can reduce the risk of our portfolio significantly by making sure that it includes a large number of assets that are dissimilar. This is called diversification. This is what people mean when they say, "Do not put all your eggs in one basket" or "Spread out your risk." It is easy to understand why diversification reduces risk.

Suppose you have put all your savings into buying just one rental property. You are taking a lot of risk because if your tenant loses his job, you may not get your rent for a few months. If something happens to the neighborhood, your property may lose a lot of its value.

If you could instead spread the same money among a few rental properties in a few different neighborhoods, you would immediately reduce your risk. Why? Because if the value of one house goes down, maybe the value of one of the other ones in different neighborhoods will go up and the two may offset each other, at least to some extent. But if real estate prices go down in general, you are still vulnerable. But what if you could find and put some of your money in assets whose return goes up when real estate prices go down and vice versa? Won't that reduce your risk further?

I am sure you are starting to see how diversification can help. Financial theory provides two important insights into the diversification process:

1. The more dissimilar the assets in your portfolio, the more beneficial diversification is because then it will be less likely that all your assets will do poorly at the same time. If your assets are diverse enough, the losses in some will probably be offset by the gains in the others.

2. As you keep adding new assets to your portfolio, the benefits of diversification diminish. And beyond a certain point diversification reduces risk by very little, if at all. If the economy really goes into a recession, probably all assets will go down as well. So you cannot get rid of such major broad risks by diversifying. You can avoid those risks by investing only in safe assets, but then you will earn only modest returns.

In practice, diversification is generally done at two levels. First, we spread out our money among several asset classes (in our case this is going to include just stocks and safe investments). This is called asset allocation. Then, within each asset class we spread out the money over a fairly large number of individual assets. Under Rule #5 we will discuss how you should do your asset allocation, that is, split your money between stocks and safe assets, to take only the amount of risk you want to take. Here let us address why diversification is particularly important for your stock portfolio and how best to diversify your stock holdings.

For your stock portfolio, diversification is extremely important because individual stocks are very risky. Every year some individual stocks go down

40%, 50%, or even more, and if you own just a few stocks and get unlucky, you can experience heart-stopping losses. Remember, neither you nor anyone else knows which stocks are so good that they will never do that to you.

But if you buy a good number of randomly selected stocks (i.e., do not deliberately pick a large number of bank stocks, technology stocks, etc.), the risk of the portfolio will go down fast. Remember our example of buying rental properties. If you buy a diverse group of stocks, when something bad happens to a few of those companies, chances are that something good will happen to a few others, and your gains and losses will even out. Studies have shown that if the stocks in your portfolio are genuinely diverse, even as few as 50 stocks will probably get you all the benefits of diversification. To be safe, however, you should go for at least 100 stocks. You may even think, "Why stop at 100? Why not buy a little bit of even more stocks just to be sure, as long as it doesn't end up costing me a lot in broker's commissions and other costs?"

That is exactly what this Rule encourages you to do. It says, go buy a little bit of every stock, that is, just buy the market (or buy at least a little bit of a large number of stocks). Conveniently, there is a very cheap way of buying the market. So you just have to follow what the Rule says, and you will bypass the entire exercise of wondering which stocks to buy, saving thousands of hours of work and an enormous amount of headache and heartache over your lifetime. Just remember that even when you buy the market by buying a little bit of every stock, you will not eliminate all your risks—you will still lose money in times when the market goes down. We will address under Rule #5 the question of what, if anything, we can do about the risk that is still left.

REDUCING THE RISK OF INVESTING IN STOCKS BY HOLDING FOR THE LONG RUN

We still have not looked into exactly how risky stocks are. How much money can we lose by investing in stocks if things go against us? The only way we can address that question is by looking at history. In doing so, we can focus on the stock market as a whole because we have already seen that we should not be holding only a few stocks. Even if we decide to own a large number of stocks instead of the whole market, our portfolio will behave pretty much like the market as long as the stocks we hold are diverse.

Let us now look at how risky the stock market has been over the years by studying Figure 6.1 and Table 6.1. They both show essentially the same information. Figure 6.1 shows the maximum and minimum compound annual returns we would have earned if we had bought and held the market or a little

FIGURE 6.1

Maximum and Minimum Real Holding Period Returns (1946–2000)

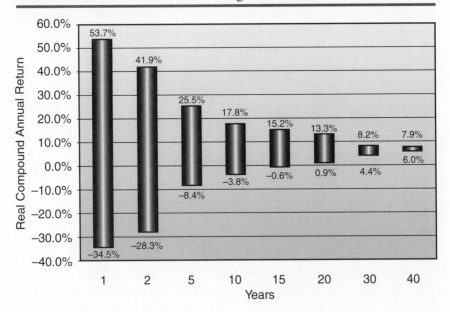

TABLE 6.1

Real Returns from Stocks for Different Holding Periods (1946–2000)

Years	Compound Annual Return			Total Return		
	Maximum	Minimum	Average	Maximum	Minimum	Average
1	53.7%	−34.5%	9.4%	53.7%	−34.5%	9.4%
2	41.9%	−28.3%	9.9%	101.3%	−48.6%	20.7%
5	25.5%	−8.4%	10.0%	211.2%	−35.5%	61.2%
10	17.8%	−3.8%	9.5%	414.7%	−31.9%	148.4%
15	15.2%	−0.6%	8.9%	738.6%	−8.0%	261.4%
20	13.3%	0.9%	7.9%	1123.0%	18.6%	357.8%
30	8.2%	4.4%	6.0%	966.2%	261.5%	480.5%
40	7.9%	6.0%	7.2%	2006.7%	942.4%	1489.2%

bit of a lot of stocks for 1 year, 2 years, and so on, up to 40 years. Table 6.1 shows the same data plus the average annual returns we would have earned as well as similar information for total returns for those holding periods. Note that the numbers shown are all real returns and are based on the period 1946 to 2000. Here are the interesting points:

- Over a 1-year period, the maximum loss stocks suffered was 34.5%. Very risky indeed.

- If we bought and held stocks for 2-year periods, the worst possible case by historical standards is a compound annual loss rate of 28.3%, which means that over a 2-year period we could have a maximum total loss of 48.6%. That's still in the heart-stopping range.

- As we hold stocks for longer and longer periods, the potential loss declines dramatically. For 10-year holding periods, the worst possible case is a compound annual loss rate of 3.8%, meaning that over the 10-year period we could have a total loss of 31.9%. That's a significant improvement over shorter holding periods in both annual rate and total terms. Nonetheless, a 31.9% total loss after holding onto one's investments for 10 years is decidedly less than exciting. If you find this worst case too discouraging, look at the best case for the same 10-year holding period: A real compound annual return rate of 17.8%, which translates to a total gain of 414.7%. That could be positively exhilarating.

- Finally, once you get past 17-year holding periods (not shown in the figure) even the minimum returns are positive, meaning none of the people who held stocks for 17 years or longer suffered a loss in real terms and, of course, many of them made very good money. By the time you get to 30-year periods the worst return was a positive return of 4.4% per year, or a total return of 261.5%.

Whether you want to invest any money in stocks or not will depend on how you feel about what the data in Table 6.1 and Figure 6.1 are telling you about the risks and rewards of investing in stocks. So take a few minutes to look through all the data carefully and make sure you fully understand them. Pay attention to both the average and maximum returns as well, keeping in mind that you are looking at real returns, to realize how big the potential rewards are.

As Figure 6.1 dramatically illustrates, if the future is going to be like the past, we can significantly reduce the risk of investing in stocks by holding them for longer and longer, which is why this Rule says that once you have bought a little bit of every stock, plan to hold them through all the ups and downs.

Warren Buffett, perhaps the greatest investor of our time, is fond of saying, "My favorite holding period is forever." You may find it comforting to know that almost everything I am saying in this book agrees with the advice he has offered to individual investors over the years.

Our intuitive understanding and the research results of the benefits of diversification, the historical evidence on how holding stocks for the long run helps, and Mr. Buffett's views all strongly support the passive investing approach. There is no point trying to pick potential winners and losers in the stock market, and there is no point trying to get into and out of the market based on one's intuition or someone else's advice. All we have to do, and the only thing wise to do, is what the Rule says to do: buy a little bit of everything and hold on through all ups and downs.

But before we move on, it is time for a little reality check again. By holding stocks for the long run or forever, you do not eliminate the risk of investing in stocks, but you significantly increase the chance of ending up making a good return over the years. However, you will still have to take some precautionary steps to be well prepared for important long-term needs such as retirement and to protect yourself against just plain old bad luck. After all, there is no law of nature that says that a stock market that goes down must come back up by a certain time. If you hit a long, bad patch and you are not properly protected, you may get hurt badly. We will address this issue under Rule #5.

THE IMPORTANCE OF IGNORING MARKET FLUCTUATIONS AND HOLDING ON FOREVER

If there is one thing predictable about the market, it is that it will continue going through ups and downs as it has for as long as it has existed. Some of these are just day-to-day or week-to-week fluctuations, but others are long term. For example, the market went down a lot in the early 1970s and then stayed depressed for the rest of the decade. It has been going up almost steadily since 1982, but there have been big ups and downs even during this steady rise. Because we keep hearing about the market's ups and downs every day or every week, it is difficult for us to keep a long-term perspective. The temptation is to react to the short term. However, no one can tell when the market is going to go down or up, so if you are going to get out anticipating a downturn, how do you know that the market will not start going up right after you sell? When they get out of the market, generally near a market bottom, most people think that they will get back in once the market starts going up. But they can never get back in on time because when the market starts going up no one can tell if it is now starting to go up for real or is it going to go down again.

The assumption behind those tempting returns for 20- or 30-year periods is that the investor held on through thick and thin. That is the only way you are going to earn those returns. It is going to be trying and painful in between. But unless you have the conviction and determination to stay in through all the market's ups and downs, you should not invest any significant amount of money in stocks because if you get lucky, you may make some money, but chances are you will lose a lot of money over the year getting in and out of the market. Let me repeat again: No expert is going to be able to get you into or out of the market at the right times. We have seen this again and again in history, most recently with technology stocks between 1998 and early 2001. You have to either decide to stay in or not get in at all. Anything else is a loser's game.

BUYING A LITTLE BIT OF EVERYTHING THROUGH INDEX MUTUAL FUNDS

Once you have convinced yourself that you want to passively invest in a little bit of all stocks (the market) or a large number of stocks, the work of investing in stocks comes down to almost no work at all because there is a special type of mutual fund that does exactly that for you at a very low cost. That's what we are going to talk about in this section, but we will start by first learning about mutual funds in general.

MUTUAL FUNDS

I am sure you have heard of mutual funds, and chances are you probably also have invested in—or own—some mutual funds. A mutual fund—most often just called a fund—takes in money from investors like you and me, combines the money into a pool, and then has that pool managed by professional money managers. The funds, of course, charge you certain fees and expenses for all of these services. In its prospectus, which is basically an information booklet that a mutual fund is required to give to every investor, each mutual fund spells out in broad terms what assets it will invest in and what investment philosophy or approach it will follow. With over 10,000 mutual funds available now, you can find a mutual fund that invests in exactly the assets you want to invest in and manages them following exactly the investment approach you think will work.

A Fund's Investment Approach

Just as there are two broad investment approaches—active and passive—so there are two broad groups of mutual funds—actively managed funds and passively managed funds. Most mutual funds are actively managed funds, but based on our discussions so far, you will be primarily interested in passively managed mutual funds and there are enough of them to meet all your needs. Within each of these two broad categories there are funds that invest in certain kinds of stocks, funds that invest in certain kinds of bonds, and so forth. Among actively managed funds, you can find many that follow any kind of investment approach you can imagine. So if there is a problem, it is not that there are not enough choices, it is that there are too many choices. Because you are going to be interested in passively managed funds of only a certain kind, your choice is going to be very easy.

How to Invest in a Fund

How do you invest in a mutual fund? It is simple. Once you decide which fund you want to invest in, you call up the fund company on its 800 number, get the prospectus for the fund and the forms for opening an account, fill out the forms, and send them back with your check. Most fund companies have good customer service, and if necessary, their customer representatives will walk you through the forms over the phone. In the future if you want to invest more money, you will just send in a check. If you want to take out part or all of your money, you only have to call up the fund and you will get a check in the mail. Most funds require a minimum initial investment for opening an account, which varies from a few hundred to a few thousand dollars, depending on the fund. There are also minimums for making additional contributions, which varies from as low as $50 to a few hundred dollars.

A Fund's Share Price

When you invest money in a mutual fund, what you actually buy is shares in the pool of money or assets the fund is managing and you become a part owner of that pool of money. You can buy (invest money) or sell (withdraw money) a mutual fund only once a day at the end of the day. The price you pay when you buy your shares or what you get when you sell your shares is called the net asset value (NAV) of the fund, which is the total value, at the end of that day, of all the assets the fund owns divided by the total number of shares of the fund. The NAV represents the value of the assets that belongs to each share. Depending on how well the managers are managing the money and what is going on with the market, the total value of the assets the fund owns, and therefore the fund's NAV, will vary from day to day. If the fund makes good investments, the value of the assets it owns will go up, so the fund's NAV or the value of your shares will go up. That's how you make money in the fund. You can check how your fund is doing by looking up its NAV or share price (same thing) in the newspaper or on the Internet a few hours after the markets close for the day.

Distributions from a Fund

Mutual funds are legally required to pay out to their shareholders any dividend or interest they earn on assets they own or any net profits they make by selling assets they had bought. The first one is called a dividend or interest distribution and the second is called capital gains distributions. Funds generally make their distributions a few times a year, but some funds make distributions once a month. To take advantage of the Magic of Compounding, you can have these distributions automatically reinvested by letting your fund company know just once. If you choose this option, the fund company will buy for you more shares of the same fund with your part of the distributions. (However, unless you are holding the fund in a tax-deferred account, you will still have to pay taxes on the distributions in the same year.)

A Fund's Investment Costs

Another important characteristic of mutual funds is the total costs of investing in the fund. The range is from a low of about 0.2% to a high of about 3% or more per year of your assets. And some funds may even charge you a sales commission—called load—at the time you buy or sell the fund. As we will see under Rule #6, because of the Magic of Compounding, high costs (anything above 0.5% per year) will significantly reduce the amount of money you make in a fund over the years. So you should almost never invest in a fund that charges you a load or has investment costs of more than 0.5% per year. Because you can find perfectly good funds of every kind that meet those criteria, there is absolutely no reason to waste any more of your money.

STOCK INDEX FUNDS

A stock index or stock average is the average price of a selected group of stocks that is used to track the performance of the group. You can say that the index tells us what is happening with the price of the stocks in the group as a whole. For example, the Dow Jones Industrial Average (affectionately called "the Dow"), the most widely watched stock index, is the average price of the stocks of 30 selected major companies. The Dow, the Standard & Poor's (S&P) 500 Index, and the Wilshire 5000 Total Market Index are all considered to be representative of the U.S. stock market and are used when we talk about what is happening with the market. There are many other indexes that people use to either look at the market in different ways or to look at specific parts of the market.

What is important from our point of view is that there is a group of funds, called index funds, that invest in exactly the same stocks that go into calculating their namesake popular indexes. So an index fund that mimics an index that is based on a large number of stocks (e.g., the S&P 500 Index) passively owns a little bit of a large number of stocks—exactly the kind of fund we would like to invest in. There are not all that many stock index funds (compared with the thousands of actively managed stock funds), and stock index funds differ from one another in only two major ways: the indexes they mimic, which determines which stocks they own, and their investment costs. Because the cost issue is readily handled, let me just say that for an index fund, you should be looking for annual costs of very close to 0.2% and never be willing to pay more than 0.5%.

You need to know about the following four types of stock index funds. Remember that in each case the fund and its namesake index mirror each other in every way so that if the index goes up by 1%, so will your fund. You can know what is going on with your fund just by following the index.

The S&P 500 Index Fund

This is the most common type of stock index fund. It owns a little bit of 500 large, leading U.S. companies (but not literally the 500 largest). Remember, by large we mean large in market value, that is, the price of the company's share multiplied by the number of shares the company has outstanding. Standard & Poor's decides exactly which companies will be included in that 500 and licenses to the different fund companies the right to use the name S&P 500 for funds that will invest in those 500 companies.

Another point to note is that the funds do not buy equal dollar amounts of each of the 500 stocks. Instead, they buy each stock in a dollar amount proportional to the company's market value. In other words, if Company A has twice the market value of Company B, then the fund will buy $2 worth of Company A's stock for every $1 of Company B's stock. This is called market-value weighting. So if an index fund is market-value weighted, then the bigger the market value of a company, the more money the fund invests in it, and the performance of the bigger companies will have lot more influence on how well the fund does. (The S&P 500 Index is constructed exactly the same way.)

Remember that no matter which fund company's S&P 500 Index fund you buy, they all own the same 500 stocks in the same proportion. In that respect they are identical. But there are differences in their costs, which you can readily check out, and also on some tax matters, which I will talk about later.

The Total Market Index Fund

The full name is the Wilshire 5000 Total Market Index Fund. It owns a little bit of every stock that is traded in the United States (about 8,000). So it owns the 500 stocks that a S&P 500 Stock Index fund owns and then another 7,500 or so smaller stocks. Because it is also a market-value weighted index, it ends up investing about 70% of its money in the 500 large stocks that are included in the S&P 500 Index and the other 30% in smaller stocks. So here also the largest companies will have the most influence on the performance of the fund, although over time the performances of a Total Market Index Fund and an S&P 500 Index fund will diverge.

Russell 1000 Index Fund

This fund is very similar to the other two except that it distributes its investments over the largest 1000 stocks. So it is also dominated by the large companies.

Russell 2000 Index Fund

It owns the 2000 stocks just below the largest 1000. So it owns stocks of only smaller companies (relatively speaking).

Some index funds that are exactly the same as the ones mentioned above do not use the same names. So if in doubt, ask the fund company for a full description and you will know for sure.

Because each of these types of index funds invests in a little bit of a large number of companies and are passively managed, buying any one of the first three will accomplish for us what this Rule recommends we do. I said the first three because the fourth, the Russell 2000 Index Fund, invests only in the smaller stocks and by itself does not provide the diversification we want. But there may be occasions when we would want to use it to complement some other investments.

Let me also point out that if for some reason you do not have access to any of these index funds, but have access to a different index fund (e.g., for your 401[k] plan at work), you should apply the following four criteria to decide whether it is suitable or not:

1. The fund should hold a large number of stocks, at least a few hundred, and include the largest stocks.
2. It should be broadly diversified and not hold any particular type of stocks (e.g., it should not be an index fund of technology stocks).
3. It should be market-value weighted.
4. It should meet the cost limits.

In addition, even though all index funds I know are passively managed, if you are being offered what looks like an index fund but does not call itself an index fund, make sure that it is passively managed.

One last bit of information. So far we have been talking about index funds that hold only U.S. stocks. There are also index funds that hold foreign stocks and index funds that hold bonds and other kinds of assets. There is also a variation on index funds called exchange traded funds (ETFs), that you may hear about. If you are interested, you can find out about them in Chapter 20.

THE LINK BETWEEN A STOCK INDEX FUND AND ITS NAMESAKE INDEX

Because you are going to invest a lot of your money in stock index funds for a long time, it will pay to understand them thoroughly. Let us look at index funds from a slightly different angle to get a deeper understanding of them.

A stock index is the average price of the stocks it comprises. But except in the case of the Dow, the average used is not the simple or familiar arithmetic average. It is a special kind of average, called a market-value weighted average, and the bigger the company, the more influence its stock price has on the average and the index. You can also view a stock index as the value of an imaginary portfolio of the stocks the index comprises where the money invested in each stock is proportional to the size or market value of the stocks. Because this is an imaginary portfolio, it has no investment cost.

A stock index fund is a real portfolio, which owns the same stocks in the same proportion as does the imaginary stock index portfolio, but it incurs a small investment cost. So the index and the index fund will always go up and down by almost exactly the same percentage, with the fund lagging slightly because of the investment costs. Also, all index funds from all fund companies based on the same index will move in lockstep except for any differences in their investment costs.

Sometimes investors get confused when they find that a given stock index has a value of, say, 900 (we do not put a $ in front of the value of an index), but one fund based on that index may have a price (NAV) of $30 and another fund based on the same index may have a price of $120. How can these prices be different? Is one better or cheaper than the other? Not at all. In all cases you are buying the same stocks in the same proportions, but you are buying them in different size packages. Because the index and all the funds will go up and down essentially by the same percentage, if you invest $1,000 in each, over any period of time you will make essentially the same amount of money in all of them. There may be only a small difference due to the difference in investments costs, if any.

Because almost all index funds are based on popular indexes whose values are disseminated throughout the day, if you own an index fund, you can easily keep track of what is happening to it throughout the day, although I strongly advise against getting into that habit. Also, for most indexes you can look up a total return for almost any period of time and it is the same as the return you will earn on its namesake index fund if you reinvest all your dividends.

ADVANTAGES OF INDEX FUNDS

By now you should be able to list all the advantages of investing in index funds. Let's see if we have the same list:

- The right index funds let you passively invest in a broadly diversified portfolio of stocks, exactly what overwhelming evidence shows you should be doing.

- If you pick the right index fund, your investment costs are going to be very low; through the Magic of Compounding, that will make a huge difference in the long run.

- Because you will pay very little taxes until you start selling your fund (if all goes right, only when you retire, and even then slowly over the years), index funds essentially allow you to defer taxes on any amount of money without any of the limitations of an individual retirement account (IRA) or 401(k)-type retirement accounts. (This is a topic we will discuss at great length under Rule #7.)

- With an index fund, you always know precisely how much of your money is being invested in what stock. There is no mystery about what stocks you are invested in.

- It is as little work as you can imagine.

Until fat-free, zero-calorie ice creams start tasting as good as regular ice creams, there will be nothing else as pleasurable and guilt free as investing in index funds. Savor them.

TWO OTHER WAYS TO BUY A LITTLE BIT OF EVERYTHING

Although using index funds to buy a little bit of everything is by far the preferred approach, there are two other approaches you may consider in special circumstances.

BUY A LARGE NUMBER OF INDIVIDUAL STOCKS

When we discussed diversification, I mentioned that if you own around 100 stocks (out of about 8,000 stocks that trade in the U.S. stock markets) and you choose them at random, that is, do not deliberately buy a large number of similar stocks (e.g., technology stocks), you will get almost all the benefits of diversification. So if you have at least $100,000 to invest and are willing to do some work, you can create and passively manage your own diversified portfolio of stocks. But I can think of only one situation in which there may be some advantage to doing so (see below), and there are several disadvantages and dangers. The primary danger is that unless you make almost a policy of not buying individual stocks, you will soon find yourself putting money into the latest hot stock or the stock you hear about at a party, and pretty soon your portfolio will not be well diversified any more and you will gravitate toward becoming an active investor.

The one situation where this approach may be worth considering is if you already own a number of stocks on which you have substantial profits and you will have to pay a lot of taxes if you sell them now. If you own a large number of such stocks and your portfolio is well diversified, then you probably should hold onto them. However, if your portfolio is not well diversified, you may want to put additional money into unrelated stocks or funds to diversify your portfolio further. My advice is that if you have any flexibility, sell the individual stocks and invest the proceeds in low-cost, broad-based index funds.

Incidentally, you should not invest any sizable portions of your money, in a retirement plan or otherwise, in the stock of your employer, even if you can buy it at a small discount and even if you think it is the greatest company in the history of civilization. It breaks the diversification rule big time because you are putting too many eggs in the same basket. Too much of your future already depends on how well the company does. By putting additional money into the company's stocks, especially if it is money you can invest in anything you want (as opposed to stocks or options the company grants you), you will unnecessarily and unwisely increase your risks. Even people at Microsoft, who thought nothing could ever go wrong with their great company, have regretted investing large parts of their savings in Microsoft stocks.

CREATE A WELL-DIVERSIFIED PORTFOLIO BY COMBINING A FEW COMPLEMENTARY FUNDS

It may occur to you, as it has to many investors, that if you invest in a few good complementary actively managed funds you can have the benefit of broad diversification and the benefits of active management simultaneously. (Complementary here means funds that hold different kinds of stocks and together cover the market.)

The problem with this idea is that it assumes there are some actively managed funds that are likely to outperform passive index funds and you can identify them. Based on the research results we have discussed, neither of those assumptions seems to be true and chances are, because of the high investment costs of actively managed funds, you will end up with poorer and not better returns. There is also the danger that soon you will be dissatisfied with the funds you have picked and become an active fund switcher. Nothing good can come out of that.

Nevertheless, there is one situation where you may be forced to adopt this strategy. If your employer does not offer a low-cost, broad-based index fund for investing your 401(k) and other retirement money, you may have to create your own well-diversified portfolio of stock funds by combining the stock funds you can choose from. Here is how you do that.

Almost all funds specialize in investing in only one specific kind or class of stocks, called the fund's style. You will have to do some research to find out the styles of the funds you have available in your employer's program and then pick funds with complementary investment styles to try to create a well-diversified portfolio for yourself. For example, you may combine a large cap and a small cap fund. Or you may combine a value and a growth fund. Your objective would be to come up with a combination that would spread out your investments as widely over the entire market as possible. You would also want to make sure that you put a lot more of your money in the bigger stocks than in the smaller stocks. Remember, the 500 stocks in the S&P 500 index, which are the large companies, represent about 70% of the total market value of all stocks. The other 7,500 or so stocks represent the remaining 30%. Do not bias your portfolio toward small stocks by putting equal amounts of money in large and small cap stock funds. To the extent you have an option, try to pick low-cost, low-turnover funds. And resist the temptation to load up on aggressive growth funds. Under certain market conditions these funds do very well, but in general they are very risky and have high costs and high turnovers.

CHOOSING AND BUYING THE RIGHT STOCK INDEX FUND

From around 8,000 stocks and 12,000 mutual funds, we have now narrowed down your choices for investing in stocks to just a few index funds. All you have to do is invest the risky or stock portion of your portfolio in one of these funds, choose reinvestment of dividend and capital gains distributions, periodically (preferably monthly) add a steady amount of saving to it, and you are done. Talk about simplifying things and following Rule #1!

We have a little more work to do to choose just the right index fund. Funds based on the same index are offered by several fund companies. They hold the same stocks, but there are some important differences among them, and because you would ideally hold the same fund with the same company (for tax reasons) for decades, you need to make absolutely sure that you have picked the right fund and fund company.

CHOOSING THE RIGHT INDEX TO GO WITH

This is the key choice. Because we want a well-diversified portfolio, the S&P 500, Russell 1000, and the Wilshire 5000 Total Market Index are your primary choices. As we saw earlier, all of these are market-value weighted. So in all cases you will be putting more money in the big companies. That's all for the good. The Total Market Index covers a larger universe, so some of your money goes into smaller stocks as well. Because of that, given a choice, I would go with a Total Market fund (that's the short name generally used for funds based on the Wilshire 5000 Total Market Index). It is unlikely that over the decades the S&P 500 and the Total Market will perform the same. But there is no way to tell which will do better. You will do fine with either. Availability and other considerations may determine your final choice.

There is also an index fund based on the Dow Industrials, and there is every reason to believe that it will do well over time. Nonetheless, because it is based on just 30 stocks, it is not very well diversified, and I would just as soon stay away from it.

Finally, if you can get only an S&P 500 index fund at work for your 401(k), and you want a broader exposure, you can invest some money in one of your other accounts (e.g., IRA) in a Russell 2000 Index fund, or in Vanguard's Extended Market fund, both of which invest in the smaller stocks. For every $100 you put in an S&P 500 fund, put about $40 in one of the small stock index funds. (I have provided specific fund recommendations in the Appendix.)

FUND COSTS

Never buy an index fund, or for that matter any fund, with a load. For an index fund look for total annual investment costs of around 0.2%, and definitely stay below 0.5%. To learn more about costs, go to Rule #6.

TAX CONSIDERATIONS

You will need to consider some tax issues before investing in a particular fund. Without some preliminary discussion of taxes it may be difficult to understand the tax issues, so I am not going to talk about them here. I just want to make you aware that you should look into those under Rule #7 before making your final choice.

THE FUND COMPANY

The crucial thing to remember here is that if you are buying the fund in a taxable account, you should plan to hold it not just for years, but decades. Otherwise you will lose a key tax advantage. Therefore, you will want to check out the fund company's reputation. Unfortunately, even good fund companies sometimes go through periods of poor management, and you cannot predict that decades in advance. Your best bet is to go with a company that has been around for some time and has an outstanding reputation in at least three areas: quality of management, commitment to customer service, and commitment to keeping expenses low. (See my specific recommendations in the Appendix.)

THROUGH WHOM DO YOU BUY YOUR FUNDS?

These days you can invest in your chosen funds through the fund company itself or through your broker. Buying funds through your broker has certain advantages, but it can get expensive, especially if you want to keep adding to your fund in small amounts on a monthly basis. So I recommend dealing directly with the fund company. (See Rule #6 for further discussion on this.)

CHOOSING AN INDEX FUND FOR RETIREMENT PLANS AT WORK

Most enlightened companies now offer at least one index fund as a choice under their 401(k) and other retirement plans. By now you know that is what I advise you to choose. There are a few little tricks to the situation. Many of the index funds offered through employers are not based on standard indexes like the S&P 500 because to put an S&P 500 label on a fund, the sponsor has to pay a licensing fee to the S&P company. To keep costs low (or earn a higher profit margin) the sponsors of the funds for retirement plans often do not want to pay that fee.

If you do not see a "name" index fund in your list of choices, ask the right people in the company if any of the choices is really something similar to an index fund under a different name. If the answer is yes, check it out. Remember, what you want is a passively managed, well-diversified (at least a few hundred stocks), low-cost fund. It does not have to be an index fund. Ask how the fund decides what stocks it will hold, if it is passively managed, and what its investment costs are. Even if it is not perfect, you may be stuck with it as the only choice. So go with it but keep asking the right people to add a better choice.

If there is nothing like a reasonably good passively managed, well-diversified, low-cost fund, you may have to make up your own following the approach I discussed.

♦ THINGS TO REMEMBER ♦

♦ There is overwhelming evidence that active investing does not work; that is, no expert and no investment method can outperform passive investing (the market) over the long run by consistently picking winning stocks (stock picking) or getting into and out of the market at the right times (market timing).

♦ You should avoid active investing and manage all your stock investments using passive investing, that is, by buying a little bit of all available stocks (the market) or a large number of stocks and holding them for the long term.

♦ You significantly reduce the risks of investing in stocks by diversifying broadly and holding for the long run.

♦ For the following reasons, you should not even experiment with active investing:
  • You will almost definitely make much less money in the long run.
  • You will incur higher tax and transaction costs.
  • You will waste a lot of time and end up paying a high psychological price for failing.
  • You will get discouraged and end up with no systematic investment program.
  • You will end up with a complex hodgepodge of funds and stocks.

♦ The best way to buy a little bit of all stocks is to invest in a low-cost broad-based index fund. Choose only no-load funds, and make sure that the fund's expense ratio is close to 0.2% and in no case above 0.5%.

♦ Holding onto your portfolio through the inevitable ups and downs of the market is going to be your biggest challenge. But to achieve investment success, you must learn to do that and be prepared to hold your portfolio for decades.

CHAPTER 7

◆

BE A SAFE, BUT NOT TIMID, DRIVER

◆

RULE #5: INVEST IN STOCKS THE MOST YOU CAN PRUDENTLY AFFORD

It goes without saying that you have to be a safe driver. That comes ahead of everything else. But that does not mean that you have to drive at 10 miles per hour or get off the road any time it even starts to drizzle. If you want to get to your destination on time and also enjoy the trip, you cannot be too timid; you have to take prudent risks.

It is the same with your investment trip. If you want to be so safe that you do not want to risk losing any money, you won't make much money on your trip. On the other hand, if you are reckless, you may get to the end of your trip in bad shape. This Rule tells you that you have to take risks, but you also have to be prudent about how much risk you take.

That brings us to an important question of investing: How much of your savings should you invest in stocks? This is called asset allocation—the distribution of your investments money among different types of assets. Most experts think, and I agree, that how you answer this question (i.e., make your asset allocation) will have a bigger impact on how much money you accumulate over time than will any stock-picking and market-timing skills.

The Rule says invest in stocks the maximum you can prudently afford. The Rule is worded to encourage you to think in terms of putting as much as possible and not as little as possible in stocks. There is good reason for this bias. Most people do not quite understand the risks of investing in stocks. So, out of fear they end up investing far too little in the stock market and miss out on making a lot of money. You should think in terms of investing the maximum and not the minimum in stocks, but as the Rule also says, you should invest only what you can prudently afford. We will devote most of this chapter discussing what "prudently afford" means and what is prudent for you.

In this chapter I will explain how you should do your asset allocation. It involves making some complex calculations, but you won't have to do any of that by hand. All you will have to do is understand the concepts and Guru, the computer program included with this book, will do all the number-crunching for you. It will be easy for you to learn how to use Guru not just to calculate the necessary numbers for your own situation but also to play "what if" games to see what might happen under different scenarios in the future. So do not get concerned here about where the numbers are coming from or will come from.

Let me admit up front that this chapter is somewhat long and complex. It is really the only complex chapter in the whole book, and, in my opinion, it is also unique and one of the most valuable. This chapter is one of the things that is special about this book. As I mentioned, how much of your money you should invest in stocks, how that should change over the years, and when and how you should sell your investments in stocks are some of the most important questions in investing. And yet, almost all books on investing skirt these issues, in part because they do not have good answers to offer and in part because they want to avoid the complexity. I also think that the "conventional wisdom" advice you get from financial planners in these matters is most often not very good.

So my suggestion is that you work through this chapter slowly if that's what it takes, and you will reap rich rewards for the rest of your life. Let me also mention that the chapter is long in part because I have explained everything in small steps and with lots of examples. You need to fully understand everything here, and if you just move along one step at a time following the examples, it won't be difficult at all.

To give you a head start let me give you a one-sentence summary of the conclusions we will reach at the end of this chapter: Put in stocks any money and all the money you won't need for the next 10 to 15 years and start selling stocks and putting the proceeds into safe investments at least 5 years in advance of when you will actually need the money to cover planned expenses. If you follow this general principle, you will automatically come very close to doing exactly what this Rule asks you to do.

We will start this chapter with a slight detour to understand how the aspect of investing we will cover here dovetails with financial planning and then move on to discussing the implications of the Rule.

THE ROLES OF FINANCIAL PLANNING AND INVESTMENT MANAGEMENT

Managing your financial affairs involves two distinct but complementary activities: financial planning and investment management. It is important to understand the roles of both and how they interact with each other.

Financial planning is the process of putting together a plan for all the financial aspects of your life, essentially for the rest of your life. It involves laying out, analyzing, and making decisions about everything in your life having to do with money directly and indirectly. During the financial planning process you raise questions such as how you are going to spend your money, what kinds of insurance and how much of each kind you need to buy, if you want to continue to live in a rented place or start saving to buy a house, how much you need to start saving for children's education and your retirement, and so forth. Then you combine all your answers to create your financial plan. In the end, a major outcome of your financial planning process is the trade-off you make between how much of your income you are going to spend on current expenses and how much you are going to save for future needs, some of which may be just a year or two away (e.g., buying a new car) while others, like retirement, may be decades away.

Investment management takes over once you have decided how much money you will save, what you will save the money for, and when you will need the money. Investment management is the process of deciding what assets you will invest the money in and then actually making and managing those investments.

The financial planning process and the investment management process have to work together because what kind of investment returns you can and do earn affect how much you have to save and invest for the future. On the other hand, you have to know how much savings you will have available for investing and when the money will be needed to decide how they should be split among safe and risky assets and to estimate what kind of investment returns you can expect to earn.

In this book, we deal primarily with investment management, but in this chapter we are also going to be addressing an area of financial planning that interacts most closely with investment management. Let me explain with an example. To plan for your retirement, you have to go through a detailed analysis of both your expected expenses and income during retirement. Once you estimate your income from Social Security, any defined benefit pension plan, and so forth, and subtract them from your expected expenses, you get an estimate of how much income you will have to provide from your savings and investments. That's where we pick up here and address the question of what should be your strategy for investing the money you save for retirement and how much you have to save to have the income from investments you will need to supplement your income from other sources. We will assume that you already have an estimate of how much income you will need; if you don't, somewhere along the line you will have to go through the financial planning process to come up with that estimate.

I will provide you with the tools for estimating how much you need to save for retirement, children's education, and so forth, which are really tools of financial planning. I am providing them here because they are not easily available anywhere else.

THE INVESTOR'S DILEMMA

Every now and then when the market goes through rough times, we all get disgusted and wonder, "Why am I putting myself through this?" The simple answer is, we all have to save and invest for our future needs. If we want to be perfectly secure, we can invest only in safe assets; but in that case we will have to save so much that for most of us that will mean significantly lowering our current standard of living. On the other hand, if we decide to invest a good part of our savings in stocks, and set our goals for savings based on the much higher return we expect stocks to earn over the long run, we will be saving much less now and have a higher standard of living now. But what if stocks fail us, and when we face those future needs we find that we have not accumulated enough money to meet them? By then we will have much less earning capacity to make up any shortfall. So what are we going to do?

Most of us cannot avoid this dilemma because the only way out of it is to have so much money already that we do not even face this dilemma. So we have to make compromises or trade-offs and in a way that's what this Rule and this chapter is all about: making the right trade-off.

LESSONS OF HISTORY ON RISKS OF STOCKS

Because stocks are going to be the only risky asset we will consider, and there are literally hundreds of myths and misunderstandings about the risks of investing in stocks, it will be best to start by looking closely at how the stock market has behaved over the years. There is always the argument that history is history, and who says the future is going to be like history. But since no one has shown any ability to see or show us the future, history is the best we have. Of course, we should not follow history blindly; rather, we should try to learn and use its lessons. We will try to derive some of those lessons here.

Let me remind you of three things about the historical data we will examine:

1. We will look at most of the historical data in real, that is, inflation-adjusted, terms.

2. We will focus on data from 1946 to the end of 2000, which is a long enough period.

3. We will look at historical results for the Standard & Poor's (S&P) 500 Index.

TWO BROAD PERSPECTIVES ON THE RISKS OF THE STOCK MARKET

Let's start off by getting a broad perspective on how stocks did in the past by looking at Figure 7.1. This figure shows how an investment of $1,000 in stocks at the beginning of 1946 would have grown over the years. That $1,000 would have grown to about $58,000—a 58-fold increase—over the period. Remember, we are looking at inflation-adjusted numbers. So your actual buying power would have multiplied 58-fold.

That 58-fold increase in real buying power is, of course, impressive. But let us look at the figure again from the perspective of risk. What is remarkable here is the almost relentless growth in the investment over the years. When observed from a long-term perspective, all those day-to-day, month-to-month or even year-to-year fluctuations in the stock market look like nothing more than small wiggles. You can see that you could have invested in the market almost at any time over the years and as long as you held on for the long run, you would have made good money. We all remember the market crash of October 1987. At that time everything looked so gloomy, it was hard to believe things would turn around ever again. And yet, look at the figure. Even if you bought into the market on the day before the largest stock market crash in the past 50 years, you would have made out just fine. In retrospect, it looks like nothing more than a small detour along the way.

We can't be sure about the future, but if the past is any indication, the risk looms so large in our minds simply because we pay so much attention to the short-term fluctuations in the market. If every one of us would put up this picture on the wall, direct our 401(k) and other monthly savings to automati-

FIGURE 7.1

Growth in Real Value of $1,000 Investment on 1/1/46

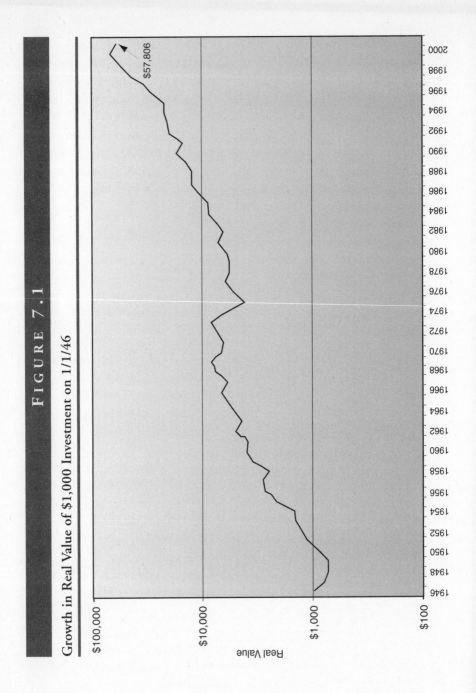

cally go into index funds, and look at our account statements once a year or may be even once every 2 or 3 years, in 15 or 20 years we would all look like investment geniuses. But, of course, in this information age we have no way of turning off the information blizzard.

Now let us look at another perspective, a short one. Figure 7.2 shows the annual return on stocks for every year since 1946. I don't know about you, but what I find most striking about this figure is how few down years there have been. Most investors worry constantly about the market going down, yet in the past 55 years there have been only 17 down years, and in only 9 of those years was the market down by more than 10%. Of course, if you were in the market in the 1970s, you vividly remember how bad everything felt for almost the entire decade, but if you were also in the market before and after, you made out just fine. (Remember that we are looking at real returns, which in down years make things look worse.)

The conclusion to be drawn from this figure is that if you are in the market for the long haul, a few bad years will come every now and then mixed in with all those good years, and we just have to take them in stride. The problem, of course, is that when the bad years come it feels like things will never turn around again. So we panic and sell out only to then miss out on all these good years that follow.

REDUCING THE RISK OF INVESTING IN STOCKS BY HOLDING FOR THE LONG RUN

By looking at Figures 7.1 and 7.2 it seems clear that the risk of investing in stocks goes down significantly if we hold for the long run. Under Rule #4 we saw how, as we hold stocks for longer and longer periods, our chances of losing money go down significantly and it becomes more and more likely that we will earn the long-term average real return of about 7%. (You may want to go back and take another look at Figure 6.1 and Table 6.1.)

Let us examine the same phenomenon in a different way. Take a look at Figure 7.3, which shows what the value of a $100 investment would have been for each 5-year holding period between 1946 and 2000. In this figure a $100 final value means you would have broken even in real buying power. The worst case for a 5-year period is a total loss of -35.5% (for 1973 to 1978), and that is pretty scary. But look how rare that was. In most 5-year holding periods you would have made good money. So even though 5 years is hardly a long holding period, your chances of losing money over even a 5-year period are not that great.

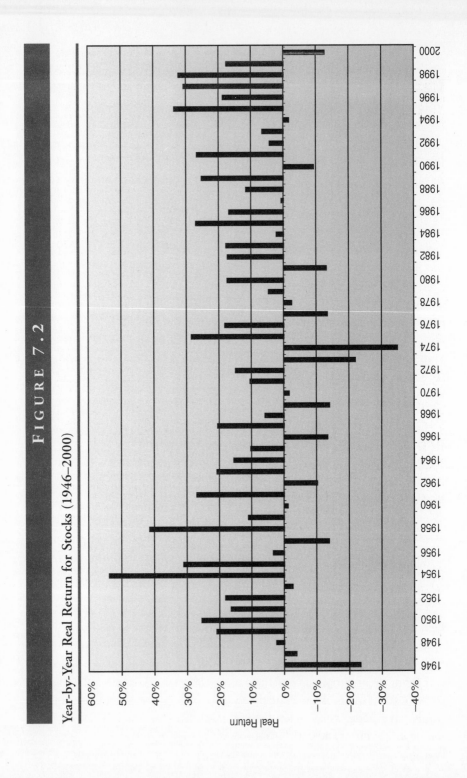

FIGURE 7.2

Year-by-Year Real Return for Stocks (1946–2000)

FIGURE 7.3

Real Final Values of $100 Investment Over 5 Years

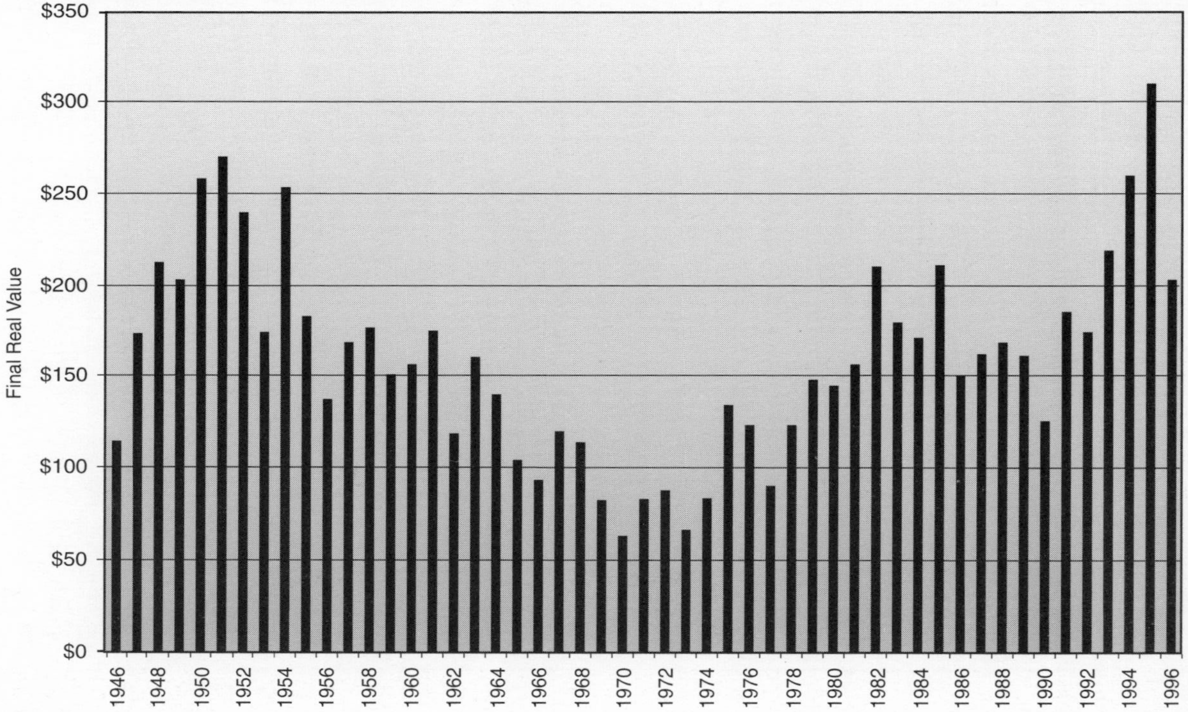

Finally, look at Figure 7.4, which is for 15-year holding periods. Here you almost never would have lost money and you would have made a lot of money almost no matter when you made your investment. (I have included nominal final values of the investment as well to emphasize again how important it is to look at real returns.)

The inevitable conclusion from all of these data is that unless the future turns out to be very different from the past—an issue we will address a little later—or you get very unlucky, if you hold stocks for the long run, you are almost certain to make very good money. To look at it another way, if you avoid investing in stocks because you are scared of the risks, you will be giving up a lot of money The key is to hold on for the long run and not worry about which way the market will go next and try to get in or out based on your own intuition or someone else's advice.

AN IMPORTANT IMPLICATION NOT TO BE MISSED

Although the data show that holding stocks for the long term is not that risky and that the longer you hold stocks the less risky it gets, the flip side of the coin is that holding onto stocks gets very risky as you get closer to the time when you will need the money.

Let's look at an example. Suppose that in 1985 you saved and wanted to invest $20,000 for something that will cost you $80,000 in the year 2000. It is something important and you will have to have the right amount of money at the right time for it. Since you believed that the stock market risks would be quite low for holding periods as long as 15 years and you had 15 years left until you would need the money, you decided to invest the money in stocks. You expected stocks to return an average of 10% per year and calculated that in 15 years the money would grow to about $83,000, more than sufficient to cover the expense. So you invested the money in a stock index fund.

It is now 1999, 14 years later. So far things have worked out exactly as you had hoped and the $10,000 has grown to about $76,000. (It is less than the $83,000 you had projected because you still have 1 year to go.) How risky is it to hold onto this position now? You may think that the risk is low because you have held this position for 14 years, and that's long term. But that would be wrong. Here is why.

We know that investing in stocks for the short term is very risky. The market can go down by 30% or more in a year, and whether and how far it will go down next year does not depend on what happened in the past or how long you have held your stock position. In the year 2000 the market may very well

Nominal and Real Final Values of $100 Investment Over 15 Years

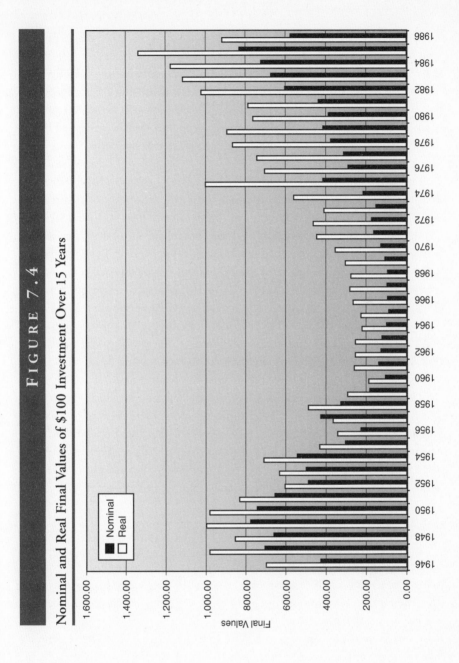

go down by 30%, and instead of ending up with the $83,000 you expected, you may end up with only about $53,000. So despite the fact that for the last 14 years the market behaved exactly as you expected, you may end up with much less money than you need because, as far as the market is concerned, in 1999 you are holding stocks for just 1 more year—it is now a very short-term investment. In fact, it has been a very short-term investment, and therefore, very risky, for quite a few years now. (In 1998 you had only 2 more years to go, and so forth.)

The key point here is that you may look at it as a long-term investment, but its risk depends on how many more years you are going to hold the position and not on how many years you have already held it. If in 1999 you thought you could hold onto the position for another 10 or 15 years, then it would be fine to hold onto the position. But if you have to have the money next year, then you should have started getting out of the market at least 5 years ago—maybe in small chunks—and put the money in safe investments. This also implies that if you really needed $80,000 in the year 2000, then saving and investing $20,000 in 1985 was not enough. You anticipated earning 10% per year for 15 years in the stock market, but in reality you were going to have to pull the money out of stocks much earlier (probably over a 5-year period) and put it in safe investments earning lower returns.

The lesson is that you cannot wait until the last moment, last year, or even last few years to pull out of the stock market money you need to cover some expense because as you get closer to the need, the risk goes up a lot. You have to anticipate such needs and pull out opportunistically well in advance and keep the money in safe investments. And you have to take this into consideration to decide how much you need to save for any future need.

WILL THE FUTURE BE LIKE THE PAST?

In retrospect it does not look like the stock market has been intolerably risky, especially in view of the huge returns one could have earned by simply putting the money in an index fund and practically going to sleep. But how can we be certain that the future is going to be like the past? We cannot be certain, but there is every reason to believe that the future should be very much like the past, not necessarily in month-to-month or even year-to-year detail, but overall and in the long run. Why? Because in the long run the future of the stock market—all the companies taken together—is very closely tied to our economy, and unless we believe that we will someday get into another great depression or worse, the stock market will continue to do well. But well means it will keep providing a reasonable return with ups and downs, not 20% or

30% returns year in and year out that many people unrealistically expect.

The tie to the underlying economy is the biggest guarantee we have for good future returns on stocks in general that we do not have for individual stocks. Even the outstanding companies of today can fall on bad times tomorrow—due to bad management, new technology coming into play, or hundreds of other reasons. That is why you cannot count on just buying and holding good companies. Too many good companies of the past have simply disappeared. But if you buy stocks of the 500 largest companies or a little bit of every stock, which is more than 8,000 companies, and hold for the long run, the bad performers will be balanced out by the good performers and the bad years will be balanced out by the good years and your investment will grow with the economy. The risk will never go away, and we will talk about protecting ourselves against it even further. But if you do not invest in stocks, especially when you are young, your risk of reaching retirement age with insufficient savings is much higher than the risk of your losing money in the stock market.

SAVING AND INVESTING FOR RETIREMENT

With a clear understanding of the risks and rewards of investing in stocks, it is now time to tackle one of the most important and challenging questions of investing: What should be your strategy for saving and investing for retirement?

We will build up the strategy by working through an example in small steps. Along the way you will understand how your strategy and the amount of money you will have to save every year for retirement will depend on how safe you want to be.

All the numbers I am using here are calculated using Guru—the software included with this book. Even before you read this section or after you have read part of it, you may want to plunge into Guru and experiment with it. It is an intuitive program, and using its extensive built-in help and explanations, you should be able to do some retirement planning right away. Even if you do not fully understand all the numbers, just trying out the program will make it much easier to understand this section and you will progress much faster.

ASSUMPTIONS FOR THE EXAMPLE

Let us assume you are now 35 years old and are just going to start saving for your retirement; you have nothing saved yet. You have decided you will retire at 65, and you want to plan for a life expectancy of 90 years.

You have also estimated that if you were to retire today, you would need to draw annually $60,000 (before taxes) from the money you are going to save and invest. In other words, when you are retired you would need to draw every year an amount of money that will have the buying power of $60,000 today. So we will have to inflate this amount for all future years. For example, if you assume that the rate of inflation will be a constant 3% for every year, then when you retire at 65, the first year you will actually draw about $146,000, the following year 3% more than that and so forth. I hope you are not surprised to see that by the time you get to 65, you will need $146,000 to match the buying power of today's $60,000. That's the effect of inflation and the Magic of Compounding. It is because inflation distorts numbers so much that you have to do any kind of long-term financial planning using a computer program such as Guru. We will keep calling that a $60,000 annual draw in retirement, always remembering that we are talking about the equivalent of the buying power of $60,000 today. (Let me remind you that this is the money you will draw from the savings we are discussing here. You also may have Social Security and other income.)

Let us assume that all your savings will be contributions to one or more tax-deferred accounts, such as a 401(k), so that you won't be paying any taxes on your returns over the years. (We will see under Rule #7 that you can save and invest an unlimited amount of money in such a way that you won't have to pay almost any taxes on the returns until you retire and start withdrawing from it.)

You do not know at this point how much you will have to contribute every year between now and the time you retire at 65 to provide for that $60,000 annual draw. That's the first thing you want to find out. But let us assume that to allow for inflation you will keep growing your contributions at the rate of inflation. In other words, if you contribute $100 this year, you will contribute $103 next year and so forth. You do not have to do that—you can assume you will contribute the same $100 every year. But with inflation, the value of $100 will deteriorate so much over the years that unless you contribute an inflating amount, you will have to start off with a very high contribution that you may not be able to afford in the early years.

You also have to make a few other assumptions. You have already assumed that the rate of inflation will be 3% per year. Let us assume you are going to earn 5% per year return on your safe investments and 10% per year on your stock investments. These are based on the 2% and 7% long-term real returns these investments have provided historically. But it will be easy to do the calculations using other assumptions to see how you will be affected if inflation turns out to be higher or stocks actually return less and so forth.

THE TOTALLY SAFE STRATEGY

Let us start off by asking how much you will have to save per year from now on if you want to be completely safe and invest all your money all the time in safe investments. The answer is, about $29,200 this year, 3% more next year and so forth. You can see right away that if you want to be totally safe and stay away completely from stocks or any other risky investments, you will have to save so much that it will most likely lower your current standard of living considerably. There is a concrete example of the investor's dilemma.

THE AGGRESSIVE STRATEGY

Let us say that after looking at all the historical data on the stock market you have come to the conclusion that the long-term risk of investing in stocks is quite low and you are going to put all your annual contributions into a stock index fund. Once you retire, you will sell only enough of the fund every year to draw the equivalent of $60,000 you will need to live on; the rest of your money will always remain invested in the stock fund.

I will call it an aggressive strategy, but I do not think it is by any means a reckless strategy. There is a good chance that you will make out very well with this strategy, especially if over the years you save somewhat more than the minimum necessary to just provide for that annual draw.

How much would you have to save and invest per year if you follow this strategy? About $7,800 this year, 3% more next year, and so forth. (If you want to contribute the same number of dollars every year instead of an inflating amount, you will have to contribute about $10,200 every year.) Compare these numbers to the $29,200 you will have to save in the first year if you were going to invest all the money in safe investments. That's how much difference the assumed 5% return on safe investments and 10% return on stocks makes.

What is the main vulnerability of this approach? Suppose between now and your retirement stocks do just fine and on average provide a return of 10%, but just after you retire it goes into a prolonged bear market. Then if you continue drawing that equivalent of $60,000 per year by selling stocks every year, as you will have to, you will run out of money long before you reach 90. So if you really live until you are 90 and the market does not turn back up sharply, you may be in serious financial trouble. Since you will have 25 years in retirement, chances are that even if there are a few bad years early on or along the way, over a 25-year span you will do just fine. But there is no question that you are taking some risk and being quite aggressive.

I want to make two important points here:

- First, you should always keep in mind what I call the "you only live once" factor. If a really bad thing has only a 10% chance of happening and it happens to you once, it may not matter that it won't happen the other 90% of the time. What do I mean? What I mean is that there may be only a 10% chance of the market doing very poorly over a long stretch of time like 10 or 15 years. But if you get unlucky and that happens to you during the first 10 or 15 years of your retirement, and you are following this aggressive approach, you will be in serious financial trouble. It won't be any consolation that it happens only rarely. So in situations where you have no other way out—as in retirement when you have almost no other way of replenishing your savings—you cannot afford to take what looks like a small chance. A financial loss that you can handle when you are 35 may be a disaster in retirement. You have to keep that in mind when planning for retirement.

- Second, when you are withdrawing money from a fixed amount of savings and the rest remains invested in a risky investment, as you are doing in this case, it matters a lot if the bad times come first. What do I mean? Suppose over your planned 25 years of retirement, the market does return an average of 10% per year. But the first 10 years turn out to be horrible and the market makes it all up in the next 15. Because you will keep selling stocks and drawing money out during those horrible first 10 years, by the time the market turns around and does spectacularly well, you will have much less money invested in stocks to benefit from the higher returns. The net effect will be that you will run out of money long before the 25 years, even if on average the market earns exactly the 10% over the 25 years, as you had hoped. Another way of understanding this serious problem is to recognize that if the market goes through a bad bear market during the first several years of your retirement, by selling and drawing out money every year you will be selling a lot of your investment at market lows. You should always try to avoid doing that.

The two points I just made are so important in understanding and dealing with the risks of the stock market that if you understand them thoroughly, you will be able to protect yourself very well over the years. If you do not fully understand them, please go back and read and think through them again before moving on.

THE MODERATE-RISK STRATEGY

Now that you understand the risks of the aggressive approach, you probably have already figured out how you can lower the risk. You can invest all your contributions in stock index funds during the years leading up to your retirement, then as soon as you retire you can sell enough stocks to raise sufficient money to last you for the next 10 years or so. You will, of course, put the money in safe investments at that point, so they will still keep earning some return. After that, in the years the stock market is unusually low, you won't sell any stocks and will draw your $60,000 from the safe investments. In the years the stock market is at normal or high levels, you will sell enough stocks to cover the $60,000 draw for the year. And in years the stock market is euphoric, you will sell even more stocks, not only to cover the year's $60,000 draw but to replenish or build up your safe investments a little bit to be prepared for some bad times. Under this strategy, you will always have about 10 years' worth of your needs safely tucked away in safe investments so you will be able to ride out a number of bad market years without having to sell stocks under bad market conditions.

I call that 10-year period your security horizon (SH) because you are completely securing your money needs for those years. Depending on how safe you want to be, you can pick a higher or lower SH and use this as one of the tools to control the amount of risk you take in the stock market.

Even before we look at any numbers, we know that to follow this strategy you will have to save more over the years because for part of the period some of your money will be invested in safe investments earning lower returns. Also, the longer an SH you pick, the more you will have to save. So you are paying to buy safety or making risk-return trade-offs. But the good thing about doing it this way is you know exactly what price you are paying and how much more safety you are buying.

Now for the numbers. If you pick a Security Horizon of 10 years, under this strategy you will have to start off by saving about $11,000 this year and then 3% more per year. Compare that to the $7,800 you had to save in the first year under the aggressive strategy. There is no question that over the years you will have to save quite a bit more to buy this additional safety.

What is the primary vulnerability of this strategy? Well, what happens if the market is doing poorly right around the year of your retirement when you were planning to sell a big chunk of your stocks to cover yourself for your Security Horizon? If you are not able to sell a good chunk of your investments at a good price early on and the market continues to do poorly for the first 5 or 10 years of your retirement, you may again face the possibility of running out of money in your later retirement years.

The problem here is that you waited until the last moment to sell stocks when some of your holdings became very short term and highly risky because you were going to need them in the next few years. What to do? I am sure you already can think of at least one solution.

THE CONSERVATIVE STRATEGY

What you can do to further reduce your risk is to recognize that by the time you are 65, you will want in safe investments enough money to cover you for your SH and start selling the necessary amount of stock 10 to 15 years ahead of retirement. With that kind of a head start you can sell opportunistically, i.e., sell some stocks in years the market is high, skip a year or two if the market is down, and so forth. The objective would be to have the necessary amount of money, that is, the money you will need to cover yourself for SH years, in safe investments by the time you reach 65. Then you will follow the same approach as you did under the moderate-risk strategy. The number of years ahead of retirement you want to start selling is your Anticipation Horizon (AH).

Remember that your goal is to have in safe investments enough money to cover you for your SH by the time you are 65. So if your AH is 10 years, at the age of 55 (or around there) you will sell or start selling enough stocks to raise the necessary money. But at that point you will still have 10 more years of contributions to make. So you will direct all those future contributions into safe investments and raise by selling stocks only the additional amount of money you will need to reach your goal for the retirement year we just discussed. This will make your stock selling less vulnerable to the ups and downs of the market because you will actually be selling fewer stocks.

Again, this will require somewhat higher contributions over the years because more of your money will be in safe investments for longer periods of time. But you are buying additional safety and you can control the amount of additional safety you buy by choosing a longer or shorter AH.

What is it going to cost you? With a 10-year AH and 10-year SH, you will now need to save about $13,600 this year and an inflating amount every year in the future until you are 65. Compare that with the $11,000 for the moderate-risk strategy and $7,800 for the aggressive strategy. You are paying more and more for buying additional safety, but you know exactly what additional safety you are buying.

Incidentally, I am sure you can see the relationships among the three strategies. The moderate-risk strategy is really the conservative strategy, with an AH of zero years, and the aggressive strategy is the same as the conservative strategy, with both SH and AH of zero years.

I went through the three strategies just to build up everything one step at a time. But now that you understand what is going on, you can see that conceptually there is only one strategy, and you take a conservative, moderate, or aggressive stance by choosing a different SH and AH. The beauty of this approach is that you can choose the SH and AH to tailor your plan to the level of risk you want to take. I believe 10 years is a good number for both SH and AH, and you can experiment with them starting with the 10-year figure to see how much more safety you can afford to buy or want to buy.

THE RECOMMENDED STRATEGY

Looking at that heading you may be thinking, "You mean there is more? Haven't we had enough?" There is just a little bit more that will give you even more flexibility to control the risk you take and the price you pay for it.

What if you look at that $13,600 first year contribution number for the conservative strategy and think that it is too much for you to handle, but you also do not like the risks of the aggressive- or moderate-risk strategies. What can you do? One thing you can do is to take another look at your annual draw goal of $60,000 and possibly decide that $40,000 of it is the money that will sustain you at the minimum standard of living you are willing to accept. The other $20,000 is something you want to have, but if part of it is not there because you got very unlucky with the market, you will be all right. In other words, you want to be conservative with the $40,000 portion—let us call it your minimum annual draw—and are willing to take more risk with the other $20,000—let us call it your additional annual draw. Once you have broken down your total draw into these two pieces, you can also split up the necessary contribution into two pieces and follow a different investment strategy for each.

Obviously this will cost you less than trying to be conservative or safe with all of the money. Here I have split up the total draw into minimum and additional draws in a 2:1 ratio. But you can pick whatever ratio you want. You should actually come up with the right breakdown by closely analyzing what costs are going to be covered by the $60,000 and what part of it you consider to be essential and what part may be optional.

Let us look at what difference this makes and see how things change if we assume a different real return on stocks over the years instead of just the 7% we have been assuming so far. The numbers for the various cases are shown in Table 7.1. As you can see, the contributions needed go up a lot as you assume lower returns for stocks, and if you want to invest all of your savings conservatively, the savings requirement may get too high for you. Also notice that the first year contribution needed for the totally safe strategy (keeping all your savings in safe investments at all times) is $29,200 and will keep escalating every year. That's where the recommended strategy with a properly broken down minimum annual draw and additional annual draw can help. Under the recommended strategy your annual savings requirement is almost one third of what would be required under a totally safe strategy. And yet, I do not think it entails all that much risk. Also, you can be even more conservative (by assuming an SH and AH longer than 10 years) with the money you absolutely want to be there and then be aggressive with the rest of your savings by putting it all in stocks.

Again, the recommended strategy really encompasses all the previous strategies, and once you understand and appreciate it, you don't have to go back to the others any more. You get all the others by suitably choosing the SH, the AH, and the breakdown between the minimum annual draw and the additional annual draw. And you pick them to match the risk you want to take.

TABLE 7.1

First-Year Savings Required to Provide for a $60,000 Annual Draw in Retirement

| Strategy | Assumed Annual Real Return on Stocks | | |
	7%	6%	5%
Aggressive	$7,800	$10,200	$13,200
Moderate (SH = 10)	$11,000	$13,500	$16,500
Conservative (SH = 10, AH = 10)	$13,600	$15,800	$18,300
Recommended			
For minimum draw of $40,000	$9,100	$10,500	$12,200
For additional draw of $20,000	$2,600	$3,400	$4,400
Total	$11,700	$13,900	$16,600
Totally safe	$29,300	$29,300	$29,300

AN EXAMPLE OF THE RECOMMENDED STRATEGY FOR SAVING AND INVESTING FOR RETIREMENT

Let us now review with the help of Table 7.2 how the recommended strategy will work in practice and the stages of saving, investing, and withdrawing money you will go through over the years. Once you enter into Guru all your assumptions, including how much money you already have saved up, it calculates how much money you will have to save and invest annually until you retire to have enough money available during retirement to make your target minimum and additional draws every year. It then provides you with the year-by-year detail shown in Table 7.2 for the minimum draw part and a separate table that we will examine later for the additional draw part. (In line with the example we have been using, this table covers the numbers for the $40,000 per year minimum draw assuming an AH and SH of 10 years. Guru assumes that you will make all contributions and withdrawals on the first day of the year, and all the numbers in the table are as of that date.)

As shown in the first row of Table 7.2, which is for today (your 36th birthday since you are 35), Annual Contribution column, you will have to make

TABLE 7.2

Detail Plan for Saving, Investing and Withdrawing Money for a $40,000 Minimum Annual Draw Managed with AH = 10 and SH = 10

Year	Birthday Number	Investment Balances Stock	Safe	Annual Contribution	Annual Withdrawal	Buy/(Sell) Stocks	Safe
Today	36	$0	$0	$9,068	$0	$9,068	$0
1	37	$9,975	$0	$9,340	$0	$9,340	$0
2	38	$21,246	$0	$9,620	$0	$9,620	$0
3	39	$33,953	$0	$9,909	$0	$9,909	$0
4	40	$48,248	$0	$10,206	$0	$10,206	$0
5	41	$64,300	$0	$10,512	$0	$10,512	$0
6	42	$82,293	$0	$10,828	$0	$10,828	$0
7	43	$102,433	$0	$11,152	$0	$11,152	$0
8	44	$124,944	$0	$11,487	$0	$11,487	$0
9	45	$150,074	$0	$11,832	$0	$11,832	$0
10	46	$178,097	$0	$12,187	$0	$12,187	$0
11	47	$209,312	$0	$12,552	$0	$12,552	$0
12	48	$244,050	$0	$12,929	$0	$12,929	$0

(continued)

TABLE 7.2 (continued)

Year	Birthday Number	Investment Balances Stock	Safe	Annual Contribution	Annual Withdrawal	Buy/(Sell) Stocks	Safe
13	49	$282,677	$0	$13,317	$0	$13,317	$0
14	50	$325,593	$0	$13,716	$0	$13,716	$0
15	51	$373,240	$0	$14,128	$0	$14,128	$0
16	52	$426,104	$0	$14,551	$0	$14,551	$0
17	53	$484,722	$0	$14,988	$0	$14,988	$0
18	54	$549,680	$0	$15,438	$0	$15,438	$0
19	55	$621,630	$0	$15,901	$0	$15,901	$0
20	56	$701,284	$0	$16,378	$0	($397,042)	$413,420
21	57	$334,666	$434,091	$16,869	$0	$0	$16,869
22	58	$368,133	$473,508	$17,375	$0	$0	$17,375
23	59	$404,946	$515,427	$17,896	$0	$0	$17,896
24	60	$445,441	$559,990	$18,433	$0	$0	$18,433
25	61	$489,985	$607,345	$18,986	$0	$0	$18,986
26	62	$538,983	$657,647	$19,556	$0	$0	$19,556
27	63	$592,881	$711,064	$20,143	$0	$0	$20,143
28	64	$652,169	$767,767	$20,747	$0	$0	$20,747
29	65	$717,386	$827,939	$21,369	$0	$0	$21,369
30	66	$789,125	$891,774	$0	$97,090	($80,104)	($16,986)
31	67	$779,923	$918,527	$0	$100,003	($82,507)	($17,496)
32	68	$767,157	$946,083	$0	$103,003	($84,983)	($18,021)
33	69	$750,392	$974,465	$0	$106,093	($87,532)	($18,561)
34	70	$729,145	$1,003,699	$0	$109,276	($90,158)	($19,118)
35	71	$702,886	$1,033,810	$0	$112,554	($92,863)	($19,692)
36	72	$671,025	$1,064,825	$0	$115,931	($95,649)	($20,282)
37	73	$632,914	$1,096,769	$0	$119,409	($98,518)	($20,891)
38	74	$587,836	$1,129,672	$0	$122,991	($101,474)	($21,518)
39	75	$534,998	$1,163,563	$0	$126,681	($104,518)	($22,163)
40	76	$473,528	$1,198,470	$0	$130,482	($107,654)	($22,828)
41	77	$402,462	$1,234,424	$0	$134,396	($110,883)	($23,513)
42	78	$320,737	$1,271,456	$0	$138,428	($114,210)	($24,218)
43	79	$227,180	$1,309,600	$0	$142,581	($117,636)	($24,945)
44	80	$120,499	$1,348,888	$0	$146,858	($120,499)	($26,360)
45	81	$0	$1,388,655	$0	$151,264	$0	($151,264)
46	82	$0	$1,299,261	$0	$155,802	$0	($155,802)
47	83	$0	$1,200,632	$0	$160,476	$0	($160,476)
48	84	$0	$1,092,164	$0	$165,290	$0	($165,290)
49	85	$0	$973,217	$0	$170,249	$0	($170,249)
50	86	$0	$843,117	$0	$175,356	$0	($175,356)
51	87	$0	$701,149	$0	$180,617	$0	($180,617)
52	88	$0	$546,559	$0	$186,035	$0	($186,035)
53	89	$0	$378,549	$0	$191,616	$0	($191,616)
54	90	$0	$196,279	$0	$197,365	$0	($196,279)

a contribution of $9,068 in the first year. In the subsequent years the contribution will keep growing at the 3% inflation rate, as assumed, and you will make your last contribution of $21,369 on your 65th birthday. If you already had some money saved up, Guru would have shown it in the columns for Investment Balances in the first row, broken down to show how much of that should be in stocks and how much in safe investments. The Buy/(Sell) columns show how much stock and safe investments it recommends buying or selling every year. In the first year, the $9,068 in the Stocks column under Buy/(Sell) means you are supposed to buy only stocks with all of the year's contributions. A positive number in these columns means you will buy and a negative number means you will sell. Whatever stocks or safe investment you buy or sell is then added to their existing balances and you earn return on those balances at the specified rates during the year. That's how you start the second year with a balance of $9,975 in the Investment Balances–Stock column. The Annual Withdrawal column shows the withdrawals once they start upon retirement.

With this understanding of what the numbers in the table mean and how the calculations work, we can now look at the stages you will go through over the years.

Stage 1: More than AH Years from Retirement

During this period all your annual contributions will go into a stocks index fund and earn return at the assumed 10% annual return for stocks. Everything will go on the same way until your 55th birthday. At that point the value of your stock portfolio will be $621,630 and you will add to it your contribution for that year of $15,901.

Stage 2: Within AH Years of Retirement

Since you have picked an AH of 10 years, on your 56th birthday you will be within AH years of retirement. Guru has looked ahead and calculated that at the time you retire on your 66th birthday, you will need to have $891,774 in safe investments to cover your necessary withdrawals for the first 10 years of your retirement (see the line for 66th birthday in Table 7.2). It also knows what contributions you are going to make between your 56th and 65th birthdays.

Taking all of this into consideration, it is recommending that on your 56th birthday you sell $397,042 of stocks and put that money along with that year's new contribution of $16,378 (a total of $413,420) into safe investments. From here on, until retirement, all your new contributions will go into safe investments because the Buy/(Sell) numbers for stocks are all zeros. As usual, both your stock and safe portfolios will continue to earn appropriate returns. Note that in actual life you may not sell all of the $397,042 of stocks on your 56th birthday. Depending on market conditions, you may sell all of it then or you may spread it out over the next few years and sell opportunistically. That is why you start to think about selling AH years ahead of retirement instead of waiting until the last moment. The key is to make sure that you will have that $891,774 in safe investment by your 66th birthday when you retire.

Stage 3: In Retirement

When you retire on your 66th birthday, you will have $789,125 in your stock portfolio and $891,774 in your safe portfolio. Because Guru picked your annual contribution by doing a complete calculation through your life expectancy of 90, these amounts together will be sufficient to cover your growing withdrawals for your 25 years of retirement and the safe money portion will be sufficient to cover you for the first 10 (SH) years of that period. However, if you look closely, you will notice that to make your $97,090 withdrawal for the year, Guru is recommending that you sell $80,104 of stocks and $16,986 of safe investments. Why is it asking you to mostly sell stocks?

Remember, our strategy is that if the stock market conditions are normal, you will cover your annual needs by selling stocks, but in years when the stock market conditions are unfavorable, you will withdraw money from safe investments and not sell stocks. Because this is a projection for 30 years into the future, Guru has no way of knowing what market conditions will be on your 66th birthday onward. So it is projecting that you will keep selling mostly or all stocks to cover your annual withdrawals until you run out of stocks by your 80th birthday. At that point you will have $1,348,888 in safe investments. From there on you will sell safe investments, and when you make your last withdrawal on your 90th birthday, all the money will be used up. It is important to note that from the time you retire to your 80th birthday Guru is making sure that all the time you will keep in safe investments enough money to cover your needs for your SH (10 years) so that if the market starts going down you will be able to cut back on selling stocks and live on withdrawals from safe investments. This is key to the recommended strategy.

As you can see, coming up with exactly how much you have to save every year, how you should invest it, what you should sell first, and so forth involve complex calculations, but you do not have to worry about any of that. Once you enter your assumptions, Guru gives you a complete plan for the future. Of course, the future will not work out exactly according to this plan, and that is why you need to understand the strategy so that you can make the necessary adjustments.

You know that there are two major areas where you will have to use your judgments. First, you may not sell all that much stock (in this case close to $400,000 of stocks) at once on your 56th birthday. At that time you will have to decide how you want to spread it out. Second, once you are retired, you will have to decide in which years you will sell stocks and in which years you won't. As shown here, when you start your saving and investment plan, you will use Guru to decide how much you have to save every year under different assumptions and choose the plan that you can live with. Then you will follow its instructions over the years and use it to track your progress.

Let us now look at how the $20,000 additional draw part works. This is shown in Table 7.3. In this case over the years you will invest all your annual contributions in stocks, starting with $2,608 today, your 36th birthday, all the way through your last contribution on your 65th birthday. Then every year in retirement you will sell enough stocks to cover the equivalent of $20,000 additional withdrawal. As before, the table shows all the detail you need. One thing you have to remember about this additional draw portion is that how much you will actually draw per year in retirement will depend, to some extent, on market conditions. In years when market conditions are not good, you may sell and withdraw less, and in years when market conditions are great, you may sell and withdraw more. The one thing you won't do is use any money from your investments for the minimum draw portion to cover the additional draw. That money is sacrosanct and has to be left alone to cover the minimum draw only.

I hope by now you find that this is fairly simple, especially with the help of Guru. If you have never looked into retirement planning before, you may not fully appreciate how powerful and simple this approach is. As long as you understand the concepts and strategy fully and estimate your minimum and additional draw requirements properly, you probably won't need any professional help to do this part of your planning and investing.

IMPLEMENTING THE STRATEGY STARTING AT DIFFERENT AGES

So far we have been discussing how to save and invest for retirement if you start young. We will now look at how you implement the recommended strategy if you are in a different age group. The basic principles do not change no

TABLE 7.3

Detail Plan for Saving, Investing, and Withdrawing Money for a
$20,000 Additional Annual Draw

Year	Birthday Number	Stock Balance	Annual Contribution	Annual Withdrawal	Buy/(Sell) Stocks
Today	36	$0	$2,608	$0	$2,608
1	37	$2,869	$2,686	$0	$2,686
2	38	$6,111	$2,767	$0	$2,767
3	39	$9,765	$2,850	$0	$2,850
4	40	$13,876	$2,935	$0	$2,935
5	41	$18,493	$3,023	$0	$3,023
6	42	$23,668	$3,114	$0	$3,114
7	43	$29,460	$3,208	$0	$3,208
8	44	$35,935	$3,304	$0	$3,304
9	45	$43,162	$3,403	$0	$3,403
10	46	$51,221	$3,505	$0	$3,505
11	47	$60,199	$3,610	$0	$3,610
12	48	$70,190	$3,718	$0	$3,718
13	49	$81,299	$3,830	$0	$3,830
14	50	$93,642	$3,945	$0	$3,945
15	51	$107,346	$4,063	$0	$4,063
16	52	$122,550	$4,185	$0	$4,185
17	53	$139,408	$4,311	$0	$4,311
18	54	$158,091	$4,440	$0	$4,440
19	55	$178,784	$4,573	$0	$4,573
20	56	$201,693	$4,710	$0	$4,710
21	57	$227,043	$4,852	$0	$4,852
22	58	$255,084	$4,997	$0	$4,997
23	59	$286,090	$5,147	$0	$5,147
24	60	$320,360	$5,302	$0	$5,302
25	61	$358,228	$5,461	$0	$5,461
26	62	$400,058	$5,624	$0	$5,624
27	63	$446,250	$5,793	$0	$5,793
28	64	$497,248	$5,967	$0	$5,967
29	65	$553,536	$6,146	$0	$6,146
30	66	$615,650	$0	$48,545	($48,545)
31	67	$623,815	$0	$50,002	($50,002)
32	68	$631,195	$0	$51,502	($51,502)
33	69	$637,663	$0	$53,047	($53,047)

34	70	$643,078	$0	$54,638	($54,638)
35	71	$647,284	$0	$56,277	($56,277)
36	72	$650,107	$0	$57,966	($57,966)
37	73	$651,356	$0	$59,705	($59,705)
38	74	$650,816	$0	$61,496	($61,496)
39	75	$648,253	$0	$63,341	($63,341)
40	76	$643,403	$0	$65,241	($65,241)
41	77	$635,979	$0	$67,198	($67,198)
42	78	$625,659	$0	$69,214	($69,214)
43	79	$612,090	$0	$71,290	($71,290)
44	80	$594,879	$0	$73,429	($73,429)
45	81	$573,595	$0	$75,632	($75,632)
46	82	$547,760	$0	$77,901	($77,901)
47	83	$516,845	$0	$80,238	($80,238)
48	84	$480,267	$0	$82,645	($82,645)
49	85	$437,384	$0	$85,124	($85,124)
50	86	$387,486	$0	$87,678	($87,678)
51	87	$329,789	$0	$90,308	($90,308)
52	88	$263,428	$0	$93,018	($93,018)
53	89	$187,452	$0	$95,808	($95,808)
54	90	$100,808	$0	$98,682	($100,808)

matter when you start. In all cases your objective is to have enough money in safe investment by the time you retire to cover your minimum annual draw for SH years and you will start putting this money in safe investments starting AH years ahead of retirement.

If You Are Over 50

As always, you will have to start off by setting your goals for minimum and additional annual draws during retirement and the SH and AH you want to target to have the level of safety you want for your minimum annual draw. Using these targets and taking into consideration the money you already have in your savings, Guru will then tell you how much you will still have to contribute per year until your retirement and how you should distribute between stocks and safe investments the savings you already have. The rest goes the same way we have seen before.

If adjusting the distribution of your current holdings of stocks and safe investments to the levels Guru recommends will require substantial switching, look ahead a few years to make sure you will not have to undo in a few years what you are about to do now. Let me explain with an example. Suppose you are now 53, you plan to retire at 65 and you pick AH and SH of 10 years. If you have a substantial part of your savings in safe investments now, your calculations may indicate that much of it should have been and should be in stocks. But you also know that in 2 years, when you reach the AH, you will start selling stocks to put enough money in safe investments again. In this case you may want to switch into stocks only the money you will hold in stocks at least until you are 65 and maybe beyond and leave enough money in safe investments so that you do not have to sell stocks in 2 years when you reach your AH. After this initial planning and adjustment, you will proceed as we have discussed before.

If you are already within the AH, then of course you will make sure you have enough money in safe investments as our strategy requires before you put the rest in stocks. As before, if you have substantial money in stocks and need to sell some to switch to safe investments, you will sell opportunistically over the next few years.

If You Are Already Retired

If you are already retired, you should first estimate if your savings will last for the rest of your life if you keep all of the money in safe investments and draw every year what you would like to draw. If that calculation shows you have enough savings, then you may just want to keep it all in safe investments and be secure for the rest of your life. If the money is not going to be enough or you are willing to take some risk to have some additional money, then you may want to set some targets for minimum and additional draws, using SH of at least 15 years for the minimum draw part and at least 5 years for the additional draw parts. That will tell you how much of your savings you should keep in safe investments and how much you can afford to put in stocks. After you make the necessary adjustments in your investments, you will draw money as before—in good years by selling stocks, and in bad years by taking it out of safe investments. Again, Guru will do all the calculations for you. You will be able to ask various types of questions, such as: If I have $1 million, want to invest it all in safe investments, and expect to live until 90, how much can I withdraw every year? Or, if I want to maintain an SH of 10 years and want to withdraw $80,000 per year, how long will my money last?

SAVING AND INVESTING FOR OTHER NEEDS

Once you have understood and taken care of saving and investing for retirement, doing the same for your other needs will get simpler, in part because the amount of money involved is not as big, and in part because you will already understand the basic principles. You can divide your other needs into two groups: specific needs and other general needs. For example, you may want to specifically save and invest for your son's college education or you may decide that you will manage it out of your general savings and investments over the years. Let us look at how you save and invest for each type of need.

SAVING AND INVESTING FOR SPECIFIC NEEDS

Take the example of saving for your son's college education. Let us assume he is 5 now. So you will need the money over a 4-year period starting 13 years from now. For simplicity, let's look at the 4 years as four separate needs. You will have to start by estimating how much you want to save for the first year in today's dollars. Note that it is safest to estimate your future needs in today's dollars and let Guru inflate it to future dollars using your inflation rate assumption. None of us can estimate in our head what something may cost 20 years later.

Because the need is long enough into the future, you will invest the money in stocks, at least for some time, to reduce the amount you will have to save. But you also have to remember that as you get close to the need, holding onto the stock investment gets very risky. So you will pick an AH as well. But in this case an AH of 5 years may be enough. Why? Because if the market goes through some difficult times as your son gets close to 18, you will probably have the flexibility to temporarily come up with the money from some other source, including your other savings, while you wait for the market to recover. But if you are not sure you will have the flexibility or want to be safer, you should choose a longer AH. Once you have decided how much money you will need and the AH, you can use Guru to calculate how much you will have to save and invest depending on whether you want to save it all in 1 year or over the years. Over the years you will invest all of this money in a stock index fund until you get within the AH period. At that point, you will start to opportunistically sell the stock holdings and put the money in safe investment until you need it to pay tuition.

Why should you consider specifically saving for some major needs? Because then you can save for it in a disciplined way on a monthly basis. It is likely that you will add to your general savings as you can afford to do so. If you take such a casual approach to saving for things that are important to you, when the time comes the money may not be there. Similarly, this will impose the discipline of selling the investments in time (AH years ahead) to keep the risk under control. Saving for specific needs does not mean that you set up separate accounts for each. All your taxable savings should be invested together in as few accounts as possible, but you will keep track on paper of how much of the total money is meant to be for what.

SAVING AND INVESTING FOR GENERAL NEEDS

As I mentioned, you may want to manage all your saving and investment needs, other than those related to retirement, together or you may handle some important needs, like money for children's education, separately and bundle together the rest. For your general saving and investing, you should follow the rule that you will invest in stocks any money you won't need in the next 10 years or so—we call it your minimum holding period (MHP)—and as you get within the AH (5 years or so in this case) of any expense you will have to cover by selling stocks, you will opportunistically sell stocks to raise the cash and put it in safe investments. As usual, you will never let yourself get into a bind where you will have to sell stocks at a time when the market is very low. Guru will do the year-by-year calculations for you.

LOOK AT ALL YOUR TAXABLE INVESTMENTS AS ONE PORTFOLIO

The part of your retirement savings that are in tax-deferred accounts will be automatically segregated from your taxable savings and investments. But when you buy and sell investments in taxable accounts, you have to look at all your savings for different purposes—the retirement savings in taxable accounts, savings for specific needs (e.g., your son's education if you are treating it as a specific need), and general savings—as one portfolio. Otherwise you may end up paying unnecessary taxes or transaction costs.

Here is why: Suppose you have $50,000 invested in stocks today, you are planning to save $4,000 per year for the next 5 years for various purposes, and you know that you will have a $20,000 expenditure coming up in 5 years. In this case you should not be selling any stocks in anticipation of that need. All you have to do is put those annual $4,000 savings for the next 5 years in safe investments and in 5 years you will have the $20,000 you will need. If you treat all the different savings separately and that $20,000 is in a separate account for your son's college tuition, you may sell stocks in that account anticipating that you will need the money in 5 years while you are buying $4,000 of stocks every year in a different taxable account, maybe as part of retirement savings. So you may end up paying taxes and transaction costs on the sales when no selling is necessary. You will have to keep track on paper of which part of your taxable saving is for what purpose. (Note that in Guru you handle the savings for the three different types of needs separately. So do not blindly follow its output for the three different types of needs. Make sure that you are not selling stocks with one hand while you are buying them back with another.)

WHEN TO BUY AND SELL STOCKS

We have so far discussed in general terms when you are going to save and invest money in stocks and when you are going to sell stocks for spending immediately or to put the money in safe investments to spend in the future. Let us now discuss in a little more detail exactly when you are going to buy and sell stocks. One thing we know for sure by this time is that you are not going to buy or sell based on anyone's advice or your own gut feelings.

WHEN TO BUY STOCKS

Your plans for savings and investment strategies we have discussed so far will determine in general terms how much money you will invest in stocks and when the money will be available. The best thing to do is to spread out your purchases over a period of time so that you buy at an average price over time and avoid investing most of your money when the market is too high. Fortunately, that is what naturally happens because we save over time as well. So just keep investing in your index funds as you are saving.

Do not try to time the market, and do not try to make judgments about whether the market is too high or too low this month, because once you get into that game, you will soon become paralyzed and not invest. You will start seeking out opinions from all sources. They will invariably be conflicting and unreliable opinions and you won't know which one to follow. Suppose you decide not to buy 1 month because you think the market is too high. Then if you are by chance right and the market goes down, you will wait to see if it goes down even further. If the market goes up, you will regret not having bought before and wait to see if the market comes back to the previous level. This is a loser's game, and millions of investors lose out on making billions of dollars in the market because they keep waiting for the right time to buy. The only right time to buy is when you have money to invest for the long run.

Should you keep buying even if the market is going down? Absolutely. That is the best time to buy. If you believe the market will do well in the long run and you are investing for the long run, wouldn't you rather buy when everything is marked down rather than marked up? Once again, do not wait around for the market to go down more and hope to buy at the bottom. You will never recognize the bottom, and chances are by the time the market hits the bottom you and everyone around you will be so panicked that you won't have the guts to buy at the bottom anyway. It is even going to take a lot of guts and faith to keep buying as the market goes down. Suspend all your judgments about whether the market is too high or too low at any point in time and keep buying regularly whether the market is going up or down. In the long run you will not just be fine, you will be more than fine; you will look like a genius.

Let me address two special situations. First, doesn't the market sometimes get way overvalued? And if at any point you think the market is way overvalued, shouldn't you wait? The answer to the first question is, yes, the market does become overvalued from time to time. But we almost always know that only in retrospect; it is hard to tell at the time. If you try to guess at any point whether the market is overvalued, you will be wrong a lot more often than you will be right. Do not play that game. If you are buying month in and month out, if you are buying a broad-based index fund, and if you are determined to keep buying even when the market goes down, you have very little to worry about. You will end up investing some money at market highs and some at market lows and it all will even out. Once you start the guessing and waiting game, you will neither buy when the market is high, nor will you buy when the market is low. Years will pass by with your money parked in money market funds and you will be missing out on the opportunity to make much higher returns.

Second, if you suddenly come into a sizable chunk of money, should you invest it right away or should you wait? You have two choices and I think for the long-term investor it is a toss-up. You can invest it right away—meaning really right away or over the next 2 or 3 months—or you can spread out the buying evenly over a period of a year or two depending on how big a chunk of money it is relative to your overall portfolio. The danger with the latter approach is that you may not follow through; you may start playing the game of guessing if the market is too high or too low this month. So, if you are going to spread it out over a year or two, set up an investment schedule and stick to it.

This is a simple message that I have expanded a lot for a good reason. People find every reason to postpone buying, especially when the market is going down or has gone down a lot, and miss out on making a lot of money. On the other hand, people are very willing to buy when the market is euphoric and at its highest level. If you think about it, it makes no sense; but that's what almost everyone does. None of us is going to have the guts or wisdom to buy only at the bottom and avoid buying at the top. So, do the next best thing and buy month in and month out.

WHEN TO SELL STOCKS

There is only one reason to sell stocks: for a current or anticipated expense. This means you are never going to sell just because you think the market is about to plunge or it has already plunged. Doing so is the easiest way to ruin the fruits of a long time of patient investing. One way to make sure you stay disciplined is to follow the rule that you will never take any money out of the market with a plan to put it back in. When you sell, you will sell because you need the money (e.g., you are retired and this is your planned annual withdrawal to cover your expenses) and you will spend it right away or you will put it in safe investments and spend it when you need to cover the expense you had anticipated.

Most people sell when they think the market is going to plunge, or has already plunged, in the hope that they will avoid further losses and will get back in when the market turns around and starts going up again. Unfortunately, if you sell thinking the market is about to plunge, you may be dead wrong and the market may keep going up. At that point you will probably wait around hoping that the market will come back to the level at which you sold your stocks, and the market may not get back there in many years or ever. So you will not know when to get back in and you may totally miss a roaring bull market.

If you sell after the market has plunged, you may be selling at the bottom. Too many people sell exactly when everyone else has panicked and the market is near its bottom only to find that the market then turns around and starts moving up sharply. Once again, in this situation you won't know when to get

144 PREPARING FOR THE TRIP

back in and miss out on big opportunities. Once you are investing in the market, knowing full well that it is going to have big swings and you will have to hold on through them to earn the long-term high returns, you cannot afford to change your game plan in the middle.

Opportunistic Selling

We have already discussed that when you have been investing in stocks for retirement or other needs, there comes a time, dictated by the AH you have chosen, when you have to start selling. You pick an AH to start selling ahead of the time when you will need the money to have the flexibility to sell over a period of time and avoid selling in a depressed market. Because this is a key aspect of our investment strategy, let me explain in some detail how you should go about it.

When you reach your AH, you should first estimate how much stocks you will have to sell every month if you were to spread out all of your sales uniformly over the AH. For example, if you have to sell stocks and raise cash of $12,000 over 10 years, you will need to sell $100 of stocks every month. That $100 is your monthly sales target. When the market is in the normal range you should sell the target amount of stocks every month. If the market starts to get depressed, you should cut back your monthly sales and if the market starts to get euphoric, you should speed it up. Remember that your objective is to complete the planned sales by the end of your AH (i.e., by the time you retire or need the money). So every 6 months or so you should compare how much stocks you have actually sold with how much you would have sold if you were selling steadily, and make necessary adjustments to your sales rates.

Before I go any further, let me reemphasize that I am in no way encouraging market timing. As I said before, you should never sell stocks with a plan to put the money back in the market when things look better. That's market timing. I am only suggesting that if you have to sell stocks and can be flexible with the timing, you probably can do better than just selling at one point in time or spreading out the sales uniformly over a period of time. This is what I call opportunistic selling.

But how do you know when the market is depressed and when it is euphoric? It is not an easy call because, as we have discussed, there are no indicators that tell us exactly when the market is over- or undervalued. There are, however, three signs or measures that you can use to guide your opportunistic selling.

- The first is a subjective measure, but in this case it may be the most reliable. Do a lot of your selling when everyone is euphoric about the market. It is as simple as that. There are times when the stock market is on the front pages of the newspapers and at the top of evening news every few days. The market makes new highs every week if not every day, everyone keeps talking about stocks and mutual funds, and stocks are the main topic of discussion at parties and around the water cooler. That kind of thing, especially if it has been going on for a while, is a sign that the market is getting euphoric and stock prices are getting too high. On the other hand, there are times when nobody wants to hear or talk about the stock market, except perhaps to complain about it bitterly. All you hear about is people selling and pulling money out of stock funds and swearing that they will never invest in stocks again. That's when the market is too depressed and since you should not be in any hurry to sell, avoid selling at those times. Just wait it out.

- The second is a quantitative measure although you cannot apply it too mechanically. Historical studies have shown that the price to earnings (P/E) ratio for the stock market fluctuates around 19 minus the rate of inflation. So if the expected rate of inflation is 3%, the normal P/E ratio for the market should be 16. You can easily find the market's P/E ratio and the inflation rate in most major newspapers. So if the market's P/E gets to 6 points or so above what should be its normal level, sell aggressively and when it gets that much below, hold off selling for a while. In between, keep selling at a normal pace. Remember, this is not a very accurate indicator; there is none. So act on it only when the market gets way above or below it. At other times consider the market to be in a normal range.

- The third is also a quantitative measure. We know that we cannot predict what the market will do in the next few years based on anything, including how the market did in the past few years. But in the long run, it is difficult for the market to keep providing real returns of much over the historical average of 7% per year because of its ties to the economy. So if the market has provided significantly higher annual returns over a 5- to 10-year period, chances are it has gotten too high and you should sell aggressively. On the other hand, if the market has been going down a lot for a number of years or returns have been much below the 7% norm for a number of years, you should slow down or hold off selling for a while.

Let me remind you that all of these are crude measures. Use a combination of them to regulate your selling, but do not get carried away with them.
Do not start watching the market every day and wondering if you should sell
today, tomorrow, or next week. Think at least in months and preferably in
years; never in days or weeks.

SHOULD YOU BASE HOW MUCH TO INVEST IN STOCKS ON YOUR RISK TOLERANCE?

Although risk (loss) tolerance and risk appetite are somewhat vague terms,
what we generally mean by both is the amount of money we can tolerate losing
before we start to have anxiety attacks and lose sleep, and ultimately sell out
our positions at large losses. Many experts believe that how much you invest
in the stock market should depend on your risk tolerance. According to them,
you should first guess what your risk tolerance is and also how far stocks may
go down in a severe bear market. Say the numbers are $50,000 and 50%
respectively. You should then invest in stocks a maximum of $100,000, be-
cause under the worst circumstances you have assumed, your loss will be
$50,000, something presumably you can tolerate.

There are a few problems with this approach.

First, people generally cannot estimate their risk tolerance ahead of time.
Second, no one knows how far the market may go down at some point in the
future, although you can take a guess based on history. Third, it is not quite
clear what you are supposed to do if the market goes down significantly and
you have a paper loss larger than your risk tolerance. Should you sell out at
that point to prevent further losses, implicitly assuming that if the market goes
down by a certain percentage, it is likely to go down even more? But there is
no basis for assuming that. If you sell out after a significant market decline,
the only thing you may accomplish is locking in a substantial loss. Fourth, if
you follow this approach and assume that the market may go down as much
as 50%, you will probably invest only a small part of your savings in the stock
market. We discussed the implications of that under the Investor's Dilemma.

This approach does not make much sense. I think that if you are not convinced that over the long run the market will go up no matter what happens
in the mean time, you probably should not invest a substantial amount of
money in the stock market no matter what investment method you follow.
Chances are whatever risk tolerance level you set, the market will go down far

enough to force you to sell out and then cheerfully go back up. The market is perverse that way. As I have emphasized throughout, your best defense against the vagaries of the market is to be a long-term investor willing to ride out ups and downs of any size and to start selling stocks opportunistically years ahead of when you will need the money.

Note that Guru's projections show how much investment in stocks you are likely to have in each future year for any investment scenario you are considering. You can use those projections to estimate how much paper losses you may face in the future years for different size market drops and try to imagine if you will be able to tolerate them. Remember that although a 50% loss may occur only once every decade or so, 15% or 20% losses—from intrayear high to low—occur quite routinely, maybe every year or every other year. Before you choose to follow an investment scenario, you have to be convinced that you will be able to ride out its potential short-term and long-term losses.

DECIDING HOW MUCH YOU CAN PRUDENTLY INVEST IN STOCKS

Our objective in this chapter was to decide what is the most you can prudently afford to invest in stocks. We have seen that you cannot pick a percentage and say, I should invest 30% of my savings in stocks. You cannot even say—as many people suggest—I should put in safe investments a percentage of my savings that equals my age (that is, 55% at the age of 55, etc.) and the rest in stocks. How much goes into stocks really depends on what you are saving for and how certain you want to be that the money will be there when you need it. And we have seen how you make that decision and adjust your positions over the years based on your specific circumstances and assumptions about how safe you want to be.

The one clear conclusion here is that the earlier you start saving and investing, the better off you are going to be. Then you will be able to afford to take more risk and put more of your money in stocks for longer periods of time. Unless you get very unlucky, your investments will probably end up doing so well that you will either have to save much less in the later years or you will end up with a lot more money than you had expected and will be able to send your son to a better school or have a more luxurious retirement. Always remember that time is your best friend in reducing risk and achieving investment success.

♦ **THINGS TO REMEMBER** ♦

♦ You have to invest in stocks as much as you can prudently afford. Otherwise the amount of money you will have to save and invest over the years for future needs will lower your current standard of living too much.

♦ You should plan to hold your investments in stocks for the long run because that significantly reduces the chance of losing money and increases the chance of earning a good return.

♦ Start selling stocks opportunistically a number of years ahead of the time that you will need the money. Risk increases the closer you get to needing the money.

♦ Plan and save for major needs such as retirement and children's education separately because you will probably want to pick a different risk-return trade-off for each.

♦ Use the following guidelines to save and invest for retirement:

   • Set your retirement goals in terms of an annual minimum draw for which you will invest conservatively and an annual additional draw for which you will invest more aggressively.

   • By the time you retire, you should have enough money in safe investments to cover your minimum draw for about 10 years. You should raise this money by starting to sell the necessary amount of stocks starting about 10 years before retirement.

   • During retirement cover the annual minimum draw by selling stocks in good years and by drawing from safe investments in years when the market is at its lows. Always cover the additional annual draw only by selling stock investments you specifically made for that part.

♦ To decide how much of your portfolio should be invested in stocks at any time you have to go through the kind of analysis we have discussed. You cannot arbitrarily decide to invest a certain percentage of your portfolio in stocks.

◆

CHAPTER 8

Do Not Go on a Long Trip Driving a Gas Guzzler

◆

Rule #6: Save Every Penny of Investment Cost You Can

You wouldn't go on a long trip driving a gas guzzler that gave you, say, 5 miles per gallon, would you? Yet most of us drive on this long investment trip on gas-guzzling mutual funds and brokerage accounts. You will be shocked to find out how much your gas bill (investment costs) will come to over the long term if you do not switch to a gas-efficient model in a hurry. If you run up high gas bills, you will get to the end of your trip with much less money in your pocket. The good news is that there are funds that run on spoonfuls instead of gallons of gas. All you have to do is drive only those.

THE IMPORTANCE OF SAVING EVERY PENNY OF INVESTMENT COSTS

The two major types of investment costs you incur are (1) the costs of investing in a mutual fund, which include the fees your mutual fund charges you for managing your money as well as other expenses the fund incurs; and (2) the commissions your broker charges you for buying and selling stocks and mutual funds (if you buy your funds through your brokerage account). If you are not careful, you also may end up paying a substantial load (sales commissions) on your mutual fund purchases, account maintenance fees, transaction fees for switching from one fund to another even within the same fund group, and so forth.

If you are a typical investor, all your life you have probably just assumed that these costs are small and mostly unavoidable, and that if your investments do well over the years, these costs would not matter. Also, you probably have looked around to find a low-cost broker and tried to avoid buying load funds, but you have not taken any of this too seriously—you have never analyzed the issue of investment costs and just how much these costs affect the amount of money you can expect to accumulate over the long run.

Well, you are in for the shock of your life. And to shake you out of your slumber and make you start paying attention, let me start with the horrendous news. (I don't even want to call this bad news because that will give bad news a bad name.)

INVESTMENT COSTS MATTER AND HOW!

Let us not beat around the bush any more. Let us go to Table 8.1 right away. This table assumes that you invest $100,000 in lump-sum today in a stock fund and expect to earn an annual return of 10% over the years. Because I think this is one of the most revealing tables you will look at in your entire life, let us understand exactly what everything in this table is.

The table has two panels. The top panel shows the results at the end 20 years, and the bottom panel at the end of 40 years. Now, here is what the various rows and columns represent:

- The first row shows the results you will have if you could avoid all costs. You are not going to be able to do that, but it is a good benchmark. The next five rows show the results of investing through five different categories of stock funds with increasing total investment costs (shown in column 2). As we will see a little later, these are representative costs for the various categories and are by no means exaggerated.

- Column 3 shows how much money, net of costs, you will have at the end of your investment period for each fund category.

- Column 4 shows how much lower the final value of your investment will be relative to the no-cost benchmark (row 1) because of the investment costs.

- Column 5 shows the percentage reduction in the final value relative to the no-cost benchmark because of the investment costs.

TABLE 8.1

How Investment Costs Affect the Final Value of a $100,000 Investment in a Stock Fund Earning an Annual Return of 10%

	Annual Costs (%)	Final Value of Investment	Reduction in Final Value	% Reduction in Final Value
At the end of 20 years				
No costs	0.0%	$672,750		
Low-cost index fund	0.2%	$648,704	$24,046	3.6%
Typical index fund	0.5%	$614,161	$58,589	8.7%
Low-cost active fund	1.0%	$560,441	$112,309	16.7%
Typical active fund	2.0%	$466,096	$206,654	30.7%
High-cost active fund	3.0%	$386,968	$285,782	42.5%
At the end of 40 years				
No costs	0.0%	$4,525,926		
Low-cost index fund	0.2%	$4,208,173	$317,752	7.0%
Typical index fund	0.5%	$3,771,940	$753,986	16.7%
Low-cost active fund	1.0%	$3,140,942	$1,384,984	30.6%
Typical active fund	2.0%	$2,172,452	$2,353,473	52.0%
High-cost active fund	3.0%	$1,497,446	$3,028,480	66.9%

Now that you understand the table, let's talk about the numbers. If you could avoid all investment costs, at the end of 20 years you would have $672,750. A very nice sum of money, especially considering that you made just one initial investment of $100,000.

If you invest through a low-cost index fund with an annual investment cost of 0.2%, the final value of your investment will be lower by $24,046 or 3.6% (relative to the no-cost benchmark.). This is not shocking, but I am sure you still find it surprising. If I had asked you before you looked at this table how much this cost could reduce the final value of your investment, you probably would have guessed 0.5% or 1% at most.

Take a look at the next two rows and let's jump to the row for the typical actively managed stock fund with an annual investment cost of 2.0%. When all costs are considered, this actually may be a little on the low side, but we will bend over backward to be fair. In this case the final value of your investment goes down by $206,654, or by 30.7% relative to the no-cost benchmark. Let us throw in two more numbers. For a high-cost actively managed fund with total annual investment costs of 3%, over a 20-year period the final value will be 42.5% lower and over a 40-year period the final value will be 66.9% lower than the no-cost benchmark.

After you are over your first shock, think about what these numbers tell you. In 40 years if you had no costs, you could have over $4.5 million, but if you invested in a high-cost actively managed fund with an annual cost of 3%, you would have only about $1.5 million, or about $3 million less. (Let me again emphasize that, as we will see soon, when all costs are considered, 3% annual investment cost is more common than you think and even if you look at the numbers for 2% annual costs, things look only slightly less dreary.)

There is nothing I can say in words that can portray the reality better than the numbers themselves do. I think just as cigarette companies are required to put a warning label on all packets of cigarettes, all fund companies should be required to send a huge poster of this table with every fund prospectus and monthly or quarterly fund statement, and investors should put it up on the wall in a very prominent place so that any time they are tempted to invest in the latest red-hot fund with a high annual investment cost, they can take another look at the poster and sober up. And until funds are required to send out that poster—which is going to be never—you probably will do well to make a copy of this table and pin it up on the wall.

Let me anticipate something you may be thinking. If you are thinking 20 or 40 years is too long a period to worry about, remember that these results do not apply to just buying and holding the same fund for 20 or 40 years. Even if you change funds 10 times during the period, you won't be able to escape these effects of costs unless you switch to very low-cost funds along the way. You may actually make things worse by trading funds because if you switch funds in a taxable account, you will pay taxes and give away some of your money every time you switch. The 20 or 40 years relate to how many years you will be investing in any fund, not just this one fund. In the context of the investing period of your life, 20 or 40 years is hardly too long for most people.

WHERE DOES THE MONEY GO?

You may find it puzzling that costs that look so small on an annual percentage basis can have such a huge impact on the money you make over the long run. So let me address two questions that are probably coming to mind.

Why will you make so much less money? The simple answer is that the 3% annual cost will significantly reduce the power of the Magic of Compounding. Remember, for compounding to work with full power, all the money you earn during a year has to be reinvested the next year to earn return on return. In this case, on your initial $100,000, in the first year you will earn a return of $10,000. But instead of $10,000, only $7,000 will be reinvested and the other $3,000 will be taken out as investment costs for the year. So in the second year you will earn a lower return than you would in the no-cost case because you will earn a return on $107,000 instead of $110,000. You will effectively earn an annual return of 7% instead of 10%. Over the years that will take its toll, and the longer the period you look at, the bigger the toll.

What will happen to the more than $3 million you won't make? Will it all end up in the pocket of the fund company? Here the answer depends on what you assume the fund company will do with the investment costs it will collect from you. Let us first note that over the years you will actually pay the fund company a total of about $600,000. That is a big chunk of money and it is so big because every year, as the value of your investment grows, you will pay more in investment costs. In the first year you will pay $3,000, in the second year $3,210 and so on until in the fortieth year you will pay about $42,000. Yes, that's $42,000 in just one year. So the fund company will do well. But the $600,000 you will pay in total is still a long way from the $3 million. Where is the rest?

Remember, the fund company will collect those investment costs from you over the years. If every year it invests all of the money it gets from you, can earn 10% return on all its investments, and keeps investing and reinvesting everything, then at the end of the 40 years it will end up with that $3 million. It will then have to thank the Magic of Compounding for the big help in getting from the $600,000 to the $3 million.

However, in practice, it will have its own costs to pay, it will have to give Uncle Sam his share, and it may not be able to earn 10% return on whatever it has left over. So it is not likely that it will end up with all of that $3 million. To you, however, all that is a small consolation. From your point of view what matters is that the fund company will end up making very good money and you will miss out on making close to $3 million that you could have easily made by avoiding the costs. Clearly, reducing or eliminating those costs has to be at the top of your list.

ANOTHER SIMPLE WAY OF LOOKING AT THE IMPACT OF THE COSTS

Another way of looking at this whole cost issue is to recognize that the 10% return we have assumed probably implies a 7% per year real (i.e., inflation-adjusted) return. On that basis, at annual investment costs of 1% you will be frittering away 14% of your real return; at annual costs of 2%, 28% of your real return; and at annual costs of 3%, 43% of your real returns, or almost half of it. Whichever way you look at it, it is bad news. But I think the way we looked at it first, in terms of the effect on the final value, is probably the most revealing.

GROWING ONGOING COSTS ARE THE WORST OFFENDERS

There are two factors working together that cause the havoc we just looked at. First, these are ongoing and not one-time costs—you pay them year in and year out. Second, the costs keep growing because the costs are calculated as a percentage of the growing value and not the original value of your investments. Clearly, the fund management company does not have to work doubly hard just because some shares they were holding have doubled in value. But that is the implicit assumption here. You will hear many different explanations of why this approach to charging fees is justified, but, truthfully, none of them hold much water. The only explanation that fits all the facts is that they do it because they can get away with it. And they can get away with it because investors don't pay attention. Most people do not mind spending two days shopping around to save $50 on buying a TV set, but they do not realize that if they take just a little time to learn how to save on investment costs, they will be able to save hundreds of thousands of dollars over the years on investment costs that buy them practically nothing.

Of course, mutual funds are not the only offenders here. Your broker, especially if he is a full-service broker, will be only too happy to charge you high commissions for trading individual stocks that can easily add up to 2% or more of your assets. And instead of just buying and holding your stocks, if you keep trading your stocks incurring that kind of expense every year, the end result will be exactly the same as the ones we have been discussing. What is worse is that the big brokerage houses are now putting a lot of marketing effort into convincing you that what you really need is a wrap account or some other similar account that will provide you a bundle of services, most of which you can do very well without, for annual fees (typically 2% or more) based on the total value of your assets in the account. At this point you should have no problem recognizing what they are after and what you are in for if you fall for this marketing ploy.

Let me also remind you that the investment costs of mutual funds are so nicely hidden that you never see them explicitly on any of your statements and you never know how much of your money is getting drained away. Unlike inflation, which is at least a visible enemy, here you are dealing with a well-camouflaged, if not totally invisible, enemy. You must be ever vigilant when faced with that kind of enemy.

WHEN IS BUYING ANYTHING OTHER THAN A LOW-COST FUND JUSTIFIABLE?

The correct answer is, "Never."

Let's bring up and dispose of an argument you may hear in favor of buying high-cost or even average-cost mutual funds. In our example we assumed that all the funds, including the high-cost funds, earn the same 10% annual return before costs. So all the high costs come out of that return and that's what makes the higher cost funds look so bad in our comparisons. But what if a high-cost mutual fund with a star money manager at the helm could earn a 15% annual return, 5% higher than the lowly low-cost index fund? Even after the 3% annual cost, you will now earn an annual return of 12%, about 2% better than the index fund. Wouldn't you then be better off investing in that high-cost fund? And wouldn't that additional annual return add up to a lot of money over a 20- or 40-year period because of the Magic of Compounding? This is what the fund people would have you believe and would offer as the justification for charging you all those costs.

Well, this really has to fall into the category of fantasy. We have talked about this before. The typical mutual fund and even the ones with the celebrity money managers at the helm have a lot of difficulty just keeping up with the market (the low-cost index fund) for long, even before counting costs. The notion that these high-cost funds over time will earn annual returns of 2%, 3%, or even more beyond the returns of the low-cost index fund is pure fantasy. You should not be willing to wager even $10 on that happening, let alone bet hundreds of thousands of dollars and your financial future on it.

INVESTMENT COSTS FOR OTHER INVESTMENT OPTIONS

The costs we talked about so far mostly apply to mutual funds that invest primarily in stocks of large U.S. companies. Let us now look at the costs associated with the safe investments and a few other investment options.

BOND FUNDS

The costs of all funds work essentially the same way as those for stock funds, that is, you effectively pay a percentage (different percentages for different categories of funds) of your investment in costs, and because the percentage remains fixed, as your investment grows, so grow your costs. All of this hampers the Magic of Compounding the same way.

The annual investment costs for bond funds as a percentage of the assets tend to be somewhat lower than those for the stock funds—0.2% at the low end for bond index funds to 1.5% at the high end. These costs do not include everything, but let us work with 1.1% as the rate of total annual costs for the average bond fund. (Many bond funds even have loads on top of these costs, and how anyone can justify paying them is beyond me.)

Unfortunately, the lower costs relative to stock funds do not make things any better because the expected return on bonds is also lower. Let us assume that the expected real return on bonds is 3%, a generous assumption by historical standards. So if costs are 1.1%, then over a third of the real return will be drained away by costs. Yes, that's over a third and that's for the average-cost bond fund, not the high-cost ones and not the ones with load.

You think that's enough bad news? Well I hate to be the bearer of worse news, but we cannot afford to forget Uncle Sam. Suppose you are holding the bond fund in a taxable account, you are in the 28% tax bracket, and the market expects an inflation rate in the future of 3%. So the nominal, before-cost return on the bond fund will be 6% (3% real return + 3% inflation rate = 6%). The return you will get after costs will be 4.9% (6% − 1.1% = 4.9%), and after paying taxes you will be left with 3.5%. So you will barely stay ahead of inflation. In the meantime, you will take huge risks because, as we have discussed, if inflation unexpectedly spikes, your bond fund may actually lose a lot of money instead of earning the 6% return we have assumed.

The economics gets a little better if you hold the bond fund in a tax-deferred account, and as with stocks, you will do much better if you invest in bond index funds, some of which have annual costs as low as 0.2%. There are also low-cost actively managed funds with annual costs lower than 0.5%. But remember there is still the risk of a higher rate of inflation. To decide whether you should buy fixed-rate long-term bonds at all, refer to the discussions under Rule #3.

You will recall our discussion under stock funds regarding the notion (wishful thinking) that a high-cost fund may be able to make up for its higher cost with superior performance. Although I do not think high-cost stock funds have any real chance of doing that, in theory it is possible. After all, the price of some stocks goes up 100% in a year. For bond funds, however, even the theoretical possibility that they could make up for the higher costs with superior performance is slim. As a practical matter, there is very little chance that an actively managed high-cost bond fund with a high front-end load would be able to consistently make up for the cost disadvantage with superior performance.

Before we move on, let me also mention that if you do decide to invest in bonds, especially with the intention of holding them for the long term, you may be able to do better in terms of costs by buying the appropriate bonds directly instead of investing in a bond fund. When you buy and hold bonds, you pay one-time costs as opposed to the ongoing annual costs for a fund. It sounds simple and logical, but you only wish life were that simple. Because it is nearly impossible for an individual to determine the fair price of a bond, chances are that you will end up paying such a high price that it will overwhelm the money you save by not investing in a fund and paying its annual costs. My general assumption is that if you are investing a small amount of money in bonds as an individual investor, you are almost never going to get a fair price unless you are buying U.S. Treasury bonds directly from the U.S. Treasury at an auction. Most of the time, a low-cost bond fund is the lesser of the evils.

INFLATION-PROTECTED BOND FUNDS

If you are going to buy bonds, Treasury Inflation-Protected Securities (TIPS) are your best choice. As I have already discussed under Rule #3, there are problems with buying them directly. But Vanguard's Inflation-Protected Securities Fund with annual investment costs of around 0.3% is the perfect low-cost fund for investing in TIPS.

TAXABLE AND TAX-EXEMPT MONEY MARKET FUNDS

In terms of costs, because of competition, most money market funds have annual costs between 0.3% and 0.5%, although there are some funds that try to get away with more. So do not let your guard down, especially if you are shopping for a tax-exempt money market fund, because there is less competition in that arena. Also, be careful about new funds that reduce or completely absorb costs for a certain period to draw in investors. They hope that when they do start charging their full fees, because of inertia most investors will stay on. If you can save money for a while, great. But once they start charging the fees and expenses, if those are too high, remember to move on.

SERIES I SAVINGS BONDS

From the point of view of investment costs, these come out ahead of almost all other options. There are no investment costs. What else could you ask for?

BANK CERTIFICATES OF DEPOSIT

From the point of view of investment costs, this is another winner because there are no costs. What you see is what you get.

OTHER CATEGORIES OF MUTUAL FUNDS

The costs I have talked about before for stock funds are really for funds that hold stocks of large U.S. corporations, that is, large cap funds. The annual total investment costs for actively managed small cap and foreign stock funds can be around 4%, and those for emerging markets stock funds can be around 9%. Such high costs are one reason I do not recommend investing in foreign stocks. Clearly, if you decide to invest some money in foreign stocks, it is even more important that you invest only through index funds to keep costs low, although the total investment costs of foreign index funds are going to be quite a bit higher than those for domestic index funds. I have not discussed the costs of some of the other categories of funds specifically (e.g., municipal and corporate bond funds) because the general discussions of stock and bond funds cover them and I do not think you need to consider them as investment choices anyway. But if you decide to invest in any of them, now that you are aware of the cost issues, shop around before you buy.

OTHER INVESTMENTS

Be they annuities, universal or variable life insurance, tax-shelter-type investments, or even something as simple as buying and renting out a house, you will need to do a thorough analysis of the specific situation. The only thing I can say in general terms is to not be lazy about doing a full analysis of all expected costs and to be realistic about your assumptions. In almost all of these cases the up-front and sometimes even the ongoing costs tend to be very high, and the justification that is always offered is that you will make up for them in higher returns or in tax savings. Be very skeptical about such claims. Most often the analysis the salespeople will show you is based on highly optimistic assumptions, and the only thing you can be sure about is that you will definitely have to pay the costs whether or not you see the expected high returns or tax savings.

BREAKDOWN OF THE COSTS OF INVESTING IN MUTUAL FUNDS

So far I have quoted total numbers for the annual costs of mutual funds of various categories. Now we will look into the five types of costs that make up that total. Of these, only two costs—load or sales commission and expense ratio—are easy to find. The others can be quite substantial, but you will almost never find out exactly what they are for any specific fund. I have to admit that this detailed discussion of costs is not very exciting, and if you decide that you will always invest only in broad-based index funds with no loads and expense ratios close to 0.2% and never more than 0.5%, then you may skip this discussion for now. But if you think you may invest in actively managed funds at one time or another, then you should read this section carefully and make sure you understand where all those invisible costs come from and how big they can be.

LOAD OR SALES COMMISSIONS

A load is simply a sales commission, charged by load funds even when you haven't talked to a salesman. This may be charged at the time you buy into the fund (called a front-end load) or at the time you sell the fund (called a back-end load) if you haven't held the fund for a specified length of time. It is charged once and can be as high as 6%. If it is a front-end load of say 4%, it means that only $96 of every $100 of your money is actually invested on your behalf. The rest is drained away up front.

For most funds the back-end load is charged on a declining schedule. For example, you may pay a 6% back-end load if you sell the fund in the first year, 5% if you sell in the second year, and so forth—ultimately nothing if you hold the fund for 6 years or longer. Although I am all in favor of holding the right fund for 6 years or longer, I do not see why you should get yourself into this bind even if you do not think you will sell in less than 6 years. Many fund families also let you switch around among their funds for free or for a transaction cost once you have paid the load for getting into one of their funds.

These funds and many financial advisors use this as an argument to justify the load. You should follow one simple principle: *Never buy a fund with any kind of load.* From the point of view of the investor, there has never been and there will never be any justification for buying a load fund. They do not perform any better than no-load funds, and you are getting nothing for the money. There are perfectly good no-load funds in any category you can think of.

If you use an investment advisor, chances are he will direct you to a load fund because a part of what you pay as load goes to him. As I discussed, there is no justification for buying load funds and that is one of the reasons you should use fee-only financial advisors. (See more on this under Rule #10.)

EXPENSE RATIO COSTS

These are management fees and other expenses that every fund automatically charges you every year. A fund's returns are reported net of these costs, so they are not as visible as a load. But a fund is required to tell you what its expense ratio is. For some actively managed stock funds, this can be over 2% per year, and for actively managed bond funds as high as 1.5% per year. Because for good index funds this is 0.2% to 0.4% per year, if you insist on buying actively managed funds, you should shoot for this benchmark.

THE FUND'S TRANSACTION COSTS

This is what the mutual funds pay their brokers for buying and selling the stocks, bonds, or other assets they hold. The numbers are buried in the fund's financial reports and are very difficult to excavate. This is another ongoing annual cost, not a one-time cost. For funds that buy and sell stocks frequently (called high turnover), this can be 0.5% or even more per year. So, to minimize this cost, you must buy low turnover funds. For an actively managed fund, a turnover of less than 15%, meaning it sells (and replaces) less than 15% of its stocks in a year, can be considered low because many actively managed funds have turnovers closer to 100%. Index funds, of course, have the lowest turnover rates, on the order of just a few percentage points.

SPREAD AND MARKET IMPACT COSTS

These are even more elusive than transaction costs and even more difficult to quantify. Because you will never find these numbers anywhere in a fund's statements or reports, I will spare you the details. You may view them as similar to transaction costs, and a fund incurs these costs on every transaction. These costs are more for higher turnover funds and for funds that buy smaller and foreign stocks.

ANNUAL TOTAL INVESTMENT COSTS FOR DIFFERENT CATEGORIES OF STOCK FUNDS

To sum up our discussion of fund costs, let us look at Table 8.2, which shows the estimated annual total investment costs for actively managed stock funds in a few different categories. Remember that these costs do not include any fund load. You should find the numbers both revealing and shocking. Because we have already looked at how various levels of costs affect the money you accumulate over the long run, there really is not much more to add. (The table is reproduced with permission from William J. Bernstein's excellent book, *The Intelligent Asset Allocator.*)

REDEMPTION FEES: THE COST THAT MAKES SENSE

I saved this one for last just so that we could end this dreary discussion of mutual fund investment costs on a slightly cheerful note. The redemption fees, which only a few funds charge, is actually a good cost. A fund that has a redemption fee will charge shareholders the fee if they sell their shares before holding them for a minimum period of time. The objective is to discourage shareholders from trading, that is, buying and selling, the fund's shares frequently. Why does the fund care? Because, when shareholders sell their stocks

TABLE 8.2

Total Investment Costs of Actively Managed Stock Funds

	Large Cap	Small Cap and Foreign	Emerging Markets
Expense ratio	1.3%	1.6%	2.0%
Fund's transaction costs	0.3%	0.5%	1.0%
Bid-ask spread	0.3%	1.0%	3.0%
Market impact costs	0.3%	1.0%	3.0%
Total	2.2%	4.1%	9.0%

in a fund, the fund may have to sell some of the assets it owns to come up with the cash. As we have seen, this costs the fund money because of transaction costs and so forth. So the redemption fee is there in part to discourage shareholders from trading the fund, and in part to ensure that if a particular shareholder does decide to trade, he or she rather than the remaining shareholders will bear the resulting costs.

Although the redemption fee may look like a back-end load, the two are very different. The back-end load is a sales commission that goes to the fund management company or someone else, never back into the fund. The redemption fee goes back into the fund itself to cover the costs of a selling shareholder's actions. It benefits the remaining shareholders. Not too many funds charge redemption fees. Some index funds charge redemption fees, and if a fund meets your other criteria and you believe you will hold it for the long term, the redemption fee will actually work in your favor. Do not hesitate to buy such a fund in that case. This is one cost that makes sense.

PARING DOWN BROKERAGE COMMISSIONS

If you decide to invest in individual stocks or mutual funds through a broker, here are my suggestions and admonitions:

- Go with what I call a semi-discount broker—someone who will charge you not a rock bottom commission but not an arm and a leg either, who will be easy to reach and can provide service reasonably promptly if there is any problem. Do not pay the high price of large, full-service brokerage houses. Neither their advice nor their hand-holding is worth the huge commissions they charge. To keep up with the competition, many of these large full-service houses are setting up low-cost arms, and these are worth considering during your search. But remember that the game everyone is playing or is planning to play is one of a modified bait and switch. They want to pull you in with low costs up front in the hope that once you are there, inertia will take over and they will be able to slowly sell you additional services or even increase their fees without your noticing or doing anything about it. Based on the numbers you have seen on the effects of investment costs, if you let inertia take over and stop paying attention, you will lose a lot of money.

- To choose the right broker, start by looking through the survey and evaluation articles in the financial magazines (especially *Smart Money*), which discuss the service quality and fees of different brokers. You need up-to-date information because in this area who is good and who is not seems to change every other day.

- If you are going to work with a broker (account executive, financial representative, etc.), make sure that he or she has your long-term interest in mind and won't try to get you to trade frequently. This is not going to be easy because the broker's income is either going to depend on how often you trade or on talking you into opening an account where you pay a high annual fee (see below). So tread carefully.

- Do not open a wrap or similar account where you commit to pay a flat annual fee of as much as 2% of your assets in return for investment advice, unlimited trades, some fancy computer printouts every now and then, and probably a free cup with a logo. As we have discussed in endless detail, that's a lot of money to pay out year after year for things you don't need. If the fee includes unlimited or a larger number of free trades, then it will become an open invitation to start trading frequently. Paying a commission per trade may sooner or later draw your attention to how much money you are wasting.

- Most brokers would be only too happy to let you buy stocks on margin, and some would even let you buy certain mutual funds on margin. The cost issue here is what interest rate they charge you. But that is minor. The real issue is that you shouldn't even let the thought cross your mind. There must be something more insane you can do; but I cannot think of it offhand. (If you do not even know what buying on margin is, I consider that to be a blessing and I feel no urge, at least here, to explain to you what that is. Feel absolutely free to enjoy your ignorance of it.)

You can also buy most mutual funds through brokerage accounts. In most cases you will pay a commission (generally higher than the commission you pay for trading stocks) for doing that. If you are planning to trade mutual funds of different fund groups frequently, doing it through a brokerage account is more convenient but more expensive. Of course, if you follow the Rules, you won't be trading in and out of funds, but you will still be adding money to your funds periodically, often in small amounts. Doing that through a brokerage account can get quite expensive over the years, especially relative to the small sizes of these periodic investments. Do some cost benefit analysis before deciding if you should deal with the funds directly or through a brokerage account. My recommendation is to deal directly with the funds because most of them will let you add to your investment in a fund in amounts as small as $100 or $250 without any cost (assuming it is a no-load fund).

Let me end by stating the obvious: The most effective and the only fool-proof method of reducing brokerage commissions is to trade less or not at all. Before you even open a brokerage account, ask yourself if you even need one. You probably don't.

THE LESSON TO TAKE AWAY ON INVESTMENT COSTS

The lesson to take away from this discussion of investment costs is very simple. As the rule says: Save every penny of investment cost you can. You already know how to do that. Invest only in low-cost funds. Look back at Table 8.1. Even when we went from the low-cost index fund with an annual cost of 0.2% to the typical index fund with an annual cost of 0.5%, it made a pretty big difference in the amount of money we could expect to end up with over a 20- or 40-year period. There is almost no chance that an average-cost or high-cost mutual fund will earn enough additional returns to compensate for the extra costs you will pay. If instead of investing through mutual funds you decide to invest on your own and spend a lot on brokerage fees, there is almost no chance that you will be able to offset with superior performance the high costs you will incur. If you ever feel tempted to invest in anything that has an annual investment cost of much over 0.5%, look back at the table, sleep on it, and hope that by the time you wake up, you will be a rational person again.

A WORD ABOUT JOHN BOGLE AND THE VANGUARD GROUP

No discussion of mutual fund costs can be complete without acknowledging the contributions in this area of John Bogle and the Vanguard Group, the fund company he founded and over which he presided as chairman. Over the years, no individual has done more than he has to raise the consciousness of both the public and the mutual fund industry of the impact of investment costs on long-term investment performance, about the importance and need of keeping fund costs down, and about the superiority of passive investing. What is most admirable is that he has had the foresight and conviction to keep speaking on these issues on behalf of the investors, even when most other industry leaders have been focused on maximizing the returns for their companies by trying to sell to the public as many varieties of actively managed funds as their marketing people can invent and charging fees and expenses as high as the market will bear. And John Bogle has led by example. Under his leadership the Vanguard Group has offered just about the lowest cost funds in almost every category, not because competition demanded it, but simply because it was and is the right thing to do for investors. While he was fighting for investors, he also managed to grow Vanguard into one of the largest fund groups. It just goes to show that good guys can finish first also, and doing the right thing by one's customers does not have to necessarily conflict with the profitability of one's business. The role he has played as a leader of the Vanguard Group and the mutual fund industry is unprecedented.

Whenever I personally have a need to look for cost and other information for a particular type of fund, my first step always is to see if Vanguard has a fund that fits the description because then I know I can use that as the benchmark for judging other similar funds. In the interest of keeping things simple and saving time, you cannot do better than starting, and probably ending, your search for any type of fund with the Vanguard Group. As we will see under Rule #7, Vanguard funds are also some of the most tax-efficient funds around, and over the years that can save you a lot of money as well. (In the Appendix on Recommended Fund Companies and Funds, I have listed, with brief descriptions, the Vanguard funds you can use to follow the Only Proven Road to Investment Success.)

♦ THINGS TO REMEMBER ♦

- ♦ No matter what you are investing in, make sure your annual investment costs are less than 0.5% of your investments—the lower, the better.

- ♦ There is almost no chance that an actively managed stock fund that has total annual investment costs of 2% or more will be able to make up for those high costs with superior performance. Such high investment costs will significantly reduce the money you accumulate over the long run.

- ♦ Pare down the costs of investing in stocks to 0.2% to 0.4% per year by investing in low-cost broadly diversified index funds.

- ♦ If you decide to invest in individual stocks, use a low-cost semi-discount broker with a good reputation for customer service and buy and hold your stocks instead of trading frequently.

◆ It is difficult to justify investing in most actively managed bond funds because their annual investment costs of 1% or more drain away over a third of the relatively low expected real return of bonds. If you want to invest in bonds at all, invest only in low-cost bond funds, whether index or actively managed.

◆ Keep an eye on the investment costs of your money market fund.

◆ Series I Savings Bonds (I Bonds) and bank certificates of deposit (CDs) have no investment costs. The I Bonds are your best choice for long-term safe investments. Use CDs of less than 2 years' maturity for the safe part of your portfolio if you can find attractive rates.

◆ Beware of funds whose investment costs are being temporarily held down for marketing purposes.

◆ Do not open any brokerage accounts, such as wrap accounts, that charge high annual fees. This kind of growing ongoing fees does the most damage to your long-term investment results. Moreover, you really get nothing of value for their generally exorbitant fees.

♦

CHAPTER 9

AVOID TOLL ROADS
WHENEVER YOU CAN

♦

RULE #7: USE EVERY OPPORTUNITY TO
REDUCE AND DELAY UNCLE SAM'S TAKE

One way to cut down the cost of a trip is to avoid toll roads and take free-ways whenever you can. On your investment trip, you will see Uncle Sam showing up every so often with his hands out to collect his tolls—income and capital gains taxes. You cannot make your whole investment trip on freeways, but if you plan well and take the right steps, you can bypass the toll roads for long stretches and save yourself a lot of money.

Taxes are similar to investment costs in that they may appear small when you look at the tax cost associated with each individual transaction, and they may even appear small when you add them up for a year, but just as with investment costs, with the help of the Magic of Compounding, over the years taxes can easily end up costing you hundreds of thousands or even millions of dollars. You can drastically reduce this drain by taking two simple steps.

TO TAX HEAVEN IN TWO SIMPLE STEPS

STEP 1: DEFER TAXES USING TAX-ADVANTAGED ACCOUNTS

The first step is to legally delay paying as much of your taxes as you can. This is formally called deferring your taxes. To encourage and help in saving for long-term needs such as retirement, politicians have deliberately created several attractive opportunities for you to set up tax-deferred (also called tax-advantaged) savings accounts. You can contribute to these accounts on a regular basis, and often it is a painless process because you do it through direct deductions from your paychecks. The great advantage of these accounts is that you do not have to pay any taxes on the returns on these investments until you start withdrawing the money, most likely during retirement. In some cases, you can even make your contributions to these accounts from your pretax money (or, what is equivalent, make tax-deductible contributions), which will give your savings a sizable additional boost.

Depending on how far you are from retirement, the combination of saving regularly, reinvesting all your returns, and not paying taxes for a long time can help you build up savings of a size that may be truly beyond your wildest dreams. You must take full advantage of saving and investing through these accounts. Although you can defer taxes only on a certain amount of money through these accounts, as we are going to see in step 2, you really do not have to be constrained by these limits. You can defer taxes on almost as much of your investments as you want.

STEP 2: DEFER TAXES BY BECOMING A LONG-TERM INVESTOR

The second step is to drastically reduce the taxes you have to pay every year if you keep switching from one stock to another, from one fund to another, or from one asset to another. All you have to do is invest in an index fund or in Series I Savings Bonds (I Bonds), keep adding to them even small amounts of money regularly, and just hold onto them. Until you start selling your stocks or cashing in your I Bonds because you need the money, the taxes you will pay will be very small. This really is deferring taxes on any amount of money you want—your own unrestricted, unlimited tax-deferred account.

Every time you switch assets in a taxable account, that is, in an account that is not one of the tax-deferred accounts we discussed before, and you have a profit on the transaction, you have to pay taxes on the profit that year. So if you do not take the action I just recommended, you may end up paying taxes of more than 2% per year on your total savings. We have already seen under Rule #6 what an annual drain of even that small size can do to the money you accumulate over the years. Take this simple step and save big money.

That's really all there is to it to the real story about reducing taxes. The rest is detail that is good to know, but do not get so lost in it that you lose sight of the big picture I have just drawn for you.

DEALING WITH TAXES REQUIRES SPECIAL CARE AND ADVICE

Under Rule #10 I will talk about the few carefully selected companions you should take along to have a pleasant and safe trip down the Only Proven Road to Investment Success. A tax advisor is going to be one such important companion. Despite all the talk about simplifying the tax codes, they have been getting thicker and more complex by the year. Hidden in those thousands of pages are quite a few opportunities to save on taxes, as well as traps you can fall into that will run you afoul of the Internal Revenue Service (IRS), cause some serious agony, and end up costing money. As you may have already learned from some unpleasant personal experience, in matters of taxes you have to cross all your t's and dot all your i's exactly. So, unless your tax situation is very simple, find and use a good tax advisor. But do not take your investment advice from him.

Also, do not let the tax tail wag your investment dog. Every now and then you may be disgusted with what you are paying in taxes. But do not let that cloud your judgment and feel tempted to try out dubious tax shelters or the latest tax gimmick. Most tax shelter ideas or tax gimmicks are dubious not because they are illegal, but because they make no sense as investments. And the fees involved are generally so high that they will have to pay off like winning lottery tickets in order for you to net any money on them.

A NOTE ON TAX LAW CHANGES

In the middle of 2000 the Congress passed and the President signed into law a new tax bill that will change many of the tax law provisions I will discuss below. These changes are going to take place over a number of years and, believe it or not, many of the new provisions are slated to expire in about 10 years unless the Congress renews them. Immediately after these changes were enacted, the Democrats gained majority in the Senate and they are already talking about changing some of the provisions of the new law. So no one knows where all of this will end up. One thing that is certain is that the tax laws will keep changing even though the basic principles I discuss here should hold for a long time. Before making any important investment decisions, you must check out the latest provisions of the tax laws. While consulting your tax advisor is the safest thing to do, generally you can also get the latest information from your brokers or mutual fund companies.

OVERVIEW OF THE THREE MAJOR TYPES OF TAXES

Over the years most of us will have to deal with three different types of taxes on the returns from our investments. It is important to understand how these taxes work because only then will you be able to take full advantage of the opportunities for reducing and deferring your taxes.

INCOME TAXES

You have to pay income taxes on your salary and most other income, including the dividends you get on your stocks and the interest you earn on investments in savings accounts, money market funds, bank certificates of deposit (CDs), and bonds. This type of income is called ordinary income, and the income tax on it is called ordinary income tax or just income tax. The major component of your total income tax is the federal income tax, on top of which you may also have to pay state and other local income taxes, depending on where you live and sometimes also depending on where you work. When all of these income taxes are combined, they can add up to pretty big numbers.

One break you get on your income from investments as opposed to your salary and wages is that you do not have to pay Social Security and a few other taxes, together called the payroll taxes, on investment income. Also, interest income on some municipal securities is partly or fully exempt from income taxes.

You cannot avoid paying income taxes on your investment income by buying mutual funds because they are required to distribute to their shareholders the dividends or interest income they earn on the stocks and bonds that they buy. They generally make these distributions once or twice a year, but some funds that are specifically intended to generate a steady stream of monthly income, generally called income funds, may even make monthly distributions. If you own shares in a mutual fund on the day it makes an income distribution, you will have to pay taxes on it in the same year you get it.

Marginal Versus Average Tax Rate

Your marginal tax rate is the percentage of your next dollar of income you will have to pay in taxes. Your tax bracket for federal income taxes determines your marginal tax rate. If you also pay state income taxes, then to estimate your marginal tax rate just add your state tax bracket to the federal tax bracket. (Your actual marginal tax rate may be a little lower, but it is a very small difference.) If you use a tax preparation program, you can use it to estimate your marginal tax rate. In your last year's tax return, increase your income by $100. Your marginal tax rate is the amount by which your total taxes (federal and state) increase. If it goes up by $35, your marginal tax rate is 35%.

Why is the marginal tax rate so important? Because, of any additional money you make, whether you get a raise or you have additional investment income, you have to pay taxes at that marginal rate. So to know how much money you are going to get to keep, you have to know your marginal tax rate. For example, if you invest some money in a money market account, expect to earn interest at an annual rate of 5%, and want to estimate how much money you will have at the end of 5 years, you need to know your marginal tax rate to do the calculations. If your marginal tax rate is 32%, then of the 5% annual interest income, you will have to pay 1.6% in taxes (32% of 5% = 1.6%) and the return you will get to keep is 3.4%. If you do your projections using the 5% return number instead of the 3.4%, you will really get to keep, your estimate will be off. If you make a long-term projection without taking out the relevant taxes, because of the Magic of Compounding, you will end up being way off. Since for most calculations like this you have to use your marginal tax rate, you need to know what it is for you.

Your average tax rate is the total taxes you pay divided by your total income. In making financial plans, you generally use it only to figure out what taxes you will have to pay during your retirement. For example, if you estimate that your average tax rate will be 20% after you retire and you expect a taxable annual retirement income of $80,000 from all sources, then you will pay $16,000 of taxes per year. In almost all other situations you will use your marginal tax rate to make future plans.

CAPITAL GAINS TAXES

If the price of a stock, bond, mutual fund, or some other investment goes up or down, that is called a capital gain or capital loss. Until you sell an asset, any capital gain or loss on it is called unrealized capital gain or capital loss; only when you sell an asset does the unrealized capital gain or loss become realized capital gain or loss.

Instead of paying ordinary income tax, you pay capital gains taxes on your capital gains, which work differently from the ordinary income tax. Most often the capital gains tax rules are more advantageous, and you may be able to use those advantages to save a lot of money or accumulate a lot more money. For that reason, whenever there is an opportunity to do so, you should try to earn the return on your investments as capital gains rather than ordinary income. The three main advantages of doing so are:

1. Capital gains are generally taxed at a lower rate than ordinary income.

2. Capital gains taxes can be deferred for as long as you want because they do not have to be paid on unrealized capital gains, that is, until you sell an asset on which you have a capital gain.

3. If you do not sell an asset during your lifetime, it may be passed on to your heirs without anyone ever paying taxes on the unrealized capital gain through the date of your death.

How Capital Gains Can Lower Your Taxes

If you sell an investment within a year of buying it, that is, hold it for less than a year, then your realized capital gain on it is called short-term capital gain, and that is taxed at the same rate as ordinary income. But if you hold the asset for more than a year, then when you sell it you realize what is called long-term capital gain, and that is taxed at a lower rate. If your income, including the capital gains, puts you in the 15% tax bracket for ordinary income, then you will pay taxes on your long-term capital gains at a rate of 10%, a tax saving of 5%. If you fall into any of the higher income tax brackets, your long-term capital gains tax rate is 20%. That is a considerable saving, and the higher the tax bracket you are in, the larger your saving. (There may be some changes to the capital gains tax rates starting with tax year 2001. Check that out before you act.)

There is one additional advantage of capital gains compared with ordinary income. If in any year you have a net capital loss, that is, your realized capital losses exceed your realized capital gains, you can deduct up to $3,000 of it in calculating your taxable income, which effectively gives you a tax break for the loss. If your marginal tax rate is 31% and you have a $3,000 net capital loss, that will mean a tax saving of 31% of $3,000, or $930. If you have net capital loss in any year of over $3,000, you cannot deduct the extra amount in that year, but you can use it in future years.

(Remember that this is just an overview of the rules of capital gains and losses. As you will suspect, there is a lot more to these rules that may apply to your specific situation.)

How You Can Benefit from Deferring Capital Gains Taxes

Now that you understand how the capital gains tax works, you can see that you can defer your capital gains taxes on any asset for as long as you want by simply not selling the asset, that is, by not realizing your capital gains. The advantage of deferring capital gains taxes, and for that matter any kind of taxes, is that you can keep earning additional return on that money—if you want to feel better, you can even call it Uncle Sam's money, although it really is your money. With the help of the Magic of Compounding, this can add up to a lot of additional money over the years.

Let us look at an example to get an idea of what kind of money we are talking about. Suppose you invest $100,000 today for 20 years and expect to earn a return of 10% per year. If all of this 10% return is ordinary income (e.g., interest), you will have to keep paying taxes on the return every year at your marginal tax rate. If your marginal tax rate is 35%, at the end of 20 years you will have about $352,000. On the other hand, if you put the money in an asset that pays no interest or dividend so that you earn all your return in the form of price appreciation or capital gains, and you just hold onto the asset for the entire period, at the end of 20 years the value of the asset will be about $673,000. If at that point you sell the asset and pay 18% tax on the long-term capital gains, you will be left with about $570,000. So it is $570,000 vs. $352,000, a very substantial difference on an original investment of $100,000.

Getting your return in the form of capital gains has the additional advantage that if you do not need the money at the end of 20 years—say it is retirement money and you are still far from retirement—you will have the option to hold onto the asset, in which case you will have the entire $673,000 working for you because you will continue to defer the capital gains tax.

Clearly, you must take advantage of this tax deferral opportunity whenever you can. But let us understand what exactly is helping us here. First, we can defer the taxes only on that portion of the return that is capital gain. If part or all of the return is ordinary income, we will have to pay ordinary income tax on that portion every year. Second, the capital gains tax is getting deferred only because we are holding onto the same asset or assets. If we keep trading the assets, then we will have to pay taxes on any profit or gain we realize every time we trade. That will keep reducing the amount of taxes we actually defer and, in the extreme, if we trade the assets every year or even more frequently, we will be back to the same situation of earning the return as ordinary income, that is, we will end up with the $352,000 at the end of the 20 years versus $570,000—no benefits of lower capital gains tax rate, and no benefits of tax deferral. Therefore, in addition to keeping your investment costs low, you must buy and hold a well-diversified portfolio of stocks or an index fund, and not keep trading.

One final point about capital gains tax as it relates to investing in mutual funds. As with interest and dividends, mutual funds also have to distribute to shareholders any capital gains they realize during the year, and if you are a shareholder on the day of such a distribution, you will have to include it as capital gains on your tax return and pay taxes on it. The fund will give you a breakdown of how much of it is long-term capital gain and how much is short-term capital gain. It depends on how long the fund held the assets it sold, not on how long you have held the fund. Because every such distribution forces you to pay some of your taxes now instead of deferring them, you really want to invest in funds that do as little of this as possible. They are called tax-efficient funds. We will talk more about how to find them later.

ESTATE TAXES

Estate taxes are payable on the value of all of your possessions—called your estate—that you leave behind when you die. Estate tax rates are quite high. But there are large exemptions. Through proper estate planning, you and your spouse can pass along to your heirs fairly substantial estates without paying any estate taxes. From the point of view of tax strategies for your investments, what is of interest here is that when you pass along an appreciated asset to your heirs as part of your estate, the appreciated value of the asset is included in the estate for estate tax calculation, but your heirs inherit the asset at its appreciated price as well. It is easier to understand the advantage of that with an example.

Suppose you bought some stocks at $100 and just before your death their market value was $150. If you had sold them just before your death, you would have paid capital gains taxes on the $50 price appreciation. But if you did not sell them before your death, they would become part of your estate at the $150 valuation, and if there are no taxes due on your overall estate (including for these stocks), the $50 price appreciation would completely escape any taxation because your heirs would inherit the stocks at the $150 value (called a stepped-up tax basis) and they will pay capital gains taxes only on any price appreciation above the $150 when they sell the stocks.

You should be aware that under the new tax law enacted in 2000, the estate tax exemption will become even more favorable over the next several years. But then again chances are that Congress will repeal some of these new provisions before they actually go into effect. Also, what I have said above applies nicely as long as we are talking about assets that are not in any tax-deferred or tax-advantaged account. If there is any money or asset left in these accounts at the time of your death, the tax situation will get complicated. So if that possibility is there, you should talk to a tax advisor well in advance to decide what steps you should be taking.

WHY AND HOW TO BE TAX EFFICIENT

Tax efficiency is a term that has come into vogue in recent years in connection with mutual funds. But it applies to your own trading as well. And being tax efficient is so important that it is a little puzzling that it has come to general attention only recently. Let us first understand what it is.

Suppose you are looking at last year's performance of two funds, and both of them reported total return of 10% for the year. On the surface it looks like they had the same performance. But suppose one fund's manager worked very hard, bought and sold stocks frantically, and, as a result, all of his 10% return consists of dividends and realized short-term capital gains. Remember, any time you or a fund sells a stock that has been in the portfolio for less than a year and has a profit on it, you realize a short-term capital gain. So if you owned that fund for the year, you would have received all of that 10% as distributions and you would have paid taxes on it. If your marginal tax rate is 30%, that's 3% in taxes you would have paid last year.

The other fund's manager showed up for work some days, played golf some other days, and sat around staring at the sky a lot. All year he was perfectly happy with the stocks he already owned and bought and sold nothing. And he has a policy of never buying any stock that pays dividends. So his 10% return came from just one source—the stocks he already owned the year before went up by 10%.

Now, leaving aside the question of whether either of the managers deserve their money management fees, the reality is that if you had held both funds in taxable accounts, your after-tax return would be just 7% on the first fund (you did not keep what you saw) and 10% on the second fund (you kept what you saw). Remember our example from Rule #6, which showed how devastating the long-term impact of a 3% annual cost can be. If in a taxable account you hold the fund that costs you 3% more in taxes every year, you will accumulate significantly less money over the years, even though from the numbers that everybody keeps reporting and advertising, both funds would seem to have the same performance.

I exaggerated lots of things to make the point. But you cannot escape the fact that if a fund trades a lot and you hold it in a taxable account, you may have to pay out a good part of its returns in taxes. That's a tax-inefficient fund—the fund manager did not think of and try to mitigate tax impacts on his investors. The second fund was extremely tax efficient. It cost you nothing in taxes.

TAX EFFICIENCY WORKS AT TWO LEVELS

Notice that even if you owned the second fund for less than a year and decided at the end of the year to sell it and move on to a hotter fund, you would incur a 3% tax bill even though you owned a highly tax-efficient fund. And finally, instead of holding funds, if you were trading stocks on your own, had a gross return of 10% for the year, but had to pay taxes on all of it, you would again have been in the same boat.

The above discussion shows that tax efficiency works at two levels—at the level of the fund as well as at your personal level. If you keep trading funds or stocks, you will find it very easy to be tax inefficient and run up your tax bills. And even if it looks small on the surface, over the years you will miss out on making so much money that there is no way the thrill of trading stocks or funds will be able to make up for it.

THE CURE FOR TAX INEFFICIENCY AND
TAX-MANAGED FUNDS

Is there a cure for tax inefficiency? Of course. Take the two steps to tax heaven. Put as much of your money as you can in tax-deferred accounts and invest the money in your taxable accounts into a low-cost broad-based index fund or I Bonds and hold onto them. No trading (especially in a taxable account), no taxes, no tax inefficiency. I know I sound like a broken record and keep coming up with the same few answers no matter what the question is, but I figure if I have a few good answers and they are simple ones, why not repeat them until you become so convinced (or tired) that you start repeating them with me as well?

Of course, once tax efficiency is recognized as important, we cannot just have tax-efficient and tax-inefficient funds. We can go a step further and have tax-managed funds that consciously manage their trading in a way that reduces tax impact. I am usually skeptical of most innovations in the fund industry, but this is one of the innovations that makes sense. Index funds and any kind of passive investing are inherently tax efficient. But as we will see, even index funds can be improved by tax management, and we are starting to see some tax-managed index funds that I will recommend you consider for your taxable accounts.

TAX EFFICIENCY OF I BONDS

In case you have missed the point, the only way to be tax efficient with your safe investments in taxable accounts is to invest as much of that money in I Bonds as you can. As long as you hold the bonds, your interest will accumulate and compound tax deferred. You will have to pay ordinary income tax on all the accumulated interest when you cash in your I Bond, but that may happen when you are already retired and are in a lower tax bracket. Remember that you can defer taxes on the interest on I Bonds for up to 30 years. Because there is no cost involved in buying and selling I Bonds, you should also get them in small enough denominations so that you can cash in at any time only the amount you need and leave the tax deferral on the rest of your I Bonds unaffected.

THE BENEFITS OF DEFERRING TAXES AND HOW TO CAPTURE THEM

We have already seen that there are three major benefits of deferring your taxes. First, by deferring taxes you can earn substantial additional returns on the tax money you are holding onto. Second, if you can defer the taxes until you retire, you will be paying them at your tax rate during retirement, which is likely to be much lower. Third, if you simply hold onto and thereby effectively defer until your death the taxes on your gains on investments whose values have gone up, you may be able to pass them on to your heirs without anyone ever paying those taxes. (See the cautionary note on this under the discussion for estate taxes.)

To encourage and help in saving for long-term needs such as retirement, the tax laws allow you to save through several different types of accounts or savings plans that let you defer taxes. They are generically called tax-deferred or tax-advantaged accounts. Your regular savings or accounts, which have no special tax advantages, are called taxable savings or taxable accounts.

The tax-deferred accounts fall into two broad categories, although, as you might expect, no two of them have exactly the same rules. In the first category, which I will call pretax contributions accounts, you make the contributions from your pretax money, all returns accumulate tax deferred, and you pay taxes only as you withdraw the money, generally during your retirement years. In the second category, which I will call regular tax-deferred accounts or just tax-deferred accounts, you make your initial contributions with after-tax money, but thereafter these accounts offer the same tax deferral of the returns as the pretax contribution accounts.

In the first category of accounts, when you withdraw the money over the years you have to pay taxes on all of the money you withdraw because you never paid taxes on the original contributions you made to the accounts or on the accumulated returns. In the second category of accounts, where you already paid taxes on your original contributions, at the time of withdrawing money from these accounts you pay taxes only on the portion of the withdrawals that comes from accumulated returns; you do not pay taxes again on the portion of the withdrawals that represents the money you had originally contributed. (Yes, the tax calculations do get complicated at that point and you will need help to do them right.)

WHAT ARE PRETAX CONTRIBUTIONS?

When you have the opportunity to make a pretax contribution, you do not pay your regular income tax on that money now. You take the money out of your pretax income or deduct it right from your gross income. In effect, it is not considered part of your current income any more. If you have a gross income of $100,000 in a year and make a tax-deductible or pretax contribution of $10,000 to a plan, that year you will pay income taxes only on the remaining $90,000. Normally, if your marginal tax rate is 35%, you would have paid $3,500 of taxes on that $10,000, which in this case you won't be paying. So you have been able to defer $3,500 of taxes. A pretax contribution is also called a tax-deductible contribution.

HOW BENEFICIAL ARE PRETAX CONTRIBUTIONS?

We have already seen (under our discussion of capital gains taxes) that the benefits of being able to defer taxes on the returns on your investments can be very significant over the years. All investments you make through either the regular or pretax contribution tax-advantaged accounts will enjoy this benefit. But for accounts in the pretax contribution category, you are deferring additional taxes (the $3,500 in our example above), and clearly that will put this category of accounts ahead of the simple tax-deferred category of accounts. How much ahead? Let us look at an example.

Suppose you contribute $10,000 to a pretax contribution account and the equivalent $6,500 to a regular tax-deferred account. You earn 10% annual return for 20 years, at which point you retire, withdraw all of the money from both accounts, and pay taxes at a rate of 20% (a lower rate because you are now in a lower tax bracket). After paying the appropriate taxes in each case, the money you get out of your first account will be about $54,000 versus $36,000 from the second account. Clearly, being able to defer the taxes on that additional $3,500 had a big impact on what you ended up with. That is why your first priority in saving for the long term has to be finding and taking full advantage of all opportunities you have to put money into tax-deferred accounts in the pretax contribution category.

DEFERRING TAXES THROUGH TAXABLE VERSUS TAX-DEFERRED ACCOUNTS

We now know that we can defer taxes on investments in both taxable and tax-deferred or tax-advantaged accounts. But what are the advantages and disadvantages of each approach?

When you invest through tax-advantaged accounts, you do not have to pay taxes on any of the returns—whether it is capital gain or ordinary income—until you start withdrawing the money. So you can switch from one investment to another or from one financial institution to another without any tax consequences. In this sense, tax-advantaged accounts give you a lot more investment flexibility. But they have a number of constraints as well. First, there are limits to how much you can contribute to such accounts every year. Second, your access to the money will be restricted to various extents until you retire. Third, a lot of these savings have to be made through plans that your employer offers you, and the investment choices may be limited.

In your taxable accounts you can defer taxes only in two ways. First, you can defer taxes on the capital gains on an asset as long as you do not sell the asset. So if you buy and hold an index fund for a long time, you will be able to defer taxes on most of the return. But any time you sell the fund to switch the money to something else, you will have to pay the taxes. That restricts your flexibility. Second, among safe investments, I Bonds provide you the only opportunity to defer taxes on interest income. All other interest income will be immediately taxable. So the opportunities to defer taxes in taxable accounts are limited. But if you are willing to just buy and hold an investment like an index fund, you can defer the capital gains taxes on an unlimited amount of money for a very long time. And, you can invest up to $30,000 per year in I Bonds (under each Social Security number) and defer taxes on the interest income for up to 30 years.

In summary, you have to take advantage of all tax-deferral opportunities, and if you play your cards right you can defer taxes on an almost unlimited amount of money.

SPECIFIC OPPORTUNITIES FOR TAX SAVINGS

We have spent a lot of time going over the tax rules and the advantages of deferring taxes because once you fully understand the rules of the game, you will be able to play it much better. Even though most people will need to get tax advice from an expert, the more you understand taxes, the better questions you will be able to ask and the more you will be able to get out of your tax advisor.

So far we have talked about four broad strategies for reducing and deferring taxes:

1. Defer both ordinary income and capital gains taxes by taking advantage of the various opportunities the government has created through the tax code to help you save for retirement and other major needs, that is, by using tax-advantaged accounts.

2. Try to earn as much of your returns as capital gains instead of ordinary income as possible.

3. In taxable accounts, defer capital gains taxes by holding onto your investments instead of trading them and defer taxes on interest income by investing in I Bonds and holding onto them.

4. Avoid ordinary income taxes by investing in tax-exempt securities.

Let us now look at the most important specific opportunities for deferring taxes.

CONTRIBUTE THE MAXIMUM TO 401(K) AND SIMILAR ACCOUNTS

If your employer offers 401(k) or other similar savings plans where you can make contributions from your pretax income, contribute to them the most you can. As we have seen, things do not get any better than this. Many employers match part of your contributions and you do not have to pay any taxes on the employer contribution either until you start withdrawing money in retirement. Make sure you are doing everything to take full advantage of that. You will ultimately pay ordinary income taxes on all the money as you withdraw it over your retirement years. But until then, it is all yours to invest. You should assume that you won't have access to any of this money until you retire, although the plans of some employers have some flexibility in this matter (e.g., in emergencies you may be allowed to borrow against them). Take the time to understand the rules of your employer's plan.

What kinds of assets should this money be invested in? Under our strategy of investing only in stocks and safe assets, in your early years, all of this money should go into a stock index fund. See the discussion under Rule #4 on how to identify an index fund in the choices you are offered and what to do if there is no index fund option. If and when your financial plan calls for putting some of your long-term money into safe investments, you will direct your new contributions here to such investments and you may even switch some of your stock index fund money to safe investments at that time. If for some reason you have decided to invest in bonds or high-income stocks, then they belong here even before the index fund because they need all the help from tax deferral they can get. As we know, an index fund held for the long term will be mostly a tax-deferred investment, even in a taxable account.

CONTRIBUTE THE MAXIMUM AMOUNT TO AN IRA

The IRA (individual retirement account) rules have become more complex over the years because of changes Congress keeps making to satisfy one constituency or another. But you cannot afford to ignore IRAs because no matter what your situation, if you have income, you can get some very good tax benefit with an IRA. You should contribute the maximum to an IRA.

At heart the IRA is a simple concept. You get to contribute $3,000 ($6,000 for you and your spouse if you are married) every year to an IRA that you can open at almost any financial institution, such as a bank, brokerage house, or mutual fund, and invest the money in almost any way you want. You get to defer the taxes on all of the returns you earn, and you may or may not have to pay taxes when you withdraw the money during your retirement years. Clearly, it is a great deal you should not pass up. Also remember that no matter who you are, at least until you are $70^1/_2$, and have that $3,000 or $6,000 of earned income (technically called compensation), you are eligible to contribute to some type of IRA.

Now here are the four ways things get complicated:

1. There are a couple of different types of IRAs. The way they work and their benefits differ to some extent, and depending on your particular situation—formally called eligibility—you may get to choose which type of IRA you want or you may be eligible to contribute to. These eligibility requirements can be complex, but you have to evaluate your situation only once a year and maybe not even that often.

2. When you withdraw your money from an IRA, in some cases you will have to pay taxes, in some other cases you won't. Calculating how much taxes you will have to pay against each withdrawal can get complicated.

3. If at the time of withdrawal you do not meet certain requirements, you may have to pay an additional penalty.

4. For some IRAs you have to start withdrawing your money by a certain age and at a certain rate.

It all sounds more complicated than it really is, especially since you do not have to deal with all the issues at one time; you just have to be aware of them. I am not going to address all these issues here because it will take pages and will probably bore you to no end. Also, the way things keep changing, my covering them here may not do you much good anyway. You will always need the latest information to do everything right. So I will cover the basics here. My recommendation is that in your early years you should invest all of the IRA money in a low-cost broad-based index fund. Then in the later years, if your financial plan calls for it, you would switch some of this money or direct future contributions to one of the safe investment choices. In view of these recommendations, I think you will do best to open your IRA at a mutual fund company.

If you call up the company where you want to open your account, the people there will walk you through the entire procedure and eligibility requirements. You can also ask them all the questions you want. That is why I have listed the four areas of complication above. You can use those to ask the right questions. The people at the major fund companies are well informed to answer all your questions, and they can also give you brochures with the most current information that you can read yourself. If you really want the ultimate, authentic detail, get IRS Publication 590, Individual Retirement Arrangements (call 1-800-TAX-FORM or go to www.irs.ustreas.gov).

Now here are the basics you need to know.

The Two Types of IRAs

There are two types of IRAs: the regular IRA and the Roth IRA. Depending on a number of factors, your contribution to a regular IRA may or may not be tax deductible. Your contribution to a Roth IRA is never tax deductible.

How Much Can You Contribute and How Do You Do It?

Both you and your spouse will have to open separate IRAs, and each of you can contribute up to $3,000 per year provided together you have at least that much earned income in the year you are making a contribution. One important point to remember is that both of you do not have to be working. As long as one of you is working and have earned income of more than $6,000, that will do. You do not have to keep opening a new account every year; you can keep adding to your account every year once you have opened it. Also, if you are eligible to contribute to both regular and Roth IRAs, you can split up your annual $3,000 contribution between the two types in any way you want, but you will need separate regular and Roth IRAs. Finally, you do not have to contribute the money for any year in a lump sum. You can make the contributions in any kind of installments and at any time during the year for which you are making the contribution, all the way up to the date that your tax return for the year is due the following year. (Note that under the new tax law these IRA contribution limits are slated to increase.)

Let me again emphasize that at least until you are 70^1/2, you can always contribute up to the total amounts I have mentioned to one kind of IRA or another, provided you have that much earned income.

What Are the Key Differences Between the Two Types of IRAs?

There are two differences that will matter to you most. First, if you meet some eligibility requirements, your contribution to a regular IRA may be tax deductible. Your contribution to a Roth IRA is never tax deductible. Second, when you start withdrawing your money from a regular IRA, you will be paying ordinary income tax on your withdrawals. Your withdrawals from a Roth IRA will be tax-free (except in some special circumstances). Your contributions grow tax deferred in both types of IRAs, that is, you don't pay any taxes on the returns until you start withdrawals.

Which Type of IRA Should You Contribute to?

For most people, a Roth IRA is likely to be the best choice. However, if you are eligible to make tax-deductible contributions to a reular IRA, you should do some analysis, with the help of the fund companies, to check if that is more attractive in your situation. If you are not eligible for either of those two, then until you retire or are $70^1/2$, you can and should contribute to a regular IRA even if you do not get a tax deduction.

What Restrictions on Withdrawals Should You Be Aware of?

For all IRAs, you can spread out your withdrawals over a number of years. The most important restriction is that, in general, if you withdraw any money from any of the IRAs before you are $59^1/2$, in addition to paying regular income taxes on your withdrawals, you will have to pay a 10% penalty. I said in general because there are some minor exceptions to this rule, and there are all sorts of other restrictions and requirements for withdrawals. That's why you always need to find out the latest information, especially before making any withdrawals.

CONTRIBUTE THE MAXIMUM TO KEOGH PLANS

If you are self-employed, you can start a Keogh plan and contribute up to 20% of your self-employment income (maximum of $30,000 per year) to it. You will earn tax-deferred return on the money until you start withdrawing from it. Even if you are employed, you can use a Keogh plan for any income you may have from a side business. Again, this is a pretax contribution account, so you should put in here as much money as you can. An added advantage of Keogh plans is that, just as with IRAs, you can set it up almost anywhere you want and get access to your favorite funds. The investment considerations are the same as those for the 401(k) accounts. Keogh accounts are a little more complex than IRAs and it may be best to get some help from a CPA or tax lawyer for setting one up for the first time.

CONSIDER ROLLING OVER YOUR 401(K) AND OTHER ACCOUNTS INTO IRAS

If you are switching jobs, you will probably have the option of leaving your 401(k) and other savings accounts with your previous employer or rolling them over into an IRA at the institution of your choice. Because this is a tax-free switch, and moving the money to a place of your choice will probably give you just the right investment options you want, seriously consider moving the money. Do not let inertia get in your way of doing the right thing. But make sure you are doing everything right to preserve the tax status of the money.

Incidentally, after you have been employed at a particular firm for a while, you may have the option of rolling over part of your savings accounts into outside IRAs even if you do not leave the company. If you have that option and if you are not happy with the investment options your employer is offering, consider doing the partial rollover.

DEFER TAXES BY INVESTING IN AN INDEX FUND EVEN IN A TAXABLE ACCOUNT

Create your own tax-deferred investment using an index fund and contribute as much as you want. This is the best way to take advantage of an index fund and the capital gains tax rules. Once you put money in an index fund, most of your return will be in the form of capital gains, on which no taxes will be due until you start selling. You will get a small portion of your fund's return every year in the form of dividend distribution and maybe even get some capital gains distribution, and you will have to pay taxes on those in the year you get them. You will still defer taxes on the bulk of the return, and you can minimize the current taxes by using the tax-managed index funds I will discuss in a moment. (Remember the Magic of Compounding. Mark your account for automatic reinvestment of distributions, and if you can at all afford to, pay the taxes on the distributions from savings.)

One of the great advantages of creating your own tax-deferred investment using an index fund is that you are in full control. You choose the fund, you decide how much to contribute and when, and you can hold onto the investment as long as you want. If you really need to, you can even withdraw money any time you want without paying any penalty. You can get the same benefits if you create your own passive portfolio of stocks or create a pseudo–index fund by combining several complementary funds, but I cannot see the advantages of doing this. Chances are, if you go that route, you will be tempted to switch stocks or funds every now and then, and the tax-deferral benefits will start to disappear fast because you will pay taxes at the time of each switch.

DEFER TAXES BY INVESTING IN I BONDS

Any long-term taxable money you want to put into safe assets belongs in I Bonds first. The inflation-protected return is just great, the opportunity to defer taxes for up to 30 years is perfect, and there is even the flexibility of being able to get your money any time after the first 6 months. (You will pay a penalty if you cash in before 5 years, but it is only 3 months' interest, small enough to justify cashing in if necessary.)

CONSIDER USING A TAX-MANAGED INDEX FUND
FOR YOUR TAXABLE ACCOUNTS

Even index funds have to distribute any dividend income they earn on the stocks they hold, as well as any capital gains they realize. This means that even if most of your capital gains on an index fund will be tax-deferred until you sell your shares, you will have to pay some taxes every year on these distributions. There are additional potential problems with funds that have substantial unrealized capital gains that I will discuss below.

Vanguard has come up with two special stock index funds, called tax-managed funds, which try to minimize these distributions in various ways. One of these, called the Tax-Managed Fund: Growth and Income Portfolio, is really a Standard and Poor's (S&P) 500 index fund. The other, called the Capital Appreciation Portfolio, is a Russell 1000 index fund. These may be attractive for your taxable accounts, especially if you are in a high tax bracket; but remember that one of the ways these funds minimize realizing capital gains is by imposing a redemption fee if you sell the funds before you hold them for a certain period. So check the fee rules and make sure you plan to hold the funds for the minimum periods required for avoiding the redemption fees.

CONSIDER A TREASURIES-ONLY MONEY MARKET FUND

Securities (bonds, notes, bills) of the U.S. Treasury are exempt from state and local income taxes. So if you live in a high–income tax state, you may earn a slightly higher after-tax return if you use a money market fund that invests exclusively in U.S. Treasuries. A number of fund companies offer such funds. To find out if it gives you higher after-tax return, you will have to compare it with a regular money market fund with a very sharp pencil. The difference may be too small and not worth it. On the other hand, you may want to go with it for the added safety, although you do not need to worry about safety with a good regular money market fund.

CONSIDER A TAX-EXEMPT MONEY MARKET FUND

There are money market funds that invest exclusively in very short-term securities. The interest income on these are exempt from federal income taxes, and there may be special funds whose income is also exempt from your state's income taxes. You can again get out your sharp pencil and see if you will do better, on an after-tax basis, using one of these instead of a regular money market fund. The calculation is simple. If your marginal tax rate is, say, 30% and you can get 5% interest on a regular money market fund, that's an after-tax interest of 3.5% (5% less 30% tax on 5% = 3.5%). So the tax-exempt money market fund has to yield more than that to be attractive.

There are far fewer tax-exempt money market funds than there are regular ones. As a result, there is much less competition among tax-exempt money market funds, and you probably will have to be in a very high tax bracket to find one that will give you a better after-tax, after-cost return.

CONSIDER A TAX-EXEMPT BOND FUND

I saved this type of fund for last because you need to consider it only if you have decided to invest in bonds outside your tax-deferred accounts and face a high marginal tax rate. As the statement implies, if you are going to invest in bonds, you will be better off putting regular taxable bonds in a tax-deferred account rather than buying tax-exempt bonds in taxable accounts. The calculation to decide whether the taxable or tax-exempt bonds provide you a better after-tax return is the same as the one I provided earlier for tax-exempt money market funds. But comparing taxable and tax-exempt bond funds is a little more difficult because there are differences in quality, maturity, and so forth. Pay special attention to the investment costs of any fund you choose in this category. High investment costs can easily eat up a third to even half of your real return on municipal bonds. (See Chapter 5 for more on tax-exempt bonds.)

POTENTIAL TAX-RELATED PROBLEMS TO WATCH OUT FOR

Let us now look at a few potential tax-related problems and what you should do about them.

DO NOT INVEST IN A FUND JUST BEFORE IT MAKES A DISTRIBUTION

Do not invest in a fund just before it makes a distribution, especially a sizable one, if you are buying it for a taxable account. If you do so, you will be effectively paying some taxes now and getting back your money later when you sell the fund—just the opposite of tax deferral. So before you buy a fund, especially toward the end of the year, call up the fund and ask if a sizable distribution is planned for the near future. Depending on how far out it is and how big it is, you may be better off waiting until the day after the distribution to buy into the fund.

Here's how it works: Suppose you invest $10,000 in a fund the day before the fund makes a distribution—dividend or capital gain, it doesn't matter—and you get your share, $500, of the distribution the next day when it is made. As a result of the distribution, the value of your fund shares will go down by $500 as well because the fund has fewer assets now and your share of the asset reduction is $500. (Since the fund's share price is likely to change that day because of general market fluctuations as well, the reduction for the distribution may not be clearly visible. Nonetheless, it will be there.) If there are no taxes involved (e.g., if the fund is in a tax-deferred account), this would not make any difference. But if the fund is in a taxable account, you will have to pay taxes on the $500 in the same year, even though all that happened is you got back $500 of your own money. You are effectively paying taxes now on someone else's dividends or capital gains and you will get back your money when you sell the fund because your capital gain at that time will be lower by $500 (remember the value of your holding in the fund has permanently gone down by $500).

TRY TO AVOID INVESTING IN A FUND WITH LARGE UNREALIZED CAPITAL GAINS

Try to avoid buying a fund with large unrealized capital gains if you are buying it for a taxable account. If a fund has substantial unrealized capital gain before you invest in it, it may be a potentially serious problem. Whenever the fund sells those assets, it will distribute the capital gains and you will end up paying taxes on someone else's gains now and get back your money later. (Similar to the situation we just covered.)

This may or may not be a serious problem with an index fund. On the one hand, because an index fund does not sell its stocks too often, these capital gains may not be realized for years or ever. On the other hand, because index funds hold onto their assets for a long time, an index fund that has been around for a while may have substantial unrealized capital gains, especially after a long bull market. In the normal course of business it won't sell those assets, and there will be no problem. But if the fund faces substantial redemptions (e.g., in a serious market downturn), it will have to sell and distribute those capital gains, and the tax problem we have been discussing will emerge. As before, if you are buying the fund for a tax-deferred account, this won't matter. But for taxable accounts, the tax-managed index funds I have mentioned offer some protection in this respect because they try to minimize this problem and try to minimize dividend distributions. Also, because the tax-managed index funds are relatively new, they have much smaller unrealized capital gains.

You can get an estimate of a fund's unrealized capital gains from the fund's annual report or from Morningstar.

DO NOT USE LIFE INSURANCE PRODUCTS FOR INVESTING

Avoid buying life insurance products (like whole life, universal life, and variable life) or deferred annuities to defer taxes. Although their fees and costs have come down some from their previous exorbitant levels, especially if you buy them through a cost-conscious mutual fund company, those investment costs are still very high. And those costs are of the worst kind, that is, of the kind that keeps draining money from your account year in and year out. You know how costly those investment costs can get. Unless you are planning to keep switching around from fund to fund, the tax deferral opportunities these products offer are not worth much. You know by now that you do not want to keep switching money from fund to fund, and you can get almost complete tax deferral on an unlimited amount of money by simply putting the money in an index fund and holding onto it. So why pay the costs? Up to a certain point in your life you will need life insurance. To meet that need, buy plain-vanilla renewable term life with as few bells and whistles as possible and you will be saving yourself a lot of money.

REMEMBER THE TAX PECULIARITIES OF TIPS

I have been recommending the Treasury Inflation-Protected Securities (TIPS) as a safe investment choice. I strongly recommend that you invest in them only through special, low-cost funds such as the Vanguard Inflation-Protected Securities Fund. There is a tax reason for making this recommendation.

You get the return on TIPS in two pieces. You get an interest income of around 3.5%, which is paid in cash, and the face value of the bond is increased semi-annually to compensate you for inflation. You will collect the latter only when the bond matures or you sell it, but tax on any adjustment of the face value has to be paid in the year it is made. So if inflation runs at 3% per year, you will be paying taxes on a total of 6.5% return (3.5% cash + 3% price adjustment) even though you will get 3.5% of that in cash now. You will have to come up with the tax on that other 3% from somewhere else. The funds sell enough bonds every year to distribute that price adjustment portion as well. So if the total return in a year is 6.5%, you will get a distribution of 6.5% and that will help pay the taxes. This problem does not exist in a tax-deferred account. But because there is at least one good low-cost fund for TIPS, you may be better off using it even for a tax-deferred account rather than buying TIPS in small quantities on your own.

◆ THINGS TO REMEMBER ◆

◆ Reducing tax costs is as important as reducing investment costs. You will accumulate significantly more money over the years if you reduce tax costs as much as you can.

◆ Take two simple steps to tax heaven:

1. Contribute the maximum to every tax-deferred retirement account for which you are eligible [e.g., 401(k), IRA, Keogh].
2. Stop trading stocks and other assets in taxable accounts and incurring ongoing tax costs. Instead, invest and keep adding to an index fund and do not sell until you need the money. Also, put in I Bonds any long-term money you want to put in safe assets and enjoy up to 30 years of tax deferral.

♦ Try to defer as much of your taxes as you can. The major benefits of deferring taxes are: (1) you can earn additional returns on the tax money that you are holding, (2) you may ultimately pay the taxes at a lower rate during retirement, and (3) you may be able to pass on some of the appreciated assets to your heirs without anyone ever paying taxes on those appreciations.

♦ In your taxable accounts, try to earn as much of your return as possible in the form of long-term capital gains. They have the lowest tax rates, and the taxes are automatically deferred until you sell an asset.

♦ When you can get an up-front tax deduction for contributing to a tax-deferred account, you get the most tax benefit over the years. Make contributing thPe maximum to such accounts your highest priority.

♦ Make sure you contribute the maximum to an IRA. The order of preference is: (1) a regular IRA with a deduction for the contribution, (2) a Roth IRA, (3) a regular IRA even without a tax deduction.

♦ You can defer taxes on an unlimited amount of money for as long as you want by simply not selling an appreciated asset. Create your own no-limit, no-restrictions, tax-deferred account by investing taxable money in a tax-managed index fund and holding onto it.

♦ Do not buy life insurance products or deferred annuities to defer taxes. You get little if any value for their high ongoing costs, which will add up to big money over time.

♦ Avoid tax shelters and other tax gimmicks. More often than not their costs outweigh their potential benefits and you will make money only if the underlying investments pay off like a winning lottery ticket.

◆

CHAPTER 10

BE PREPARED FOR ROAD WORK AND TRAFFIC JAMS

◆

RULE #8: HAVE REALISTIC EXPECTATIONS

If you take an important trip and want to get there by a certain time, you have to always allow for road work, traffic jams, and other possible problems along the way. Without a realistic plan, you won't get there on time. It is the same with your trip to investment success. You will invariably encounter problems along the way; you cannot expect that over a 30- or 40-year period everything will go smoothly. So you have to make realistic plans with realistic expectations.

Studies have shown that in making judgments and decisions in almost all areas in our lives, all of us give more weight to what we have experienced and, on top of that, we give lot more weight to our more recent experiences. This can seriously bias our views as investors because very few of us have long-term or broad personal experience with the market. So when this Rule says, "Have realistic expectations," if we base them on just our own limited experiences, or even worse, just on our most recent experiences, they may look realistic but they may not be realistic at all. To determine what are realistic expectations about investing, we have to seek a broader perspective and learn from history and other people's experiences as well. We all know that, but unfortunately, most of us are not very good at learning from other people's experiences, especially from other people's mistakes. We somehow insist on learning the hard way by repeating other people's mistakes. Still, let us try to set some realistic expectations based on history and whatever else we know and hope this will help us become better investors and avoid making some painful mistakes of our own.

THE MOST UNREALISTIC EXPECTATION ABOUT INVESTING

The most unrealistic expectation people have about investing—especially investing in stocks—is that if they work hard and smart or can find the right advisor, they can improve their investment returns. They believe higher returns are out there—they just have to find a way to get at them. I think this unrealistic expectation has been responsible for the failure of more people as investors than any other single factor.

If you are investing poorly, making the mistakes I have warned about, you can improve your returns by correcting those mistakes. But once you have done that, you will earn what the market gives you. You may not have thought of it that way, but this is the flip side of all these research results that show that no one can beat a simple index fund with any consistency. The simple index fund is the market, and that is the return the market gives us.

At times when the market is doing poorly or going nowhere and money market funds and other safe investments are providing paltry returns, I have people come up to me and ask, "I am making no money at all. What can I do now to do better?" The honest answer is, "There really isn't much anyone can do. And, if you have been investing correctly, doing something else now will be the wrong thing to do." The stock market is not going to tell you ahead of time how much return it will give you; it won't tell you if you will get a big lump of return every 7 years and nothing on the other 6 years or if you will get your returns uniformly over the years; it won't even tell you if it will give you any return at all. You will just have to sit there patiently hoping that over the long run you will earn the return that you can realistically expect.

Do not gamble with your future by having and acting on the unrealistic expectation that you can do much about what returns you will earn in the market.

WHY HAVE ANY EXPECTATIONS AT ALL?

Since I just finished effectively saying, "Whatever will happen, will happen—just learn to live with it," you may wonder, "In that case, why have any expectations at all?"

The primary reason is that you have to plan for the future. You have to have some idea about how much money you need to save and invest for college tuition, retirement, and so forth. Whether you call them expectations or assumptions, you have to have some numbers to make your plans.

AVOID RECENCY IN SETTING YOUR EXPECTATIONS

Many studies have shown that in thinking or making predictions about the future, we tend to depend a lot more on our more recent experiences than on what happened in the distant past. This is called recency. And this does not apply just to ordinary people like you and me; even so-called experts fall victim to it again and again. Many of our investment mistakes can be directly traced to the influence of recency on the expectations we set for our investments and the investment decisions we make.

In recent years when it looked like the stock market could not go anywhere but up, investors surveyed said that they were not greedy, they would be happy with 20% annual returns on stocks. None of them even had any idea how unrealistic that expectation was because they were only looking at recent history—they were suffering from recency.

The only way any of us can avoid recency is to look at long-term data. We often hear the argument that things have changed, that we are in a new era, that 30- or 40-year-old history is not relevant any more. I am sure there is some truth to the claims of change. But also remember the well-worn adage, the more things change, the more they remain the same—history, even long-term history, is often more relevant than we think. And human nature, the driving force behind it all, probably has not changed one iota in thousands of years. So if we choose to ignore history, it is only at our own peril.

REALISTIC EXPECTATIONS ABOUT INFLATION

In setting your expectations about all investments, inflation is the key, the big unknown because the value of the wealth you accumulate over time will depend on how much of the returns you earn on your investments get eroded by inflation. But we have already said in Rule #3 that no one can predict what the rate of inflation will be in the future. So our most realistic expectation about inflation is, "We don't know."

That sounds like a big problem, but it isn't. Remember, following Rule #3 we have been carefully choosing only investments that are likely to keep us ahead of inflation. So in making our financial projections, we will set inflation at a reasonable rate (say 3%) and set our expectations or assumptions about the returns on the other investments relative to inflation. This way even if the inflation rate goes up to 6% or something else, it will matter much less and our plans will not be seriously affected.

Let us be careful here. We are saying higher or lower actual inflation won't matter much because we are assuming that the inflation-protected investments we have chosen will actually earn higher returns to compensate for higher inflation. That's an assumption, a realistic expectation, but it is not carved in stone. Let us keep that in mind. (If the inflation rate turns out to be different from the 3% or whatever you use in making your plans, there will be some other effects because of taxes and compounding. But let us not get bogged down in that.)

REALISTIC EXPECTATIONS ABOUT INTEREST RATES

Investors have to deal with two interest rates: short-term and long-term. The short-term interest rate is what you earn on your money market funds, short-term bank certificates of deposit (CDs), and short-term bonds. Here a reasonable expectation is that the real return will be between 2% and 3%, that is, the nominal return will be that much higher than the short-term inflation rate. So if you make your financial projections using an inflation rate assumption of 3%, you should assume that your safe investments will have a return of between 5% and 6%. As we have discussed before, this is not a great return, and after taxes it will help you to just keep up with inflation or, if you want to look at it another way, it will just preserve the buying power of your money. Whenever you feel impatient with that paltry return, remind yourself: This is my safe money. I am at least keeping up with inflation. And I have money invested in stocks to earn better returns.

Incidentally, it is easiest to establish return expectations for the inflation-protected securities—Treasury Inflation-Protected Securities (TIPS) and Series I Savings Bonds. At the time you invest in them, you will know for sure what returns they will earn over and above inflation.

For long-term interest rate you can make fairly reliable assumptions about the nominal return you will earn, but not about the real return. Since the nominal return will remain fixed, the real return you earn will depend on what the actual inflation rate turns out to be. If the inflation rate goes up enough, you may even end up with a negative real return, that is, a loss in buying power. So, unless you can predict future inflation rates very well, you may get seriously hurt investing in long-term bonds. That is why I have advised you to stay away from long-term bonds. If you do not invest in long-term bonds, you won't have to worry about having the right expectation or assumption.

REALISTIC EXPECTATIONS ABOUT STOCK MARKET RETURNS

This, of course, is the biggie. To help you set your expectations right, I want you to go back and look at Figure 7.2. It shows what your real return would have been for each year between 1946 and 2000 if you were invested in a Standard & Poor's (S&P) 500 index fund. During this period you would have earned a compound annual real return of 7.8% per year, but just imagine how it would have felt had you been along for that ride. I have avoided making any predictions so far. But now I am going to stick my neck out and predict: The ride is going to be bumpy in the future as well. I cannot tell you if it will be more bumpy or less. But once you have decided you are getting on a really scary roller coaster, does it really matter if it is the scariest of them all or not?

So my recommendation is, have absolutely no short-term expectations about the stock market other than "It will vary a lot," and do not get impatient or scared when it does.

Now for the long-term expectation. I think a real return of 7% or slightly lower is the best you can go with. It will be very unrealistic to expect a continuation of the over 12% real annual return we enjoyed for the 1982 to 2000 period, despite all that talk you keep hearing about this being a new era and the Dow is going to 100,000 or whatever. In fact, a very strong case can be and has been made that given the high real returns of the recent past, returns in the next decade or two may be much lower than that 7%, in the 0% to 4% range. I have nothing against being conservative. But if you are talking about the next 30 or 40 years, I feel reasonably comfortable with the 7% number, but nothing higher. What this implies is that if you are going to do your planning assuming a 3% inflation rate, you will assume a nominal total return of anywhere between 7% and 10% per year for stocks. If you are planning for the next 10 years or so, you should also do a few alternate sets of calculations assuming lower real returns—maybe down to 4%—as well.

◆ THINGS TO REMEMBER ◆

◆ Form realistic expectations about your investments by learning from history and other people's mistakes. Do not get overly influenced by your personal, recent experiences.

◆ The most unrealistic expectation investors generally have is that they can somehow earn higher returns than the stock market in general. Learn to accept the fact that you will earn what the stock market gives you, and there is nothing you are going to be able to do about that.

◆ Because you have to make plans, you have to have some expectations or make some assumptions. But make sure they are realistic.

◆ You should make no assumptions about future inflation rates because they are unpredictable. Instead, you should choose investments that provide reasonable protection against inflation and have expectations only about their returns relative to the inflation rate, that is, real returns.

◆ Your realistic expectation for safe investments should be real returns of 2% to 3% per year.

◆ You cannot form any realistic expectations about the real returns on medium- and long-term bonds and should avoid investing in them.

◆ You should have no expectations about short-term and year-to-year returns on stocks. Learn to live with the fact that they will vary widely.

◆ Your realistic expectation about long-term investments in stocks should be a real return of around 7% per year, and probably lower for the next decade or two. Do not expect the recent exceptionally high real returns on stocks to continue, and do not buy into the stories that "we are in a new era now."

CHAPTER 11

♦

KNOW YOUR ROUTE AND STICK TO IT

♦

RULE #9: INVEST WITH CONVICTION, INVEST WITH DISCIPLINE, INVEST WITH PATIENCE

Before you get started on a trip, you need to know your route. Otherwise, if you get lost, the weather gets bad and you ask for directions from a stranger, he may point you in the right direction, but he may send you off in the wrong direction, too, and you may not find out until it is too late. In investing, whenever the market gets depressed (or even when it starts going up sharply), it will be very easy to think that you are lost. But you cannot afford to ask for directions from any of the gurus who are keen to offer you advice. We already know that they will invariably send you off in the wrong direction. So before you get started, know your route well, and once on the road, stick to it. Be your own guide.

Over the years, millions of investors have received the same kind of investment advice that I have offered you. And yet, most people never become successful investors because of one simple, or maybe not so simple, reason: they fail to heed this Rule. Most people generally earn on their investments only a fraction of the return they could because they fail to realize that investment success depends at least as much on psychological factors and their own behavior as it does on technical knowledge of the markets. Even a mediocre investment method will probably earn a decent return over the years if followed with conviction, discipline, and patience. But even the best investment method will fail miserably in the hands of an investor who does not really believe in it, who will not keep doing year after year what he decided to do when he got started, and who will not give the investment methods enough time to work.

In investing, we are our own worst enemies. Of course, all of us want to be successful investors and earn a lot of money. But our emotions get in our way. We are constantly buffeted by fear and greed, two powerful emotions, and after suffering through months or even years of pain caused by market downturns, we throw in the towel just at the worst possible time. What is most ironic is that emotions can get in our way even in good times. After the market has gone up for a while and we have made some good money, we start to get so worried about protecting what we have made that we sell out prematurely only to watch the market keep going up.

I am going to discuss the roles of conviction, discipline, and patience in successful investing and how you can use them to help you. But the real conversation has to take place between you and the person in the mirror. You have to come to an understanding with him or her about how you are going to prepare yourself psychologically to jump over this major hurdle on your way to investment success.

INVESTING WITH CONVICTION

To succeed as an investor, you have to have a true, unshakable conviction in the investment method you are going to follow, because no matter which investment method you follow, your conviction is going to be severely tested. For investing, we almost need an investor's version of Murphy's law that says, "Everything that can go wrong with an investment will go wrong starting with the day after you commit a big chunk of money to it." Once you invest for a while, you will become almost convinced that there is a major conspiracy going on against you. At some point it may even get so bad that you will start thinking that you are so wrong so much of the time that you will be better off doing exactly the opposite of what you are about to do. So, if you do not have the conviction to carry you through all those bad times, you will have no chance of being a successful investor.

Of course, it would be disastrous to have an unshakable conviction about an investment method that is fundamentally flawed. The question then is, how do you truly convince yourself that the method I recommend in this book is the best one you could choose for the long run. If what you have read so far has not convinced you, you should read Chapter 19, and if necessary you can even pursue some of the additional references I have provided there. The point is that you have to first develop a true conviction in an investment method before you commit to it. Otherwise, you may as well not get started with it. Without such conviction you will have no defense against the greed to chase the latest hot stock or the fear to bail out when everything looks hopeless and everyone has only gloomy things to say about the market. If you are not going to stick to your chosen investment method through thick and thin, there is almost no chance of your succeeding as an investor.

We all form our convictions in different ways, and we actually have very few deeply held convictions. Look inside yourself and try to understand how in your case those convictions developed, what it took to convince yourself. See if you can apply some of that understanding to help yourself in forming the unshakable conviction in your chosen investment method you are going to need as an investor.

INVESTING WITH DISCIPLINE

Discipline here means doing the right thing at the right time month after month, year after year, decade after decade, fighting off fear, greed, laziness, and every other excuse and emotion. It takes discipline to keep reinvesting the dividends, it takes discipline to keep sending in that check to your mutual fund as you assumed in your plan, especially when the market has been going down for a few years, and it takes discipline to keep taking any of the other actions your financial plan stipulates, ignoring what you think and what others think the market is going to do in the future.

In this connection let me again remind you of the importance of keeping everything as simple as possible (Rule #1). If you get into an investment method where you need to study charts for 30 stocks and make a new decision every day, dig through Morningstar reports on mutual funds every month, and so forth, even if you are a person who regularly gets up at 5 A.M. five days a week—winter, summer, rain, or shine—to go to the gym, you will have difficulty being disciplined about managing your investments. You see, to you going to the gym must be fun or you would not be pursuing it with that kind of discipline. Working at your investments when the market has been going down for a few years is no fun at all. By following this book's simple investment method that eliminates the need to dig through a lot of information, the need to spend a lot of time managing your investments, and, most of all, the need to make new decisions frequently, you will automatically bypass many of the discipline problems most investors face. So, keep it simple. Keep the work to a minimum.

You will still face two major tests of being disciplined. First, you have to be disciplined about saving and investing every month the money you have promised yourself to save. Remember, discipline in this respect helps the Magic of Compounding to work its magic most. If either out of fear or lack of discipline you fail to make your periodic investment in the periods when the market is low and end up investing only when the market is high, you will accumulate much less money in the long run.

Second, when you get close to major expenditures or retirement, you will have to start selling stocks opportunistically as our strategy specifies. It will be very easy to postpone selling if the market is high and sell in a hurry if the market is low. And yet, you will have to be disciplined to do just the opposite. This won't be easy, but it will be essential for your success. If you do not take out of the market and put away safely the money you will need in the near future, you may lose much of the fruits of your years of disciplined and patient saving and investing.

One thing that will help a lot in being disciplined is having your financial plan in writing and having your spouse or someone else close to you as your investment partner. Both will help a lot with holding onto your conviction and being patient. Review and update the plan and the performance of your investments together every year or so and make sure that when one of you starts to lose conviction, discipline, or patience, the other (or the two of you together) brings up all the reasons for staying the course.

INVESTING WITH PATIENCE

No investment method does well all the time, and all investment methods need to be given time to work. Throw in the variability of the market, and investing will test the mettle of even the most patient person. What are your defenses?

First, remember our discussion about not having any short-term expectations about the market. If you have no expectations, you cannot complain that things are not working out and be impatient about it. Of course it is easier said than done, but even if the market has gone down for 3 years in a row, do not throw in the towel. We do not know what will happen in the future, but if you look at the yearly returns of the Standard & Poor's (S&P) 500, you will realize that whatever is happening to the market at the moment is not something new under the sun; it has happened before.

Second, recognize the interrelationship between conviction and patience. If you have conviction, you will find it much easier to be patient. So work on your conviction. Have a full understanding of how much risk you are taking and what plans you have made to control it. For example, by the time you get to retirement you will have the next 10 to 15 years of your minimum draw requirement in safe investments. So if the market takes a sharp downturn, remember that you are fully secured for 10 to 15 years, and that's a long enough time for the market to turn around. The more you understand the investment approach you are following and the more comfortable you are with it, the easier it will be for you to be patient. On the other hand, if you do not fully understand what you are doing, you will find it very difficult to wait patiently. All you need to do to take a successful trip down the Only Proven Road to Investment Success can be summarized in probably less than five pages. But almost no one will be able to stick to it over the long run by just knowing what to do. That is the reason we have spent so much time talking about the "whys." Your patience will have to come from your understanding of the "whys."

Third, work with your partner. Try to focus on other things in life, things over which you have some control, and do not obsess over the market and your investments. With the barrage of investment information that gets hurled at you every day from every direction, it is difficult not to know what is going on with the market. But you will be better off if you find out what is going on only every 6 months or every year. Just keep that in mind. Try to ignore the news as much as you can. Every piece of news is going to sound relevant, but you really do not know how it is going to affect the future in the long term. Acting on any of that information will almost certainly do more harm than good. As we have discussed before, in the end you will make on your investments what the market gives you. There is almost nothing you can do to improve on that. So be patient and hope for the best.

TAKE ONLY THE RISKS YOU CAN AFFORD TO TAKE

One of the main reasons people's convictions get shaken and they lose their discipline and patience is that they often take more risk than they can handle or they thought they could handle and then they suddenly find themselves sitting on a loss of a size that threatens their financial future and security. It happens to people again and again. Too many people do not give much thought to saving and investing for a big part of their lives. Then one morning they wake up in a panic realizing that they have fallen way behind and try to compensate for that by suddenly plunging into the market with everything they have. Or, maybe greed takes over and they just cannot resist the temptation of throwing a large chunk of money (sometimes including some margin or borrowed money) into a hot market or a few hot stocks that seem to be getting everyone else rich. Before they know it, the market or the stocks turn around and plunge, leaving them with the prospect of having to take out a second mortgage on the house to pay off the lost margin money.

Follow Rule #5 to decide how much risk you will take and how you will manage it.

♦ THINGS TO REMEMBER ♦

♦ Even if you are following the best investment method, you will fail as an investor if you do not apply it with conviction, discipline, and patience.

♦ You need a true, unshakable conviction in the investment method you decide to follow. Otherwise greed, fear, and other emotions will force you to abandon your investment method exactly at the wrong time.

♦ Before you get started with this book's investment method, make sure that you are convinced that this is the right investment method for you for the long run.

♦ To succeed, you must follow your investment plan with discipline, year after year, decade after decade. The simpler your investment plan, the easier it will be to stay with it.

♦ Be patient with the market and your investment results. You have to give any investment method ample time and opportunity to work.

♦ Take only as much risk as you can afford. If you overinvest or take too much risk, it will be impossible for you to hold onto your convictions and continue investing with discipline and patience.

♦ Have a written investment plan and work with your spouse or someone else as your investment partner. Both will help in getting through the inevitable trying times.

♦

CHAPTER 12

Do Not Take Along Freeloaders and Distracters

♦

Rule #10: Choose the Right Companions for Your Trip

Would you want to take along freeloaders and distracters on a long trip? Free-loaders can cost you a lot of money, and distracters can be even worse problems. They can talk you into taking a different and less desirable route, can get you lost, and, at worst, can even distract you enough to get you into accidents. And all this for what? You didn't need them in the first place. The situation is pretty much the same with your investment trip, except that your costs can be much higher and there are just too many people from the investment management community interested in coming along and distracting you. The more successful they are in influencing you, the less successful your trip is going to be.

On your trip down the Only Proven Road to Investment Success you need to take along only a few companions to have a pleasant, safe, and successful trip. Let us start off by discussing the categories of companions you really need and how to choose the right ones in each category. After that I will give you an overview of the investment management community and discuss what each of its members claim they can do for you and what their goals and motivations are. If you are careful, you can get a lot of useful information and help from many of them at reasonable costs; but if you let your guard down, your dealings with many of them may end up being very expensive and seriously damaging to your financial future. I will give you the guidance you need to make the best of what they have to offer.

THE COMPANIONS YOU REALLY NEED

There are three categories of companions you need to take along on your trip:

1. A broker or a mutual fund company through which you will make most of your actual investments and who will provide you with certain current information. You may end up dealing with more than one brokerage house or mutual fund company, but to keep things simple, the fewer the better.

2. A financial planner to help you prepare and periodically update your financial plan.

3. A tax advisor to help you make sure that you are taking advantage of all the opportunities to reduce and defer taxes and following the requirements of tax laws and rules.

I hope you are not surprised to see that an investment advisor and manager is conspicuously absent from the list. A key message of this book is that you can and should be your own investment advisor and manager, and the book is designed to help you do just that. I think you should stay away from investment advisors not just because it will save you a lot of money in fees over the years, but also because instead of being a help on your trip, an investment advisor is likely to keep trying to divert you from the Only Proven Road. There are two main reasons for that.

First, if all you are going to do is invest in one of the five safe assets and in one or two stock index funds, what is the investment advisor going to do? To justify his fees, he will have to keep trying to persuade you to create a portfolio of stocks or actively managed mutual funds, change your asset mix from time to time based on market conditions, and so forth. Second, even if he does not have any financial motives, like almost everyone else in the investment management community, most investment advisors are trained to believe (and most of them really do believe) that one can achieve better investment results by picking individual stocks and mutual funds, and by getting into different kinds of stocks and funds under different market conditions and in different phases in one's life. All of this is contrary to the overwhelming evidence and contrary to the approach you are going to take. So you not only do not want to take an investment advisor along on your trip, as I will discuss later under this Rule and under Rule #11, one of your major challenges is going to be staying away from such advisors and their advice.

In addition to the three essential companions mentioned above, from time to time you may need help from a few other people, and I will talk about them when we discuss the various members of the investment management community. They do not need to be permanent companions on your trip.

Let us now look at what kind of help you will be seeking from each of these companions and how you should choose each.

CHOOSING THE RIGHT FUND COMPANY

The one choice here that may have important long-term consequence is the choice of the fund company and the stock index fund for your taxable savings. Remember that the most important strategy for deferring taxes on your taxable savings will be to invest in a stock index fund and hold that position for a very long time, probably decades. If you want to or have to change a fund company or fund along the way because the quality of its management deteriorated or some policies changed (especially with respect to fees and costs), you may have to swallow a fairly large tax bill.

Unfortunately, most fund companies, even the major ones, seem to go through good and bad times in terms of management quality. For your investment in stocks in taxable accounts, your best bet is to stay with large companies that have been around for some time and have a stellar reputation, at least for now. My first choice here would be Vanguard, and I also would not hesitate to use the right T. Rowe Price and Fidelity funds. (See more about this in the Appendix on Recommended Fund Companies and Funds.) Do not use a new and untested fund company, even if it has low fees and offers other benefits. If for some reason things change for the worse with the fund company you choose now, your first step would be to direct new savings into a fund at a different company. Depending on how serious the problem is and your tax situation, you may ultimately have to swallow the tax consequences and move the money to a different fund company. Because of long-term uncertainties, you may even consider using two or at most three different companies for your taxable savings that go into stocks through index funds, especially if you have sizable investments.

In selecting a fund company, although the company's attitude toward holding down costs should be a major criterion, do not settle for less than the highest quality of service. A good fund company should be able to provide you with good quality and up-to-date information on rules for retirement accounts, walk you through and promptly handle your paperwork, and be helpful in every other way possible. As we have seen, over the years even the lowest cost fund will make a lot of money from you, and you deserve nothing less than excellent service. The large companies definitely have an edge here. To help with your selection, keep an eye on the evaluations of fund companies published periodically in magazines such as *Smart Money*. Ignore their ratings on investment performance of the different fund companies. That is a useless number, and if you are investing in index funds, it makes no difference to you. Over the years keep an eye on the costs of your funds and stay informed about any big changes taking place at your fund company so that, if necessary, you can take action.

As for any of the other money you invest in funds, the choice of the fund company is less critical. Here you won't be stuck with your decision if something changes. You will be able to move all your other taxable money and tax-deferred money to a different fund company without any consequence. It is a matter of some time and effort. So pick the best fund and fund company you can for now and be prepared to move if things change.

For the money you have in your 401(k) and other similar savings accounts with your employer, you do not have much of a choice. You are stuck with the fund companies your employer has decided to patronize. But if they do not have the right kind of index funds or their service is poor, make sure you bring it to the attention of the right people at your company. One point to keep in mind if you are not happy with the fund choices you are being offered is that after you have been with an employer for a number of years, you may have a choice of moving out some of your savings to a rollover individual retirement account (IRA) at a financial institution of your choice. If you decide to go this route, make sure you understand all the consequences, especially any tax consequences (although there should be none), before you do that. If you have any tax-deferred retirement account money with any past employer, you also may want to move that into a rollover IRA so that you can deal with the fund company of your choice and invest in just the funds you like.

I have already discussed (under Rule #6) the pros and cons of dealing with fund companies directly and investing in funds through your brokerage account. My recommendation is that you deal with the fund companies directly, especially if you may want to make periodic contributions to or withdrawals from these funds. Otherwise you could end up paying a lot of unnecessary brokerage fees.

CHOOSING THE RIGHT BROKERAGE HOUSE AND BROKER

If you strictly follow the recommendations of this book, you won't need to have a brokerage account. This will not only simplify things in general, but it will provide you with at least one layer of protection against the temptation to buy the latest hot stock or fund. If you have to first open a brokerage account before you can jump into the stock or fund, your inertia may work in your favor and prevent you from getting involved.

If you decide to open a brokerage account, go with a good semi-discount broker—someone who will charge you a reasonable commission and has a good reputation for service. To make your selection, use the evaluation articles that *Smart Money* and other financial magazines publish from time to time on brokers. Make sure that you pay attention to only the aspects of the evaluation that matter to you and not just the overall score of the broker. (For example, whether you can do after-hour trading through a broker is of no consequence to you. You are hardly ever going to do any trading, even during regular hours.)

I will have a lot more to say about brokerage houses a little later. But let me mention here that you need to watch out for a few traps in making your selection. Stay away from the major full-service brokerage houses. They still charge exorbitant commissions for buying and selling stocks and even higher commissions for buying and selling mutual funds. Do not get persuaded by the argument that they charge no commission for investing in their own mutual funds. Because of high investment costs, you probably will never want to invest in those mutual funds anyway. There are a few other problems with these big players. Their dominant strategy is to sign you up for a big bundle of services—called a wrap account or something similar—for an annual fee based on the size of your portfolio. As we have seen, that kind of fee structure is the worst offender in the long run, and you should never sign up for any of them, especially because you don't need most of the services the packages include.

Another big problem is if you open an account at one of these places, especially if you sign up for one of those service bundles, you may end up with your own broker or "account executive." I think good service is great in most areas of life except here. If you have your own account executive, you will start getting calls about all kinds of new investment opportunities, most of which will offer you no real value. But if someone you know keeps calling you, sooner or later you will feel obligated to do some of the things he suggests. And this can be a small or a big problem. So if you do open a brokerage account somewhere, you may be better off not knowing anyone there as long as you can find someone to fix problems promptly. Even some so-called discount brokers have been going upscale, charging pretty high commissions, and planning to sell you all kinds of bundled services. Beware of such motives, which may not be evident up front.

CHOOSING A FINANCIAL PLANNER

This is going to be an important and difficult decision. I have already discussed under Rule #5 what financial planning involves. For reasons I will discuss in a moment, I think most people will be better off working with a financial planner if they can find the right person at the right price. And there is the rub. From my experience, unless you have or are contemplating having savings of a few million dollars and, therefore, can justify paying fairly high fees, you will have to get very lucky to find the right person at the right price. But I think you should try to find the right person because, in the long run, it can make a big difference. Look at it this way: You have to spend the time to find the right person only once in your lifetime or maybe once every 10 years or so. If you do get lucky and find the right person, the time will be well spent.

Of course, you must first decide whether you really do need a financial planner. Why can't you do all of your own financial planning yourself? If you are willing to spend some time at it, are not afraid of numbers, and have the discipline, you may be able to do it on your own by reading books, taking a course somewhere, and using Guru. If you can pull that off, that will be great because once you acquire the necessary knowledge, you will be able to create and update a customized plan in a way that no one else will be able to do.

But many people who think that they have the qualifications to do it on their own actually don't and most people go through life without a systematic financial plan. That can have expensive consequences. You may find yourself without the right kind of insurance when you need it, you may find out after you retire that you had made mistakes in calculations and you have not saved enough for retirement and so forth. Doing proper financial planning is actually much harder than investing. It takes quite a bit of knowledge in many different areas, and you have to keep up with many changes that happen all the time in all those areas. However, your worst enemy will be discipline. You may never get the whole thing done on your own. You will work at it for a while, then something else more urgent will come up and you will set it aside. By the time you get back to it, you will have forgotten much of what you were doing. So my advice is that you should make the effort to find a good financial planner.

Now let us talk about what kind of a person you should seek. First and foremost, he (or she) should be really good at it. Most financial planners are not. Most of them have just taken a few courses and dole out nostrums that may do you no good.

Second, you want someone who is exclusively a financial planner. He should have no interest in selling you or recommending to you any specific product, and he should not be directly or indirectly compensated from any product or service you buy on his recommendation. Fees from clients like you should be his sole source of income.

Third, he should not be an investment advisor as well. You do not need an investment advisor, and you do not want him to influence your investment decisions.

Fourth, if he is also knowledgeable about or is an expert in taxes, that's good. Be a little skeptical here and find out more. If he is really a tax expert, then he may be doing financial planning on the side. He may not be that good at financial planning and know enough about insurance and other things a financial planner needs to know. But there are exceptions.

Fifth, he should not be part of a financial conglomerate that sells all kinds of financial products. The financial planners associated with most such places are biased toward recommending products that the organization offers. Generally you are not going to get unbiased recommendations.

Finally, you should feel comfortable with him. Ideally, this is a person with whom you will work for many years and to whom you will reveal a lot of financial and other details of your life. If you do not feel comfortable enough to discuss these things openly with him, he is really not going to be able to help you.

Why is it so difficult to find a person who will meet these requirements? Because good financial planning takes a lot of knowledge and experience, and people who are good at it charge high fees. Because the fees can easily get into the $5,000 to $10,000 range, most people cannot afford to or do not want to pay these fees. Most financial planners who charge you much lower fees use financial planning as a front to sell you all kinds of other products on which they earn commissions, and what you get as a financial plan is the printout from a standard computer program customized to some extent based on your answers to a series of questions. Even major financial conglomerates use the same approach to bring in customers, to whom they then try to sell other products.

One final recommendation I will make is that even if you do not want to do your own financial planning, you should learn more about what is involved and what kind of help you are looking for before you start your search. The more you know, the better chances you will have of identifying the right person and getting just the kind of help you need.

CHOOSING A TAX ADVISOR

If your financial matters are not complicated, you may be able to get away without a tax advisor. But most people will be better off establishing a long-term relationship with a tax expert. You will need his help only from time to time. So it should not cost all that much over the years, and chances are you will save many times the cost by actually saving on taxes, deferring taxes, and avoiding mistakes you could have made otherwise. It is money well spent.

What you are seeking is someone who is good at tax planning, and who can help you create a tax strategy that fits your situation. To do this, the person has to be knowledgeable about rules for retirement plans, IRAs, estate taxes, and so forth. Tax professionals are generally either certified public accountants (CPAs) or lawyers. There are some CPAs who also become qualified financial planners, called personal financial specialists (PFS), by taking some special course. If you can find one of these people who is also knowledgeable about taxes, you may have to deal with just that one person. But remember that you still need to check him out thoroughly. Just because someone has a certificate at something does not mean he is good at it.

THE INVESTMENT MANAGEMENT COMMUNITY

I use the phrase *investment management community* to include all the groups with whom you may need to interact in connection with managing your investments. The primary players are the brokerage houses, mutual fund companies, financial news media (which include financial news TV channels, business newspapers, and financial magazines), financial advisors, and investment gurus.

The reason you need to know something about all the different players in the investment management community is that even though you need to take along only a few of them as companions on your trip, the rest of them are not going to leave you alone. You will be constantly bombarded with information and solicitation trying to convince you that you need the services they offer, and if you are not well protected by knowledge, you may end up wasting a lot of money.

The most important thing you need to remember about the investment management community is that investment management is a business like any other business. Everyone is in this business to make money for themselves. Saying that they do not have your best interest in mind may sound a little harsh, but the reality is that your well-being is not the highest priority for most people in this community. Your well-being is not a priority at all, although you will hear phrases like "the customer comes first" bandied around all the time.

Because our investment costs are their income, for them to make a good living, they have to charge you and me a great deal of money. On the surface this may not look very different from many other services we buy. But there are two major differences. First, unlike many other services, the investment management community does not have that much real value to offer for the money they charge us. Think about our investment plan. If all you need is a money market fund, a few certificates of deposit (CDs), and one or two index funds, why would you spend much money on anyone in this community? Second, we are talking about big money here. There is no comparison between what you can waste on a few dinners even at the most outrageously priced bad restaurant and what you can waste over the years by paying even 0.5% higher annual investment costs.

So you have to watch out for yourself very carefully, and be a discriminating consumer.

BROKERAGE HOUSES

We have gone through almost a complete cycle here. In the bad old days, brokerage fees used to be almost fixed and sky high. Then we had deregulation and the commissions came down a lot because discount brokers got into the business. But for a while now the commissions, especially at the big brokerage houses, have been creeping up and have again reached outrageous levels. Because the stock market was doing so well until recently, all these costs remained sort of hidden and most investors were not paying attention. But as we have seen, these fees can drain away so much of your return under normal market conditions that if you deal with any of these houses, you will end up with a lot less money for retirement. And do I have to remind you that the advice, which is supposedly what you are buying, is really worth nothing?

You should be aware that there is also a serious conflict of interest at play here. Most brokerage houses, including some of the so-called discount brokers, are now part of big financial conglomerates. These conglomerates earn huge amounts of money from their corporate clients and, consequently, the analysts at these places are almost never willing to say anything bad about their corporate clients—many of them are actually out promoting the stocks of these client companies, even though they claim to be offering completely unbiased recommendations. So you will get tons of "buy" recommendations but you will hardly ever get a "sell" recommendation even when a company is performing very poorly and its stock is going down everyday. Their recommendations are seriously biased. Even when you are not dealing with them directly, you may see their representatives on TV or quoted in the financial press, and you should be skeptical about what they are saying.

I have already cautioned you many times against signing up for wrap-type accounts with them. You now know that their investment advice—their list of top-10 recommended stocks, stock of the week, etc.—is not just seriously flawed but biased. And you also know that you can really do without them. So what do you need a brokerage account for?

MUTUAL FUNDS AND FUND COMPANIES

I think what mutual fund companies could be and what most of them have ended up being is one of the saddest stories in the development of our financial institutions. There was the potential that they could provide the ordinary investor with a valuable service at a low cost and the investors would be able to turn over to them the responsibility of managing their savings prudently. Instead, most funds have set out to make the most money they can for themselves, and they continue to mislead the public through their enormous marketing efforts, by holding out hopes of high returns when there is no way that they will be able to deliver them. Instead of coming up with the type of investment funds from which the ordinary investor could benefit, they keep offering funds that push the poorly informed public more and more in the direction of gambling with their money. There are now over 10,000 mutual funds, more than there are stocks, and for the public it now takes more work and knowledge to analyze and find the right fund than it takes to analyze a stock because the funds' managers keep changing, they keep turning over their portfolios rapidly, and so forth. I would guess that over 90% of the funds out there are not just bad and useless funds, they are even dangerous for investors. That's not an achievement an industry can feel proud of.

Yet, you are not going to be able to get away from dealing with the fund companies, and they are a good source of all kinds of free information. So use their web sites and free literature as much as you can, take full advantage of their well-informed customer service representatives, and stick to investing only in the few types of funds I have recommended (see the Appendix for recommendations.)

FINANCIAL ADVISORS

Almost anyone can be a financial advisor—to the extent there are any requirements, they are not very meaningful or stringent. First let's look at the difference between financial advisors and financial planners. Although, strictly speaking, there is a difference in their functions, most financial planners are also financial advisors because it is difficult to make a living by doing just financial planning, and most financial advisors do financial planning on the side because that gets the customers coming through the door. Financial advisors primarily advise—*sell* may be a more descriptive word—clients on what insurance policies to buy, which mutual funds to invest in, and so forth. They generally charge the clients a fee based on the size of their portfolio, and they also get commissions from the insurance companies, fund companies, and others on the products they sell. As you can sense right away, that's a situation fraught with potential conflict of interest. Even the most honest person will have difficulty being unbiased when put in that situation. On top of that, as I have said, to justify their fees, they have to convince you that you need to pick the right stocks and actively managed funds and then keep making changes as times change. This is not a winning recipe.

So my advice is, as before, if you decide to work with a financial planner, find one who is not a financial advisor as well and stick to your own investment advice. Financial advisors—whether they work for a big firm, a financial conglomerate, or just for themselves—are a group of people from whom you will not benefit much.

THE FREELANCE INVESTMENT GURUS

By freelance investment gurus, I mean the people who sell to the public investment advice for a few hundred to a few thousand dollars a year through their investment newsletters, telephone hotlines, and Internet sites. The good thing about many of the gurus in this group is that they have a track record, that is, performance history, that you can research. A newsletter called the *Hulbert Financial Digest* keeps track of how well you would have done if you had followed the advice of the best known of these gurus over the years. As you might suspect by now, the track records of essentially all of them who have been around for a while are absolutely horrible. In fact, the track records are so bad that you have to wonder how they became well known in the first place and how they have survived in this business for any length of time.

None of this would matter much if these people did not flood every potential investor's mailbox with solicitations for subscriptions, each of which seem to proclaim the sender to be America's number one investment advisor with a spectacular track record. Everything in these solicitations is so exaggerated—sometimes even outright fraudulent—that sometimes even experienced investors fall for their claims. If you fall for any one of them, it is not the annual subscription fee for their services of a few hundred dollars that will hurt you, it is the thousands or even tens of thousands of dollars you may lose following their investment advice. Even if you do not subscribe to their services, every now and then you may see one of the gurus on the financial news channels or see them quoted in magazines or newspapers. None of them have anything good to offer you, and you should completely ignore all of their advice.

THE MAINSTREAM INVESTMENT GURUS

As opposed to the freelance investment gurus, the group of people I call mainstream investment gurus are actually investment professionals who work at major brokerage houses, mutual funds, and money management companies—the mainstream of the investment management community. They either manage money themselves or advise money managers and financial institutions. In terms of credentials, they have it all.

Advising the public on investing is not their day job. They do it mostly for fun and fame. And in this business fame or celebrity almost directly translates into dollars in the pocket. These days they seem to be everywhere all the time, on TV, in newspapers and financial magazines (sometimes even in general or celebrity magazines), on the Internet, you name it. They are always ready with definitive opinions on where the market is going, exactly how far a stock is going to go by the end of next month, and so forth. People even call them while they are on TV and ask for their opinions about specific stocks and the market.

What should warn you against this entire guru business is that every stock market cycle gets its own gurus, and even within the same cycles gurus come and go. They generally have their 15 minutes of fame and all the media exposure that goes with it, and then they go back to their regular jobs. The problem is that because they make specific predictions about individual stocks or the market, once those get on tape, it becomes easy to verify them, and then it does not take that long to find out that they do not have any better predicting ability than do you or I. They are just able to surround their predictions with exotic-sounding mumbo jumbo, and many people fall for this gibberish and then regret it. As you can imagine, the more vague or long-term a guru's prediction, in general, the longer he or she lasts. But all good things have to come to an end, and the world has to move on to the guru in waiting. (In all fairness, I have to admit that there are some gurus who have shown enormous staying power and have been around for years. I cannot explain that. Their track records are so poor that there must be something else at work here. In any case, from your point of view, they are not any different.)

If you have not guessed already, my advice is that you totally ignore them—all of them. You won't be missing anything worthwhile.

THE FINANCIAL NEWS CHANNELS ON THE TV

After struggling in obscurity for many years, the financial news channels on TV finally caught the public's imagination in the recent bull market and they are taking advantage of it in every way they can. They deserve much of the blame for turning investing into the circus it has become. Their minute-by-minute breathless coverage of every up and down of the market or individual stocks has been primarily responsible for convincing the public that every little up and down means something, that investors should pay attention to them and act on them. Few things have been more harmful to the markets or the public than this impression.

What is worse, to fill their air time and attract advertising dollars, these channels have to keep parading through an endless number of investment gurus who are right only for 15 minutes, 15 days, or maybe 15 months. As I mentioned earlier, none of their predictions is any good, but many unsuspecting investors seem to believe that if someone has put them on TV, they must know something. So they act on their advice and get burnt. I think it is really irresponsible to put these people on TV and give their useless advice so much publicity. Even the anchorpeople on these channels realize how useless this advice is, and once they have moved on to the latest guru, they do not hesitate to make fun of the past gurus whom they themselves had promoted.

Let me cite one outrageous example and show how harmful this practice can be. For a number of years one financial TV channel heavily promoted a guru who kept predicting that the Nasdaq would keep going higher and higher. By the time it got to 5,000, he was a major celebrity and predicted Nasdaq would go to 6,000. Of course, the Nasdaq collapsed after that, and those who bought technology stocks when Nasdaq was at 5,000 will probably regret it for a long time to come. The sad part of the story is that most of these people would never have heard of this guru or his prediction if the news channel had not given him so much exposure, and at least some of them may not have bought technology stocks at those unjustifiable levels. The guru has now admitted that he was wrong, but when someone predicts that the market will go up to 6,000 and the market actually goes down to 2,000, no admission is really necessary. The channel rarely puts him up any more and has moved on to new gurus. But I am not sure how the people who lost so much money can help blaming the channel to some extent. I am sure—just as the regular broadcast channels keep arguing that there is sex and violence on TV because the public wants it—that the financial news channels will argue that they put up these people because the public wants them. I am not sure if that absolves them of their responsibilities.

In any case, TV is a very powerful medium, and most people have been conditioned to believe that investing is complex. So they get easily influenced by what they see on TV, especially if it is repeated again and again. Your best defense is to never turn on these channels. You will miss little of value.

THE FINANCIAL AND BUSINESS MAGAZINES

It is time for me to stop pointing out how useless everyone's stock-picking, fund-picking, or market-timing advice is. I think I have made my point. So after mentioning that you should totally ignore all advice of this nature in the financial and business magazines, let me say that they are still the best source of news about the investment and business world. You do not need advice on which stocks or funds to buy, but you do need to know about changes in tax laws, you need to know which fund company is having management problem, and you need to know what if any worthwhile new financial products have come to the market. If you can filter out the bad or useless stuff, of which there is plenty, these magazines do offer some good stuff. The two major financial magazines are *Money* and *Smart Money*, and the three major business magazines are *Fortune*, *Forbes*, and *Business Week*. Of these I find *Smart Money* and *Fortune* to be the most informative and interesting, and because on a subscription basis all of them are fairly inexpensive, you can try them out to see which ones appeal to you most.

Let me end by reminding you that when one of these magazines pronounces that a bull market or a bear market, which has been in place for years, will probably continue for the rest of our lives, savvy investors take that as a sign that things are about to turn around and start moving in the other direction. That has to say a lot about the reputation of these magazines or of the savvy of the savvy investors. I will leave it to you to decide what it says about whom.

♦ THINGS TO REMEMBER ♦

♦ Everyone in the investment management community is keen to offer you advice at as high a price as possible. You need to be on your guard all the time because much of this advice, even when free, can do serious damage to your financial health.

♦ You need only three companions on your trip down the Only Proven Road to Investment Success:

1. A fund company or broker through which to make your investments.
2. A financial planner if you can find one who is capable and is a fee-only professional so that your interest will be his top priority.
3. A tax advisor, whom you will need only at times.

♦ You should ignore most of the investment advice dispensed by the brokerage houses, investment gurus, financial news channels on TV, and the rest of the investment management community. There is too much evidence to show that none of this advice is useful.

♦

CHAPTER 13

IGNORE THE GLITZY BILLBOARDS AND STAY ON YOUR ROUTE

♦

RULE #11: RESIST THE LURE OF THE SIREN SONGS

You are driving along on your trip and you pass all these glitzy billboards that become more and more enticing. What do you do? You know if you get off your route and start checking them out, you will be late and it may even be dangerous—you never know just by looking at the billboards. On your trip down the Only Proven Road to Investment Success you will come across lots of glitzy billboards—or hear siren songs—and most of them are going to be dangerous to your financial health.

Everyone in the investment management community is going to try hard to get you off the Only Proven Road because none of them will make any money off you unless they can get you to stray. So they will sing their siren songs to lure you into trying one of their newfangled investment methods or schemes or maybe even one of the old ones that has been thoroughly discredited.

How are you going to defend yourself? Your only defense is to know enough to not fall for any of them. If you know something has been tried before and failed, often with disastrous results, then it should be much easier for you to resist falling for it. Unfortunately, it is essentially impossible to cover even a fraction of the dangerous ideas people have promoted or still promote as legitimate investment methods. I am going to choose and discuss only a handful of them and hope that after you get to know them for what they are, you will become skeptical enough to resist the lure of the others as well.

I have broken down this discussion into two sections. First I will discuss a few broad themes that are used to compose new siren songs almost every day, and then I will discuss some actual siren songs that are so good that they have gone platinum. I regret I cannot cover them all, because it is fun to talk about them and maybe even to read about them, as long as you have no money riding on them.

Before getting started let me share with you one of my fears—I hope that it will not come true. The investment management community has too much to gain from getting you to stray, and it has too many resources at its disposal to give up easily. So over the years most people do stray, and sooner or later they regret it and get back on the Only Proven Road. But they can never recover the time they have lost and the money they have missed making. I hope that if you have come this far, you will stay the course for the rest of your life.

(If you are sure that you will be able to stay on the Only Proven Road no matter what, you may skip this chapter, at least for now, without missing anything useful. Someday in the future you may read it just for entertainment. Also, if you hear about a new investment idea and feel tempted to try it, check here to see if it is one of Wall Street's super-hit siren songs.)

SOME BASIC THEMES OF SIREN SONGS

MOMENTUM INVESTING AND THE GREATER FOOL THEORY

On Wall Street this may be the most popular theme of all time because more hit siren songs seem to have been based on it than any other I can recall. The idea behind momentum investing is that once a stock starts moving up for whatever reason, right or wrong, or for no reason at all, it will gain momentum (hence the name), attract attention and buyers, and will keep moving up faster and faster. You are supposed to make money by getting on the bandwagon early on. You may ask why a stock would just keep going up like that without good reason, and why, sooner or later when people found out that there was no good reason for the move up, wouldn't it collapse?

Well, that's where the greater fool theory comes in. It holds that it is not your role in life to question if there is a reason for a stock to go up or if a stock's price can get so high that it is ridiculous to even think of buying it. The theory preaches that for you to justify buying a stock at any price all you need is to make sure—or believe—that there will be a greater fool around to buy it from you at a higher price. And as we all know, a fool is born every minute. So, at least in theory, there should be no shortage of fools to buy your stocks. Of course the stock will eventually collapse. But you or your money manager is smart enough to get out in time and not end up being the last greater fool. Aren't you?

Put as bluntly as I have here, you may have difficulty even believing that I am being serious and not just pulling your leg. But actually hundreds of billions of dollars continue to be invested based on this theme and its variations. You may think that no self-respecting money manager would even admit that this is his investment philosophy, but in reality many money managers and fund companies are proud to claim that they are great momentum players and even become celebrated for that expertise. And there are probably 10 times as many closet momentum player money managers who try to dress up their basically momentum investing approach in more respectable-sounding mumbo jumbo.

This has been going on almost forever, and the reason it has had this staying power is that in a red-hot market nothing succeeds like momentum investing. When the markets get into a frenzy and stock prices start moving up so fast and to such heights that no rational explanation can justify either, only the siren song of momentum investing supported by a belief in the greater fool theory can lure investors into throwing more money into the market. There are actually some momentum player money managers who know when to get into a moving stock or market and for a while their funds do spectacularly well while all other cool-headed people are sitting out scratching their heads and making no money. The problem is that sooner or later all these great momentum players end up being the greater fools and are left holding the bag when the stock or the market ultimately collapses.

This is one of Wall Street's most enduring themes, and you will hear songs based on this theme many times during your investing career. If you fall for it even once, especially in a big way, the money that you have accumulated over many years through hard work and patience will vanish in almost no time. Don't listen to the chant that this time it is different or this is a different era. There rarely is anything new under the sun, and most new investment ideas are just new variations on discredited old themes.

GROWTH AND VALUE INVESTING

When we were discussing investment methods, I said there are two main approaches to investing: active investing and passive investing. I did not go into any of the dozens of different ways in which the active investors do their thing because there is not enough evidence to show that any of them work. But almost everyone in the investment management community believes in active investing, and all your life you will hear new siren songs based on the two most popular active investing themes: growth investing and value investing. You should know what they are and why you should not fall for either.

Growth investors believe in finding and buying stocks of companies that will grow fast. Because everyone concedes that ultimately the value of a company and its stock should depend on how much money the company makes, there is no question that the companies that actually grow fast and make a lot more money in the future will be worth a lot more in the future. So if you can identify them now and buy them at reasonable prices, how can that be bad? Of course, that can't be bad; that would be just great. But can anyone really tell now which companies will keep growing fast in the future? And can anyone determine whether the prices of their stocks today are reasonable for the growth the companies will actually be able to generate?

Well, there is the rub. The evidence shows that growth investors grossly overestimate the growth potential of good companies and, based on that, pay too high prices for these companies. They actually drive up the prices of these stocks by piling into them with a herd mentality. But in the real world so many things change so often that not even the managers of these companies can predict how well they will do in the future, let alone these outsider analysts who know very little about what is really going on inside the companies. So when almost invariably the companies fail to live up to the highly inflated expectations, their stocks collapse. Growth investing is a good theme, but in the long run it is essentially impossible to earn returns higher than those of the general market based on even the prettiest song written on this theme.

Value investors take almost the opposite attitude. They believe that investors tend to neglect the unglamorous companies (the ugly ducklings), companies that have sinned by not growing as fast as they were expected to grow (the fallen angels) and companies that are in such bad shape that they may even go bankrupt. So they believe that these companies tend to get significantly underpriced. Now you can figure out for yourself where this line of reasoning is leading. Why not buy these stocks dirt cheap, wait until the companies fix themselves, and once they get back into the good graces of investors, who will then pay high prices for these stocks, sell them your stocks at a nice profit and move on to the next ugly duckling? Value investors even acknowledge that they can be wrong about many of these companies. Many ugly ducklings can grow up to become just ugly ducks, and many companies that are close to bankruptcy actually go bankrupt. But value investors believe that if they pay very little for them in the fist place, how much can they lose? And if even a few of their picks work out well, they will make up for all the bad ones.

Right off the bat let me admit that of all the themes on Wall Street, this is the one that I and people whose opinions I hold in high esteem find remotely believable. And there is also some evidence that the value investor's arguments do hold some water. But making money is never easy. And even if value investing is basically a good concept, that's only half the story. To make money it has to be put into practice with a lot of finesse, and that's not easy. Few people seem to have the talent to identify the ugly ducklings that will grow into beautiful ducks, and even fewer have the ability to know when the price is low enough to get into one of these companies.

Another major problem is that value investing generally does poorly during bull markets and makes up for that by losing less money than growth investing during bear markets. So if you want to be a value investor, you will have to sit around year after year holding onto your faith and making at most modest returns while your neighbor the growth investor and even the index fund investing nerd across the street are making good money. This is going to be so difficult to live with that chances are you won't last long as a value investor. Only die-hards do.

Let me assure you that there is not much evidence to show that value funds do better than index funds over time, so there is no reason for you to go off in search of great value funds or value fund managers. In fact, most value fund managers with great track records have fallen by the wayside because of the problems value funds have in bull markets. And what if, after your patient waiting for years during bull markets, they end up not doing well in bear markets either? So when you hear the songs based on the value investing theme, feel wistful but don't get lured.

GOOD COMPANIES VERSUS GOOD STOCKS

One story you will often hear is that you must buy the stock of this company or invest in this industry (sector is the official name) because this is a great company or this is the industry of the future. The second part of the story is often even true. There are great companies and they are not hard to spot. And every so often a new industry or technology does come along that truly has the potential to revolutionize our lives. But that does not make the stock of the company or the stocks of the industry great buys.

There are a few more questions you have to answer before declaring a stock a good buy. Even if you are convinced that a company is a great company, if its stock is already overpriced, it won't be a good investment. And there is the rub. How do you know it is not overpriced? How do you know what the right price should be? Those are the questions that money managers and analysts spend their lives trying to answer, and clearly they are not able to come up with very good answers or they would be earning great returns on their investments. Demonstrably, they don't.

The problems with evaluating a new industry or technology are even more complex. Is this really going to revolutionize life or is it just another fad? How long will this revolution take? Are the companies that are pioneers right now going to be the ones that survive and prosper or are they, as is so often the case, going to be driven out of business by newcomers? There are many more questions, and they all are difficult to answer. No one seems to have enough foresight to be able to answer them with any reliability. Consider the Internet revolution. Most of the pioneer companies have fallen by the wayside, and there is no assurance that even the pioneers of today will survive and prosper. Yet, there is little doubt that the Internet is revolutionizing our lives and is going to keep doing so for some time.

So, remember the distinctions between good companies and revolutionary industries or technology and good stocks worth buying. Too many new investment ideas blur the distinction. Do not fall for them. Stocks that will be good investments are essentially impossible to spot ahead of time no matter how obvious the choice may seem in retrospect.

And this ties back to our discussion of growth and value investing. Stocks of good companies are often not good investments because they tend to be overpriced and get hammered when they fall short of the overinflated expectations that no one could live up to. On the other hand, stocks of poorly performing companies may be underpriced because no one wants them. But buying the right ones at the right price and waiting around with infinite patience may be not only difficult, but may not even be worthwhile.

SIREN SONGS THAT HAVE GONE PLATINUM

Because I can cover only a few of these super hits, I have chosen the few that are most popular and dangerous.

SECTOR FUNDS

A sector fund invests only in the stocks of companies in one specific industry or even one particular part of an industry. In investment language that is called a sector. All sector funds are designed to be concentrated, that is, hold stocks that will go up and down more or less together. That makes them highly risky and diametrically opposite of diversified funds. As we have discussed, extensive research has shown that investors can significantly reduce risk and get much better risk-return tradeoffs when they hold diversified funds or portfolios.

If sector funds are by design highly risky and offer poor risk-return tradeoffs, why should anyone invest in them? The argument fund companies offer is that if you believe that a particular sector, let's say the personal computer sector, will do well in the future but are not sure which personal computer companies will do better than others, then you can invest in a personal computer sector fund. The fund's manager, who has access to all kinds of information and resources, will figure out for you which personal computer companies have the best prospects.

This strategy sounds attractive until you have to figure out which sector is going to do well in the future. Studies have shown that just as with stocks, no one can consistently pick the winning sectors of the future.

So how come Fidelity has over 40 popular sector funds and every other day someone seems to come up with another sector fund? One explanation is that almost always a few sectors appear at the top of the list of the best performing funds of the past 3 months, 6 months, 1 year, etc. because the market goes through cycles, and every sector sooner or later gets its day in the sun. And what a day it generally is! It seems there is always a sector fund or two that was up 50%, 100%, or even more in the past year. That kind of performance, of course, catches people's attention. In retrospect it seems so obvious why a particular sector did so well that people can even convince themselves that they could have predicted it a year ago. So they feel they have to either invest in that sector fund right now or at least bet on the sector fund they now think is going to be the star next year. If only it were that simple!

By now you know that evidence shows that no one can figure out beforehand which sector fund will do well next. If you invest in a sector fund, you will take an enormous amount of risk because every year a large number of sector funds also appear on the list of the worst performing funds of the year. And if you invest in sector funds, you will have the additional privilege of paying high investment and tax costs. For the fund companies, sector funds are a good way of luring more investors and their money. For you, they are siren songs whose lure you must resist.

HOT NEW FUNDS

In a roaring bull market everyone wants to buy a red-hot fund, and there never seems to be enough of them around when people want them. So to meet the demand, fund companies have figured out a way to create new funds with great records of past performance. That almost sounds contradictory, doesn't it? How can a new fund have a record of past performance at all, let alone a great one? Here's how:

A fund company interested in playing this game starts a few tiny funds and stuffs them with lottery ticket–type stocks (known in the industry as aggressive growth stocks). Just as happens in a lottery, most of these stocks end up losing a good part of their value, but a few end up doing extremely well. After some time the fund company closes down the funds that do poorly—the ones that ended up holding the losing lottery tickets—and trots out with great fanfare the fund that happened to own the winning stocks (or winning lottery tickets) as the next great fund run by the next great investment genius. Now you have a tailor-made red-hot fund you can buy.

Of course, it is not likely that the fund's great performance will continue for very long, because no one really has the talent to keep picking winning lottery tickets. Also, when a new fund is small, it holds a small number of stocks and if even a few of them do well by chance, the fund ends up with great performance. But once a fund starts to grow (in size) rapidly because investors are pouring money into it, it has to buy many more stocks and now just a few stocks doing well by chance do not help its performance all that much. So it is difficult for a fund that has grown in size to duplicate the performance it had when it was tiny.

Even when no one tries to mislead you, you still face a similar situation with almost all new funds. Scores of new funds are started all the time. However, unless there is some kind of a hook (e.g., a new fund managed by a manager with a stellar record at another fund), you hear about only the new funds that happen to do very well early on. All the others are ignored by everyone and are sooner or later closed or merged into other funds. But the ones that do well early on and are widely promoted do well for essentially the same reasons I mentioned in connection with the new red-hot funds created by design. And for the same reasons, these new funds do not do well for too long, especially after they grow in size.

What you need to remember is that you will hear about tiny new funds with spectacular records of past performance all the time. But do not get tempted and throw money at them because, in a short time, especially if everyone keeps pouring money into them, they will end up with spectacularly poor or at best average performance. And remember, average fund performance is generally quite a bit worse than the performance of a simple broad-based index fund, and the index fund is nowhere near as risky as one of those red-hot new funds.

BUYING OR SELLING OPTIONS ON STOCKS

By now you probably have heard of options on stocks in one context or another and have been given the impression that one can make a lot of fast money in options with limited risk. Very little of that impression is true, even though trading in options has exploded in the past 10 years. In reality almost all individual investors who get involved with options lose most of the money they use to trade options. I cannot offer you one good reason why you should ever get involved with options; but I can give you several reasons why you should never go even close to them. Here are a few from the top of my list:

- Your broker will charge you significantly higher commissions for buying and selling options (compared with stocks). Also, if you get involved with options, you will almost certainly trade them much more frequently—easily five or ten times more frequently—than you trade stocks. So the investment costs you incur will soon make the 3% annual investment costs I have been grumbling about look like peanuts. A big part of your money will go straight into your broker's pocket.

- You can make money in options over time only if you can correctly and consistently keep predicting which way and how far a stock or the market is going to move in the next few days, weeks, or months. No one can do that. Despite what you are told by different people, there is no option investment strategy—absolutely none—that has even a fair chance of making money over time if you cannot make that kind of prediction. If you trade options, you may get lucky every now and then and have a winning streak of a few months. But if you keep at it, you will invariably lose most of your money (just as almost all gamblers do).

- Although options are related to stocks, they are much more complex. Unless you put a lot of time and effort into understanding exactly how they work, someone unscrupulous or someone who himself has limited knowledge can easily convince you to try a dangerous option investment strategy by telling you only part of the story. So until you become very knowledgeable about options, don't even listen to anyone's stories about options. And if you do become very knowledgeable about options, you will stay away anyway.

I have not even tried to explain what options are and how they work because even explaining the basics would take pages and get you nowhere. So instead of going into that, I will leave you with one final story that, I hope, will reinforce my admonitions. There is one fairly well-known investment guru who has been claiming for years that he is the number one advisor in the country on options trading. Over the years he has been forced to change the name and format of his advisory service a number of times because in every incarnation he managed to lose so much money for his clients that to stay in business he had to pretend that he was reborn with new wisdom. If that's the performance of the number one options advisor—even if that "number one" part is self-proclaimed—what are your chances of succeeding?

DAY TRADING

Day trading is another investment trend that has gained a lot of notoriety in recent years. I actually should not even call it an investment trend because if the definition of investing is to make a financial commitment with a reasonable expectation of making a reasonable return over a reasonable period of time, then day trading fails on all counts to qualify as an investment method. People get involved in day trading with the unreasonable expectation of making a spectacular return over a very short period of time. That's pretty much what most of us think of as speculating or gambling. Because you should be interested in investing and not gambling, you should never have any interest in day trading. But in the spirit of this chapter, let me tell you some things about the dark side of day trading so that you will be able to resist the lure of its siren song.

Let us start off by understanding what day trading is. Ideally, if you are a day trader, you buy a stock just before it starts going up for a short time and then you sell it once it turns around and starts going down in a few minutes or, at most, a few hours. In the process you make a small profit per share—which can amount to a big chunk of money depending on how many shares you bought—and then you move on to the next stock or the next trend. As a day trader you almost never hold a stock overnight; you trade it off within the day, and that's where the name *day trading* comes from. So instead of trying to cash in on those boring decades-long up trends in stock prices, you try to cash in on the exciting minutes-long trends. Fair enough.

But the question is, are there really any minutes-long trends that you can cash in on, or is that all in your imagination? From all the evidence, it seems that those patterns are all in the minds of the day traders and those who try to cash in on them only succeed in losing all of their capital, most of which ends up in the pockets of the brokers as enormous trading costs. Most people get lured into day trading by TV ads of companies that offer to train them and provide them with a desk, computer, and trading software, all for free, for the privilege of being their broker. They are willing to spend all this money because they know that as brokers, they are guaranteed to make a lot of money. If you get unlucky, you will lose most of your capital very quickly, and a big chunk of it will go into their pockets. And if you get lucky and hit a winning streak for a time, they will make even more money because a good part of your winnings will end up in their pockets, too. Sooner or later your luck will run out, your winning streak will end, and you will be wiped out.

Your best defense, of course, is to stay away from it all. But remember that even if you do not fall into the hands of one of these companies, with fast Internet trading anyone can become—or slip into becoming—a day trader right from home. Be very careful about getting involved in the market on a day-to-day basis. Be a long-term investor and leave the day trading to the pros.

BUYING ON MARGIN

If you think a stock is a particularly good buy but do not have enough cash available to buy as much of it as you want to buy, you can buy it on margin. When you buy stocks on margin, you put up only half of the money and your broker lends you the other half on which you will pay interest. This significantly magnifies both your profit and loss potential. For example, if the price of the stock doubles, you will triple the money you had put up or invested; but if the price of the stock falls by half, you will lose all of the money you had put up. Actually, even before the stock's price falls by half, your broker is legally required to ask you to put up more money—called margin call—and if you cannot come up with it quickly, he will sell off the stocks, take out the money he had lent you and the interest on it, and you will get back only what is left over.

Buying on margin is playing with fire. A margin call from a broker often feels worse than an audit notice from the Internal Revenue Service, if that is possible. People have even lost everything they have as a result of margin calls. Remember, there is no stock that you absolutely, positively know will go up. So do not get caught in a market frenzy and buy a few of the latest hot stocks on margin. Those are the ones that are most likely to plunge at a moment's or a day's notice and take down with them the decent life you have put together with years of effort. Investors learn this lesson every few years through horrible experiences, but somehow, as time passes, another group of investors comes along to learn it all over again by making the same mistake for themselves.

Buying on margin is so risky that even most brokers will not suggest it to you. But you may still hear about it from someone else or from your investment guru. Doesn't matter where you hear it, give it a firm pass. (I have not explained exactly how buying on margin magnifies your risk because I hope I have convinced you never to get involved with buying on margin.)

SHORT SELLING

Suppose you are sure that a stock is overpriced and will collapse any day now. You can bet on that by selling the stock now at the high price and then buying it back at a lower price when the stock collapses. This is making money by selling high and then buying back low. But how can you sell stocks that you don't own? Most often your broker can lend you the stock you want to sell and you can return the stocks to him when you buy them back. This is called selling short or short selling because you are selling something you do not have (you are short of it).

You can make a neat bundle of money selling stocks short if your intuition is right and the stock goes down or, better even, collapses. And you can lose a pretty big bundle if you are wrong, the stock goes up, and you have to buy it back at a much higher price to return to your broker what you had borrowed. All of this is the opposite of buying a stock you expect will go up. But one big difference is that when you buy a stock, the most you can lose is what you paid for the stock because its price cannot fall below zero. When you sell a stock short, you may lose more money than you expected to because your loss will depend on how much the stock goes up and, at least in theory, there is no limit on that.

What is really sad about short selling is that often people who sell short are right and the stock ultimately does collapse. But in between it goes up so much that most short sellers have to get out at huge losses only to sit on the sidelines and watch the stock finally collapse as they expected.

The plight of the short seller is one of the saddest on Wall Street. There is just no way you want to be any part of that story. Like buying on margin, this is so risky that most brokers will never suggest it to you. But your investment guru or adventurous friend just may. Wherever the idea comes from, it deserves nothing more and nothing less than a firm no.

BEAR FUNDS

Because the fund companies are ready to cater to your every need, they have come up with some specialized funds that mostly or exclusively sell stocks short. They are called bear funds because, at least in theory, they make money in bear markets, that is, in declining markets, when none of the other funds make money. Such funds will, of course, lose money—sometimes a lot of it— if the general market or the stocks it sells short go up. You will hear some investment advisors or gurus suggest that you put some of your money in such funds so that you will be protected, at least to some extent, if the market goes down. This is another piece of advice you should not hesitate to completely disregard.

If someone could tell you for sure when the market would go down and by how much and for how long, you could profit from investing in a bear fund. But because no one can tell you any of those things with any certainty and on average the market goes up rather than down, over the long run a bear fund should work out to be a very reliable money-losing machine. The managers of bear funds would tell you that they are great at picking losers—they can pick out stocks that will go down even when the market is going up. Their claim is no more reliable than the claims of the managers of the regular funds who claim they are great at picking winners. Take a pass on both. In case you need another reason to pass up bear funds, they have some of the highest investment costs. The talent of picking losers, even when unproven, does not come cheap.

234 PREPARING FOR THE TRIP

♦ THINGS TO REMEMBER ♦

- ♦ Steadfastly stay on the Only Proven Road to Investment Success because once you stray from this safe road, you will be in a dangerous jungle about which you know very little.

- ♦ Most new investment ideas you will encounter are actually old ideas that many people have tried before and have profoundly regretted trying.

- ♦ Keep in mind that no investment can make you rich overnight, and that anything that promises to do so is speculation, where your chances of losing are many times higher than your chances of winning, if there is a chance of winning at all.

- ♦ A few super-hit siren songs you should resist are momentum investing, investing in sector funds, investing in red-hot new funds, trading options, buying stocks on margin, short selling, and day trading.

◆

THE ELEVEN POTHOLES THAT RUIN MOST TRIPS

◆

In investing, as in everything else in life, if you can keep doing all the right things all the time, you will certainly be successful. But that is not easy to do, especially in investing, where too many people will be constantly offering you wrong advice and tempting you to do the wrong things. So in addition to keeping in mind all the right things you should be doing, you also need to be mindful of all the wrong things you should not be doing. The Only Proven Road to Investment Success is full of small and big potholes. Here is a description of the most dangerous ones you must avoid. This will be equally crucial to your investment success.

1. FAILING TO CREATE AND STICK TO A LONG-TERM INVESTMENT PLAN

This without a doubt is the deepest and largest pothole that ruins the trips of millions of investors. And the reason it gets the number one billing is, if investors avoid this pothole by creating and sticking to a well-conceived long-term investment plan, then they will almost certainly avoid all the others. Most investors never take the time to systematically learn the basics of investing and

235

create and stick to a long-term investment plan because they think investing is too complex. Because they never quite make up their minds about what investment approach they are going to follow and never develop enough confidence in what they know, they lurch from one pothole to another on a trip that is neither enjoyable nor successful. Take the time to learn the truth about investing, create an investment plan, and stick to it.

2. INVESTING TOO LITTLE IN STOCKS FOR FEAR OF RISK

After investing for a number of years and suffering through a series of stock market traumas, most investors end up believing that the stock market is too risky and drastically cut back their investment in stocks. Most often the problem is not that investing in stocks is too risky but that they were investing the wrong way with the wrong expectations. People overinvest in a high-flying market or market sector, and when the bubble bursts and they get badly hurt, they blame the wrong culprit—the risks of the stock market—for their failure. Over the long term, how much money investors make depends more on how much they invest in stocks than on almost anything else, provided they invest the right way. Reduce the risks of investing in stocks by passively holding a well-diversified portfolio of a large number of stocks (preferably an index fund) for the long run, and invest in stocks as much as you can prudently afford.

3. ACTING ON NEWS AND THE MARKET'S UPS AND DOWNS

In this day when minute-by-minute coverage of the latest news and the ups and downs of the stock market are everywhere and every bit of news is over-analyzed and oversensationalized, it is difficult for investors not to react by buying and selling stocks frequently. And yet, this is exactly the wrong way to invest in stocks because no one can make money investing this way. Good and bad news keeps arriving at random and buffeting the market, but no one really knows what the long-term impact of any of this news will be on the market or what other news is waiting around the corner. Learn to ignore the news all the time and hold onto your stock investments through all the ups and downs of the market.

4. IGNORING VISIBLE AND INVISIBLE INVESTMENT COSTS

The investment management community does a very good job of hiding all the large investment costs they charge investors and downplaying their impacts on the returns investors earn. But the costs an average investor incurs drain away a significant portion of his investment returns. Pay attention and eliminate all investment costs you can because it is the simplest way to increase your investment returns by a lot without taking on an iota of additional risk.

5. FALLING FOR THE LATEST FAD AND JOINING THE HERD

Every so often the market goes crazy for one fad or another. Sometimes it is technology stocks, other times it is biotechnology stocks or a money manager who is hot. Everyone recommends them to everyone else, the newspapers and magazines scream about them on their covers, and a frenzy is created. The herd mentality takes over, and everyone piles into them with the total confidence that they will not be the last "greater fools" buying in at exorbitant prices. And yet, some investors invariably end up being the last "greater fools" because the fad and the frenzy always end. Even veterans get caught in these cycles again and again, and neophytes get so badly burned that they swear off the market for a long time, if not forever. Do not fall into one of these potholes and ruin your trip.

6. LISTENING TO "EXPERTS" WITH NO IDEA OF THEIR TRACK RECORDS

Investors are so used to listening to experts in every field or watching experts perform superbly in sports and other arenas that no matter how much they are warned, they cannot resist the temptation of taking the words of so-called investment experts as gospel and investing money on that basis. No one ever inquires into their track records, which for the best ones are mediocre and for the rest are invariably abysmal. Investors get persuaded by their "expertise" simply because they are on TV or some other public forum, hold impressive job titles at major organizations, and offer endless persuasive explanations of why what they are saying is right. Unfortunately none of these really count for making money on investments. The only thing that may count is an impressive track record based on proper evaluation over at least a few market cycles. Until you have checked that out, do not listen to an "investment expert."

7. TRYING TO PICK STOCKS OR TIME THE MARKET

Millions of investors drive into this pothole every day. Despite all evidence to the contrary, people just cannot seem to accept the fact that no one or no investment method can consistently identify the stocks that will be winners in the future or predict which way and how far the market is going to move next. Even when they give up their search after a lifetime of wasting time and money, most investors still remain convinced that the right method or right guru is still out there; they just have not found them. Like believing in Santa Claus, some fantasies are probably worth holding onto. But do not waste your money or stake your future on such fantasies.

8. JUMPING AROUND FROM ONE INVESTMENT METHOD TO ANOTHER

To find out if an investment method really works, you have to give it a long try. Jumping around from one investment method to another is like jumping around from one diet to another. In the latter case you end up gaining weight or hurting your health; in the former case you end up losing money and hurting your self-confidence. You gain nothing from these short-term experiments. You should not try any investment method that does not have a good long-term verifiable track record with real money, not paper money. If it does and if you really want to give it a try, be prepared to give it a long enough try or don't try it at all.

9. BEING OBLIVIOUS TO TAX CONSEQUENCES

Uncle Sam has spread around numerous little potholes all over the road. None of them is huge or too dangerous by itself, but all those bumps along the way will make for a very unpleasant and much less profitable trip because every profitable trade in a taxable account incurs a tax penalty. Bypass these potholes by holding onto your stocks instead of trading them frequently.

10. ACTING ON TIPS FROM FRIENDS OR STRANGERS

It is unlikely that your friends or people you meet at parties and other places know any more than you do about investing successfully. If they brag about all the money they have made in the market, they probably got lucky or are suffering from selective amnesia—forgetting the much bigger losses they suffered in other stocks or at other times. In either case, do not ask for or take their investment advice.

11. INVESTING IN COMPLEX EXOTICS

Most investors do not even recognize exotic investments, like options, as potholes because they are mostly told about their upside. Investing in them is a lot more complex and a lot more risky than investing in stocks, and in the long run, investors lose most of the money they invest in them. Unless you are convinced that you fully understand both the pros and cons of an investment and are also convinced that there is a good chance the investment will be profitable, stay away from it. Remember that there are no sure ways to make a lot of money fast; but ways to lose a lot of money fast abound.

CHAPTER 15

◆

MAKING THE LAST
KEY DECISION ABOUT
YOUR TRIP

◆

You have now learned everything you need to know to be a successful investor and manage your money well for the rest of your life. If you are new to investing, I hope you will enjoy a great sense of relief and think, "So, that's all there is to it. I can do that." That really is all there is to it, and your sense of relief is well justified. As I promised at the beginning, taking a trip down the Only Proven Road to Investment Success is not complex at all.

But before starting on your trip, you still have to make one last major decision and answer for yourself the following question: Do I really want to invest in stocks? You are probably surprised that after spending so much time and effort trying to convince you that you must invest in stocks, I am now raising this question. I have a good reason for bringing this up.

I am convinced that if you have money that you can invest for 10 or 15 years or longer, you should invest it in stocks—it won't be that risky and you will most likely earn a very good return. But I also know from personal experience and from studying the history of the stock market that investing in stocks, even if you do it exactly as I have recommended, is going to be a trying experience.

Very few people are able to stick through the ups and downs of the market. If you panic and bail out when the inevitable market downturns come or get caught up in the market frenzies that will sweep away almost everyone

241

from time to time, then you will be much better off not investing in stocks at all. Unless you are totally convinced that you want to invest in stocks and will be able to stick to your conviction through the market's ups and downs, do not even get started investing in stocks: it will end up being a disaster.

Most people have no clear idea about what they should expect when they start investing in stocks. They have some vague notion that they may lose some money. They think they will get enough notice and will get out before things get too bad. None of that works. You now know the true story about the stock market, and if at this point you decide it is not your cup of tea, you may be making one of the best decisions of your life. So give it some serious thought, and go back and look at some of the history again. To the extent possible, put yourself in some of the worst times in the history of the stock market and try to imagine how you would have felt if you had a big chunk of your money invested in stocks at those times.

Remember that you can reduce your risk and control how much you invest in stocks by choosing a longer anticipation horizon and security horizon. So it is not an all-or-nothing proposition. But you have to be prepared to stay in the market with whatever you decide to invest. Changing your mind is what is going to do the most damage to your investment portfolio.

You have some important decisions to make. Take some time to make them, but do not put them off for too long. (For help in making your decision, you may want to review the section "Should You Base How Much to Invest in Stocks on Your Risk Tolerance?" near the end of Chapter 7.)

WHAT IF YOU DECIDE NOT TO INVEST IN STOCKS?

Even if you decide not to invest in stocks, you still have to invest for the future. I recommend that in that case you stay with the safe investments we have discussed. Do not get tempted and try to earn a little higher return by trying anything else. For example, you will hear again and again that you should put part of your money in bonds. You should put them in short-term corporate bonds, Treasury Inflation-Protected Securities (TIPS), which are also bonds, and Series I Savings Bonds. But do not invest in medium- or long-term bonds, convertible bonds, junk bonds, or any other kinds of bonds. None of them provide enough protection against inflation, and if inflation picks up, you will end up losing a lot of money. I do not think they are suitable for individual investors. Also, do not go out and buy annuities or other life insurance products to provide income for the future. They all have the same inflation-related problems, and on top of that, they have high costs.

If you invest in assets other than the safe investments, chances are you may or may not make a little more money, but you will definitely be taking a lot more risk for no commensurate benefit. If you have decided to avoid risks by not investing in stocks, then stay safe and do not invest in anything else that is risky.

WHAT IF YOU DECIDE TO INVEST IN STOCKS BUT STILL WANT TO TRY SOME ACTIVE INVESTING?

If you have been investing for a while, your experience probably confirms most of what I have told you. You have searched out and tried different investment methods, different mutual funds, and even different investment gurus; but they all have disappointed you. The performance of your investments so far has been far from satisfactory. But you are not ready to give up on your search yet. You are still not ready to settle for the boring average return. You still believe the superior investment method is out there, the genius fund manager is soon going to be discovered, or the prescient investment guru is on his way down from the mountaintop.

I can understand you and I have a suggestion for you. Why don't you take 90% or 95% of your money and send it down a trip on the Only Proven Road to Investment Success and try out whatever else you want to try with the other 5% or 10%? That way you can indulge your curiosity about the market and enjoy the excitement of riding through the ups and downs of the market and individual stocks without putting too much of your financial future at risk. At times you may even get to enjoy the thrills of owning a stock that goes up 300% in a year. I have to admit that the stock market is intoxicating, and if you have been bitten by the investment bug, it is an excitement you don't want to give up. You don't have to. Try what I just suggested, and if after a few years you really find an investment method or fund that provides superior returns, you can always put some more of your money into it.

But before you do that, make sure that the superior result of any of these other investments is not just a fluke. In investing, deciding if someone's superior performance is the result of true genius or sheer luck is one of the most difficult things to do. For example, sooner or later all segments of the stock market enjoy their 15 minutes of fame. Large-cap value stocks do well for a while, then maybe large-cap growth stocks do well for a year or two, then small-cap stocks get their turn and so forth. So if your large-cap value fund does very well for a few years, before you conclude that you have finally found the genius money manager you have been seeking and move a big chunk of your money into his fund, make sure that these were not the years when large-cap value stocks were in favor. Because if that is the reason the fund did well, it will do poorly when the spotlight inevitably moves on to the next market segment.

Indulge yourself if you want to. Enjoy the excitement of being involved in the market. Just let most of your money earn that boring average return year after year. In the long run you will be impressed with your own wisdom and investment genius.

PART III

GETTING ON THE ROAD AND HAVING A SAFE TRIP

This part covers the nuts and bolts of managing your money using this book's recommended investment method. It starts by summarizing for you the overall investment strategy and then takes you through the four steps of actually investing and managing your money. There is also a chapter on how to use Guru to do the calculations you need to plan and manage your investments and to get answers to your "what if" questions.

CHAPTER 16

◆

A REVIEW OF YOUR
PLAN FOR THE TRIP

◆

You are now ready to begin your trip. You know the road you are going to take; you have learned the rules of the road; and you are even aware of the potholes you must anticipate and avoid. But as you would do with any long and important trip, let us take one final look at your plan for the trip before you actually get on the road.

This is the "how to" part of the book. I will review here how you are going to make your decisions and make and manage your investments. If you need to refresh your memory on why you will do things in a certain way, you can do so by going back to the relevant Rule or to Chapter 2, which is a summary of the "whys." As part of telling you exactly how to implement our investment strategy, I am going to recommend specific funds that you may want to use. I explained at the end of Rule #6 and in the Appendix "Recommended Fund Companies and Funds" why I consider Vanguard to be one of best fund companies, and all the funds I will name here are Vanguard funds. They are all excellent funds, but other fund companies have similar funds as well. As long as you stick to the criteria I have discussed for choosing fund companies and funds, you can substitute other similar funds for the funds I recommend here. (The Appendix also has a description of all the funds I recommend.)

Finally, you will have to use the software, Guru, to do a lot of your financial planning and to manage your investments. It is essentially impossible to do the necessary calculations by hand. Guru is specifically designed to do the necessary calculations and to answer your "what if" questions. It is intuitive

247

and easy to learn and use. Take the time to play around with it and you will have a lot of fun.

ASSETS YOU WILL INVEST IN

Over your lifetime, you have to invest in only two kinds of assets: risky assets and safe assets. The only risky asset you will invest in is stocks. Once you have decided how much of your money should be invested in stocks (using methods we will discuss below), the rest of your money should be invested in one of the five safe asset choices. We call them safe assets because they are safe in two ways: they provide complete or near-complete protection against inflation, and your chances of losing any of your principal, that is, your original investment, in any of them are very small.

TAXABLE AND TAX-DEFERRED ACCOUNTS

Accounts such as 401(k)s, individual retirement accounts (IRAs), and so forth are called tax-deferred accounts because you do not have to pay taxes on your return on investments in them until you start withdrawing the money. To some of these accounts you can even make contributions from your pretax income—same as saying the contributions are tax deductible at the time you make them—which makes them even more attractive.

All other accounts are taxable accounts, meaning you will generally have to pay taxes on any investment returns in these accounts in the year you earn the returns. There are four exceptions:

1. You do not have to pay any taxes on capital gains on assets even in a taxable account until you actually sell the assets and realize the capital gain.

2. You do not have to pay taxes on the interest on a Series I Savings Bond (I Bond) until you cash in the bond.

3. You do not have to pay any federal income tax—and sometimes any state income tax—on tax-exempt bonds.

4. You do not have to pay any state income tax on debts of the federal government, such as I Bonds, Treasury Bills, Notes, and Bonds, including Treasury Inflation-Protected Securities (TIPS).

INVESTING IN SAFE ASSETS

In safe assets we have five choices: money market funds, bank certificates of deposit (CDs), short-term corporate bond funds, TIPS funds, and I Bonds. It is a little difficult to put down hard and fast rules about how you choose from among these. But once you understand these well, making your choice should be easy. (For quick reference, use the table "Comparison of Safe Investment Alternatives" in the Appendix.) Here are some broad guidelines:

- *Money you want to keep readily accessible and may need within the next 6 months:* Put this money only in money market funds.
- *Money you can invest for 6 months to 2 years:* Choose from bank CDs, short-term corporate bond funds, or TIPS funds, depending on which is offering a higher return.
- *Money you can invest for 2 to 5 years:* Again, choose from bank CDs, short-term corporate bond funds, or TIPS funds, with higher preference to TIPS funds.
- *Money you want to invest for longer than 5 years:* Here your primary choices are I Bonds and TIPS funds, with a preference for I Bonds for taxable accounts because of their tax deferral as well as automatic interest reinvestment features.

Here are specific recommendations of funds. You may not have access to all these options and funds for your tax-deferred savings accounts at work. In that case, use a money market fund or a short-term corporate bond fund. Make sure the bond fund holds bonds of less than 5 years' maturity.

MONEY MARKET FUNDS

You can use the Vanguard Prime Money Market Fund or, if you are in a high tax bracket, for your taxable accounts you can use one of Vanguard's tax-exempt money market funds. If you live in a large state such as New York or California, you should consider one of Vanguard's state-specific tax-exempt money market funds, whose returns will be exempt from your state's income taxes as well. Another choice is the Vanguard Treasury Money Market Fund, whose returns also will be exempt from your state's income taxes (but not from federal income tax).

BANK CDS OF UP TO 2-YEAR MATURITY

Sometimes CDs of up to 2-year maturity pay returns that are 1% or more higher than money market funds. If you can find a CD with an attractive yield and can afford to tie up the money for the maturity period, consider it. Although generally lesser-known banks offer the higher yields, as long as you stay within the FDIC (Federal Deposit Insurance Corporation) limit ($100,000 for an account in your name and $200,000 for a joint account with your spouse), your money will be safe in any of these. Keep the maturity to less than 2 years. You can always roll it over at maturity if the new rate at that time is attractive.

SHORT-TERM BOND FUNDS

You can use the Vanguard Short-Term Corporate Fund, Vanguard Short-Term Bond Index Fund, or similar funds at other companies. If you are in a high tax bracket, for your taxable accounts you can also consider the Vanguard Short-Term Tax-Exempt Fund. Make sure that the expense ratio of any fund you choose is below 0.5% and it hold bonds of less than 5-year maturity.

TIPS FUNDS

The Vanguard Inflation-Protected Securities Fund is a good choice here. In case it closes down, other choices may come up. Check out the expense ratio of any new choice before investing. If you want to consider buying TIPS directly in taxable accounts, remember their tax quirk: you will have to pay taxes every year even on the part of your return that you won't actually get in cash until you sell your TIPS or they mature.

SERIES I SAVINGS BONDS

These are your best choice for safely investing long-term taxable money. Buy them in small enough denominations so that you can cash them in as you need them.

INVESTING IN STOCKS

Although investing in individual stocks is risky, you can reduce the risk significantly by diversifying, that is, by investing in a large number of diverse stocks and holding them for the long term. Also, there is overwhelming evidence that neither stock picking nor market timing works. So you will invest in a broadly diversified portfolio of stocks at a low cost and passively hold it for as long as possible (that is, until you need to sell stocks to pay for current or anticipated expenses). You have three options for investing in stocks.

INDEX FUNDS

You can pick almost any broad-based low-cost U.S. stock index fund. Over the long run they won't perform exactly the same, but you can't tell ahead of time which will do better. The most common choices are Standard & Poor's (S&P) 500 Index Funds, total market index funds, and Russell 1000 Index Funds. Of these, a total market index fund is preferable because it is the most broadly based. Use only no-load index funds with expense ratio of less than 0.5%. For taxable accounts, consider a tax-managed index fund to minimize your tax bills.

Two good choices for your taxable account are the Vanguard Tax-Managed Capital Appreciation Fund and Vanguard Tax-Managed Growth and Income Fund. Remember that both charge redemption fees if you hold the fund for less than 5 years. For both taxable and tax-deferred accounts you can use the Vanguard Total Stock Market Index Fund and Vanguard 500 Index Fund. Finally, if you hold a large-cap index or nonindex fund (e.g., if at work you cannot find funds that are more broadly diversified), you can use the Vanguard Small-Cap Index Fund or the Vanguard Extended Market Index Fund to broaden your holding. The Vanguard Extended Market Index Fund combined with an S&P 500 Index Fund will duplicate a Wilshire 5000 Total Market Index, and the Vanguard Small-Cap Index Fund combined with a Russell 1000 Index fund will duplicate the broad-based Russell 3000 index. Make sure that you buy only $30 to $40 of small cap index for every $100 you have invested in large cap stocks.

A SIMULATED INDEX FUND

You can create your own simulated index fund by buying a number of low-cost, low turnover, actively-managed U.S. stock funds that complement one another and together provide a well-diversified coverage of the U.S. stock market. Make sure that a larger proportion of the investments go into larger-cap stocks. In general there is not much advantage to this approach. But if you are convinced that certain active fund managers can do better than index funds, then you can play your hunch this way without taking too much chance with your money. However, if your company's 401(k) program does not offer a suitable index fund, you will have to use this approach to create your own simulated index fund from the funds available.

A PORTFOLIO OF INDIVIDUAL STOCKS

You can buy a group of at least 50, preferably closer to 100, individual stocks, making sure that you have a well-diversified portfolio with a larger proportion of the investment going into larger cap stocks.

Of the three choices, using an index fund is the easiest and recommended approach, especially if you have a small amount of money to invest.

YOUR INVESTMENT STRATEGY

Because you are going to invest in only two kinds of assets—safe assets and stocks—the only questions you have to answer are: (1) how much money you will invest in stocks, (2) how you will vary that over time, and (3) when you will sell your stocks. You will automatically invest in safe investments any savings you do not invest in stocks.

There are three characteristics of stocks that will be the basis of our strategy for investing in stocks: (1) Over the long term, stocks have provided the highest inflation-adjusted return of all investment choices; (2) short-term investments in stocks are very risky; and (3) the longer stocks are held, the lower their risks.

To take advantage of these characteristics, you will invest in stocks only money you will not need for the next 10 years or longer, depending on what you are saving for and how safe you want to be. And you will sell stocks opportunistically starting at least 5 years ahead of when you will need the money so that you are not forced to sell stocks under unfavorable market conditions at the last moment.

What you are saving and investing for will determine when you will need the money and how certain you want to be that the money will be there. To decide how much money you have to save and how you should invest it, you will categorize your needs as follows: (1) money for retirement, (2) money for other specific needs, and (3) money for general expenses. We discussed under Rule #5 (Chapter 7) how to decide how much you need to save and invest for each category and how you should manage the money. You may want to refer back to the material there from the section "Summary of Strategy for Saving and Investing for Retirement" through the end of the chapter. You will use Guru to calculate the numbers. Guru will also help you decide at the beginning and then every year how much of your money should be invested in stocks and how much should go into safe investments and when and how much stock you will sell.

THE FOUR-STEP INVESTING PROCESS

To implement the recommended investment strategy, initially you have to go through a systematic, three-step process. Then you will use a fourth step to review and adjust your plan and portfolio annually. I will first define the four steps to give you an overview and then discuss each in detail in the next chapter.

Step 1: Taking your financial inventory. The objective of this step is to end up with a comprehensive picture of what investments you currently have, how much you expect to be able to save annually in the future, and what future needs you want to save for.

Step 2: Creating your investment plan. The objective of this step is to find the tradeoff between what you can afford to save and what future needs you will be able to fund with those savings. You will end up with a plan for how much you will save for each kind of future need, how much of your savings you will put in taxable versus tax-deferred accounts and then how much you will invest in stocks and how much in safe investments.

Step 3: Making your investments. The objective of this step is to move your investments in both taxable and tax-deferred accounts into the right assets at the right funds or brokerage houses and end up with a streamlined portfolio of very few investments and accounts reflecting your investment plan.

Step 4: Reviewing your progress and making adjustments. Once a year and also whenever there is a major change in your life, you will review your plan and the status of your investments. Most importantly, as you get closer to one of the future needs for which you have been saving, you will have to start selling stocks opportunistically or take other steps to raise the money you will need.

A FEW IMMEDIATE ACTIONS YOU CAN TAKE

Going through the four-step process will take some time and work. I recommend that you take the time soon to go through these steps because they are important for your financial future. But if you are not going to be able to do that soon, here are a few actions you should consider taking right away.

Pay Off Any High-Interest, Credit Card–Type Loans

If you have any high-interest credit card–type loans, you should pay them off as soon as possible. The interest rates on these are always much higher than the returns you will be able to earn on any investment. Paying them off is the highest return investment you can make without taking any risk. If you do not have enough money to pay them off right away, then paying them off should probably be your second highest priority right after making the maximum contributions to all the tax-deferred accounts you can contribute to. I am saying "probably" because it will depend on your specific situation. Because you cannot make up in later years any contribution you miss making to tax-deferred accounts, you should try to contribute the maximum to them every year. On the other hand, if you have a lot of these high-interest loans, it may be worthwhile to pay them off first, even if you have to pass up making contributions to tax-deferred accounts for a year or two.

Move Your Stock Investments to Index Funds

You should switch all your investments in stocks to index funds as soon as possible, after giving proper consideration to any tax consequences. There is, of course, no tax consequence in tax-deferred accounts. And as long as you are not getting out of the market but rather switching from individual stocks or actively managed mutual funds to index funds, there is not much reason to wait. If you have a lot of investments and large losses in any particular sector (e.g., technology), you may be tempted to hold on until the sector turns around. The problem is, how do you know that the sector will turn around and not keep getting worse? It is never wise to hold concentrated positions, such as a lot of technology stocks. I think you will be much better off taking your losses and moving on.

As for stocks in taxable accounts, taxes do matter. If you are holding stocks with large capital gains on them and also have some stocks on which you have losses, you can sell both kinds to offset losses against gains and minimize the tax impact. As I have made clear throughout this book, if you have made substantial money on individual stocks or actively managed funds, you just may have been lucky and the luck may run out soon. Make your decision keeping that in mind.

If you are 15 years or more away from retirement, switch all of your nonstock investments in tax-deferred accounts to stock index funds and direct all future contributions to the same funds. On the taxable side, any money you won't need in the next 10 to 15 years should also go into stock index funds. (In deciding what money you do not need in the next 10 to 15 years, remember to keep aside an emergency fund in safe investments and to take into consideration any cash needs you will have in the next 5 years or so.)

◆

CHAPTER 17

ON THE ONLY PROVEN
ROAD TO INVESTMENT
SUCCESS

◆

It is now time to start on your trip down the Only Proven Road to Investment Success—a trip that will probably last for decades and, I hope, will be fun and profitable. You have prepared well for it. It is now time to put in practice what you have learned by following the four steps I will describe below.

STEP 1: TAKING YOUR FINANCIAL INVENTORY

You have to start off by taking an inventory of your savings, loans, and investments. This will mostly involve pulling together information from different statements, pay stubs, tax returns, and so forth. Before I list the information you need to gather, two things.

First, do not spend a lot of time and effort trying to get all the information right to the last dollar. It is not necessary. Remember, the errors inherent in making the very long-term projections and plans you will be making are so large that trying to get all these numbers precisely right will be a waste of time and may be unnecessarily frustrating. Depending on your income level and the size of your portfolio, getting the numbers right to within a few thousand dollars will be adequate.

Second, those of you who are familiar with a spreadsheet program such as Excel will immediately recognize that you will be able to organize the information and do the necessary calculations much more easily if you use one of those programs. But if you want to or have to do it by hand with paper and pencil, you will have no problem whatsoever. The calculations are quite simple and you won't need anything more than a simple calculator.

Now let us look at what information you need to gather. Remember that if you are married, "you" here means both of you.

- A list of all the investments you have in tax-deferred accounts, including their current values and breakdowns of what they are invested in.
- A list of all the investments you have in taxable accounts, including their current values and breakdowns of what they are invested in. If you have investments in individual stocks, bonds, or mutual funds, find the information on their tax bases so that you can estimate how much tax you will have to pay if you sell them.
- The balances in your checking and savings accounts (only if they are large).
- A list of all the debts you have with remaining balances and interest rates.
- An estimate of how much you are saving each month broken down by your contributions to the various tax-deferred accounts and the amount available for investing in taxable accounts.
- An estimate of your marginal income tax rate and capital gains tax rate.

ESTIMATING MONTHLY SAVINGS

Unless you have been saving systematically and have a budget, estimating how much you are saving today may be somewhat difficult. What is important is to decide how much you can and should be saving in the future. If you do not have the time now, you may want to take your best guess for now, but as soon as you have the time, you should prepare a budget so that you can regulate your spending and have a better estimate of what you can save. In estimating how much you can save each month, remember to deduct the payments on mortgages or other installment loans that you will have to keep making. As I discussed before, you should pay off any high-interest credit card–type loans as soon as possible. In any case, your estimate of what you can save per year has to be made after providing for payments on all loans that will remain outstanding.

ESTIMATING FUTURE NEEDS

You also need to decide what future needs you want to save for and how much each will cost. In estimating costs, estimate them in today's dollars, that is, estimate what they will cost today and let Guru figure out how much they will cost in the future when you will actually need the money. Otherwise, you may make substantial errors.

For these you will need to be specific. That means, for each you will have to put down how much money you will need and in which year. Estimating the need for retirement is going to be the most difficult, in part because it is the largest chunk and in part because it is so far away (for most of us) that it will be difficult to guess.

Here are a few things you should keep in mind with respect to retirement savings. First, if you are far from retirement, you can estimate it as a percentage of your current monthly expenses (e.g., 60%). But as you get closer, you need to make a much more detailed analysis of what your expenses will be during retirement to establish your retirement needs. Gross estimates may be quite a bit off. Second, for the purpose of your saving and investing, what you really need to know is how much retirement income you will have to draw from these savings. So after you estimate your total retirement needs, you will subtract from them the retirement income you expect from other sources such as Social Security, expected payments from defined benefit pension plans, and so forth. Third, as we have discussed before (and will address again in Step 2), you should estimate your retirement needs in today's dollars and in two pieces: a minimum annual draw piece and an additional annual draw piece. You should estimate these for the first year of retirement and let Guru grow them for the years after that at a rate you specify. Trying to make year-by-year estimates for something so uncertain and so far away is not worthwhile.

STEP 2: CREATING YOUR INVESTMENT PLAN

Most of this step will involve working with Guru. The objective of this step is to make the tradeoffs you need to make for yourself to decide how much you are going to save for each future need, how the money is going to be invested over the years, and, if all goes well, how much money you will have available when the time comes. You may start off with certain goals for retirement and find that for the degree of safety you want, you will have to save a lot more money annually than you can afford to save. You will then make adjustments to either the retirement income or the level of safety you want to target until you reach the right compromise for yourself. Of course, you will have the opportunity to make adjustments over the years based on changes in your financial condition as well as how the market does.

One thing you have to keep in mind is that the degree of safety you actually achieve will crucially depend on your starting to opportunistically sell stocks at the time specified in your plan. If you do not do that and hold onto stocks too close to the time you need the money, you will substantially increase risk. If you get lucky, you may end up with lot more money; but if you get unlucky, the money you need just may not be there. Unless you start selling and putting the money away in safe investments in time, most of this planning will be useless.

The details on how to use Guru to do your planning are covered in the next chapter. Once you have completed the planning process, make sure that you save the Guru files that contain your plan under suitably descriptive names for future reference. As we will see in Step 4, it will be helpful to keep track of the revisions you make to your plans over the years. You also may print out your plan for your records.

STEP 3: MAKING YOUR INVESTMENTS

The objective of this step is to end up with your money invested exactly the way the plan calls for. If the changes required are large, you may find it psychologically difficult to go through all the changes at once. But unless there are compelling tax reasons that I will discuss below, try to get on with it soon. If you have decided that you want to follow the Only Proven Road to Investment Success, you will be better off making a full commitment.

We will look at tax-deferred and taxable accounts separately because of the differences in their tax treatments and the possible differences in the available investment choices. In all cases you will follow what your investment plan tells you to do.

SAVINGS PLANS AND OTHER TAX-DEFERRED ACCOUNTS AT WORK

Because there are no tax consequences here, you should aim to end up with the balances in safe and risky investments in accordance with your investment plan.

If you have less money invested in stocks than the plan specifies, you can immediately switch to an index fund or a simulated index fund all the money you currently have invested in actively managed stock funds or in individual stocks. If you have substantial losses in some stocks or funds, my recommendation is to sell them and switch instead of waiting to see if things turn around. You can never tell if things will change for the better or worse.

Because in this case we assumed you have less money invested in stocks than your plan specifies, you will also have to move some money from safe investments to stocks. Unless it is a large amount, just do it and get on with it. If the amount involved is large, you may decide to do it over a number of months on a schedule, but make sure you go through it. Do not stop if the market starts going down. Remember that if you are investing for the long run, the best time to buy is when the market is going down.

If you are close to retirement, your plan may actually call for you to start selling stocks opportunistically. Refer back to the discussion under Rule #5 on how and when to sell and start looking for the right opportunities.

INDIVIDUAL RETIREMENT ACCOUNTS

If you already have some regular or Roth individual retirement accounts (IRAs) with a mutual fund or brokerage firm, check to see if they offer the right funds. If the money is invested in anything other than the right kind of index fund or safe investments, you should move the money to the right kind of funds. This will also be a good time to consolidate the money into as few accounts as feasible, but before combining money you now have in separate accounts, make sure that this will not create any tax problems in the long run. Money from different kinds of IRAs (regular, rollover, Roth) often has to be kept separate. Also, make sure that you move all of this money through fund-to-fund transfers. Otherwise you will have to abide by certain rules or you will end up paying unnecessary taxes. The people at the fund company you are moving the money to can get you the necessary forms and even help you fill them out properly.

As for switching money from stocks or funds you are currently holding to index funds, follow the recommendations I made above.

TAXABLE INVESTMENTS

Here the first thing to check is how many different accounts you have at how many different places and how many different funds and stocks you are holding. If you have a clutter of funds and stocks, you need to ruthlessly trim things down to probably just one index fund and one money market fund. Choose your funds carefully using the criteria we have discussed, and move the money.

In Step 2 you have already figured out how much of the money in your taxable accounts should be in risky assets and how much in safe assets. (Remember to pay off the high-interest loans first.) Chances are you will have to sell some individual stocks or stock funds to switch the money to a stock index fund or a safe investment. This is probably going to be psychologically the most difficult part, especially if you have substantial losses on some funds and stocks. Although the situation with every individual and his portfolio is different, under most circumstances you will be better off cleaning up house, taking the losses, and putting the money where it belongs: either in a stock index fund or a safe investment. In selling, try to offset gains and losses to minimize tax consequences. But irrespective of the tax consequences, for the long run you will be much better off putting your risky investments in a stock index fund, and once you switch to it, your money will be able to grow tax deferred for a long time. Unless you have a very well-diversified portfolio now, holding onto it just because of tax considerations can be very risky and unwise.

STEP 4: REVIEWING YOUR PROGRESS AND MAKING ADJUSTMENTS

Unless there is a major change in your personal life and financial conditions, you have to review your investments and investment plan only once a year and make necessary adjustments. If at all possible, you should totally ignore the market in the interim. As you already know, you are not going to get into or out of stocks because of market conditions. So what is this annual review going to cover?

The most important thing to check is your savings rate. Are you saving what you had planned to save? If you are not, you have to get yourself back on track. And if it seems you had set too ambitious a goal, then you have to lower your savings goals, but then you will also have to go through your plans again to see which future need you are going to save less for and if you will be able to live with the smaller amount of money you will have. You will need to review and make adjustments for a few other things, as discussed below.

HANDLING DIFFERENCES BETWEEN ACTUAL AND ASSUMED MARKET RETURNS

In making projections, we assume that the market will provide a steady return year in and year out. Real life does not work this way. So what do you do after a few years of much better or much worse than expected market performance. Nothing really. Unless your plan calls for you to start to sell stocks because you are getting close to needing some money, you are not going to sell stocks. On the other hand, if you are in a period when you are supposed to be opportunistically selling stocks, then take advantage of good market conditions and pull back if the market is doing poorly. You will find both hard to do because our natural instinct is to hold on when the market is doing well and everyone is optimistic and sell when everything looks gloomy. This is when you have to be disciplined and do the right thing. (Refer back to the discussion under Rule #5 on when to sell and when to pull back.)

You have to anticipate and be prepared for another problem. Once a year you will enter your current balances for each category of savings (e.g., retirement) into Guru and see how much money you will have or you will be able to draw when you need the money. After a few bad years Guru will show that you will have much less money in the future than you had anticipated because the current balance of your savings will be less than expected. This is natural and again an effect of the fact that the market does not go up steadily, whereas we (Guru) assumed that it would move in a straight line. There is no way of getting around this problem. It is inherent in the nature of risk. If you have been saving what you had planned to save, keep doing the same and things will work out alright.

REVIEW OF INVESTMENT PERFORMANCE

Because you will have only safe investments and investments in stock index funds, chances are that not much will change in 1 year or even many years and your review will cover only a few items. (There is not much to review in bank certificates of deposit other than reinvesting the money on maturity.)

Safe Investment Funds

With respect to these, the most important thing to check is each fund's performance in the past year relative to similar other funds. If the fund is doing much better or much worse than the others, call up the fund company to find out why. Much better performance may indicate higher risk—the fund may be investing in derivatives or somewhat longer maturity securities. Worse performance, among other things, may indicate an increase in the fund's expense ratio, especially the elimination of a promotional low management fee. The latest expense ratio is something you should always monitor. Among other things, ask the fund company representative if there have been any changes in the fund's investment and other policies. Because for these funds there is generally no tax consequence of switching to similar funds even in taxable accounts, if you are uncomfortable with what you find out about a fund, switch to a different fund.

Stock Index Fund

For the stock index fund, check its latest expense ratio and how well it is tracking the index it is supposed to mimic. If anything seems out of line, check with the fund people. Any time you move taxable money from one index fund to another there is likely to be some tax consequence. So you should consider a switch only if something looks seriously wrong. For example, a small change in tracking error for a year with an explanation that makes sense to you is, of course, no reason for concern.

Funds in Savings Accounts at Work

The performance of funds in your savings accounts at work needs closer monitoring, especially if you had to create your own simulated index fund by combining a few funds. Check the performance of your portfolio against the broad market index you are trying to emulate (e.g., the S&P 500 Index or the Wilshire 5000 Total Market Index) and try to understand the cause of any significant difference. It may be the poor performance of one particular fund or it may be that you are too heavily weighted in one type of fund. There may not be room for doing much, and this kind of checking and readjusting may take up quite a bit of time and effort without really getting you anywhere. So, do not try to do too much fine tuning. These are the reasons why you were looking for an index fund in the first place, and if one has come along and seems to meet the criteria we have discussed, switch in a hurry.

♦

CHAPTER 18

GETTING THE BEST
ADVICE FROM GURU

♦

Once you have understood this book's investment method, Guru will be your
personal guide on your trip down the Only Proven Road to Investment Success and help you plan and manage your investments. It will take the necessary data and assumptions from you, do the thinking (calculations), and give
you precise advice (output) on what you should do now and in every year in
the future. It will also show how your portfolio will look, that is, how much
money you will have invested in stocks and safe investments, by year. In this
chapter I will cover a few things you need to know to use Guru properly and
get its best advice.

But do not start reading this chapter yet. Guru is an intuitive program, easy
to learn and use. There is also extensive help built into every step of it. The
file "User's Manual for Guru" on the CD-ROM contains instructions for
installing and running Guru. You can read and print out this simple text file
using the WordPad program built into Windows or using Microsoft Word.
Once you have Guru running, put in some data and assumptions about yourself, and let Guru show you what kind of advice you can get from it. You need
to develop an understanding of how various assumptions affect Guru's output, that is, your financial plan. It will be much easier to do that by playing
around with Guru than by reading pages of description and discussions.

Guru provides its output in the form of a table (similar to Table 7.2) with
year-by-year projections of everything you need to know and do. Take a few

minutes to understand every column of data in the output tables. If something is not clear, use the help. You can print out the tables to review or keep for future reference. Also, you can save any analysis you do—called a scenario— in a file with a descriptive name. You will then be able to look it up when you need it or to create a new scenario starting with one you had created before.

Come back and read this chapter after you have familiarized yourself with Guru. At that time it will be much easier to understand. (Most of what Guru does is based on the discussions we had under Rule #5. If necessary, reread the relevant sections there to refresh your memory.)

THE FOUR TYPES OF ANALYSIS GURU CAN DO

Guru handles the following four types of planning:

1. *Planning for Retirement:* Use this to find out how much you will have to save annually until retirement and how you should invest the savings over the years to have the retirement income you would like to have.

2. *Planning in Retirement:* Use this if you are already retired and want to find out how you should invest your money over the years and (1) How long your money will last, (2) How much you can afford to withdraw annually, or (3) How much savings you need to have to be able to afford certain minimum and additional draws for the rest of your retirement years.

3. *Planning for Specific Needs:* Use this to find out how much you will have to save in one lump sum today or in annual installments and how you should invest the savings over the years to provide for specific major future needs like children's education.

4. *Planning for General Needs:* Use this to find out how you should invest your other savings over the years and if you will have enough money to cover your other nonroutine general needs like replacing a car, taking a vacation, etc.

All the four types of analysis are based on the two basic principles we have discussed: (1) You will invest in stocks only the money you will be able to keep invested for a long time, and (2) you will start to sell stocks opportunistically and put the proceeds in safe investments a number of years in advance of when you will actually need the money to cover expenses.

To do its analysis, Guru needs certain data and assumptions from you. (A particular set of data and assumptions defines a scenario that you can save for future use.) Let us now first look at some of the data and assumptions that are common to most of the analyses, and then we will look at each type of analysis in some detail. To keep our discussion short, I won't cover here anything that you can figure out easily by working with Guru and using the help there.

SOME COMMON CONVENTIONS AND ASSUMPTIONS

Here are my recommendations for the assumptions you will have to enter for most of your analysis. Remember that you will always enter estimates for savings and investment in today's dollars and Guru will inflate them appropriately for the future year to which they apply. For example, if you tell Guru you want to save $20,000 for a need 15 years away, it will figure out and use how many dollars you will need then to have the same buying power $20,000 has today.

COUNTING TIME

Guru does all calculations annually, starting its count "today," meaning the day you are doing your calculations. So unless you are doing your calculations on January 1, Guru will not be using calendar years. For example, if you are doing your calculations on April 20, 2002, the first year for the calculations will be April 20, 2002 to April 19, 2003, the second year will start on April 20, 2003, and so forth. You will have to enter the current year and your current age. If you are doing your calculations in the first half of a year (e.g., April 2002), enter 2002 as the current year. If you are in the second half of the year (e.g., August 2002), enter 2003 for the current year. Similarly, if your current age is 35 years and 4 months, enter 35; for 35 years and 7 months, enter 36. (Remember, your age is 35 on your 36th birthday.)

TIMING OF MONEY FLOWS

Guru assumes that all money inflows and outflows take place on the first day of the year (as it counts year, not calendar year).

ASSUMPTION FOR INFLATION RATE

Guru uses your assumption for inflation rate to estimate future costs based on estimates of costs you enter in today's dollars. For example, if your target for minimum draw is $40,000 per year in today's dollars, you are 25 years from retirement, and your assumption for inflation rate is 3%, Guru will provide for about $84,000 of draw in your first year of retirement, 3% more for the second year and so forth. Unless you have reason to assume otherwise, use 3%, the long-term historical average inflation rate. Remember that you should use an estimate of the average inflation rate for the period the plan will cover and not for the next year or two.

ASSUMPTIONS FOR RETURNS ON STOCKS AND SAFE INVESTMENTS

Enter estimates of these in nominal terms, that is, not in real or inflation-adjusted terms. But base your estimates on assumptions of real returns. So, if you expect stocks to earn a real return of 7% over the time horizon in question, and you are assuming an inflation rate of 3%, then you would enter 10% (7% + 3% = 10%) for return on stocks. Similarly, for return on safe investments, if you want to assume a real return of 2%, enter 5% in nominal terms. These are the numbers I recommend using. You may decide to use somewhat different numbers. At the very least, you should do a few "what ifs" using different assumptions.

PLANNING FOR RETIREMENT

The most important inputs here are the minimum annual draw and additional annual draw you want to target. You will specify the pretax amounts you will want to be able to draw. In setting these targets, keep in mind that these draws will get combined with your income from other sources such as Social Security, and you will have to pay taxes on the combined income.

You also have to specify the anticipation horizon (AH) and security horizon (SH) you want to use to control your risks. Once you enter these assumptions and other data, Guru will tell you how much money you will have to contribute every year to your retirement savings to achieve those goals. You can try out different scenarios by changing the assumptions. For example, if the required monthly contribution is too high for you, you can reduce your desired minimum and additional draws in steps to find out what you will be able to have for the amount of annual contribution you think you will be able to make. Note that Guru allocates all the savings you already have at the time of planning toward funding the minimum draw because that is more important.

Whether Guru assumes a constant or growing annual contribution will depend on what you enter for contribution growth rate. You should make it zero if you think you won't be able to grow your annual contributions over the years. But this may not be realistic. If you are far from retirement and assume you will annually contribute only a constant amount, you will have to save a lot more in the early years. A growth rate equal to the inflation rate may be a more reasonable assumption.

For both AH and SH, I recommend you use 10 years, but you may choose to be more conservative by making either or both longer. Play around with different values to see how they affect your contribution requirements.

For life expectancy, 90 years may be a good assumption unless you have reason to choose something different.

You can set SH equal to your remaining life expectancy at retirement (i.e., 25 years if you plan to retire at 65 and want to use a life expectancy of 90), and leave AH at 10 years. This will force all your investments into safe assets 10 years before retirement, a very conservative approach. You can shorten AH to be somewhat less conservative. Finally, if you want to be totally safe or want to find out how much more you will have to save every year if you want to be totally safe, set AH equal to the number of years you have left till retirement and SH equal to your remaining life expectancy at retirement. Guru will then put all your savings (starting from the very beginning) into safe investments.

PLANNING IN RETIREMENT

If you are already retired, Guru can answer for you the three most common questions people in retirement want answered:

1. How long will my money last? (For this you will have to tell Guru how much money you have in your savings, what SH you want to maintain, and how much you want to withdraw per year.)
2. How much can I afford to draw per year? (For this you have to tell Guru how much money you have in your savings, what life expectancy you want to use, and what SH you want to maintain.)

3. How much savings do I need to be able to afford certain minimum and additional draws? (For this you have to tell Guru your desired draw amounts, the life expectancy you want to use, and the SH you want to maintain.)

As usual, Guru will provide a year-by-year analysis showing how you should invest your savings over the years and you will be able to play around with your assumptions to choose the plan that best suits your needs.

PLANNING FOR SPECIFIC NEEDS

You will use this part of Guru to plan and save for specific future needs that are important to you and for which you want to specifically save and invest in a disciplined way. It is likely that you will add to your other general savings as and when you can afford to do so. If you take such a casual approach to saving for things that are important to you, the money may not be there when the time comes. Also, handling important needs separately will impose the discipline of selling the investments in time (starting AH years in advance) to keep your risk under control.

The key inputs here are the target amount you want to save, the year you will need the money, and the AH you want to use. Once you enter all the data, Guru will tell you how much you need to save if you can save it all in a lump sum today and also how much you will have to save annually if you want to save the money over the years. You can use the contribution growth rate to specify if you want to save a constant amount of money every year or you want to make growing contributions.

You should use a minimum AH of 5 years. The longer you make it, the earlier you will switch your investments to safe assets, and the lower the risk you will take. You can set AH equal to the number of years you have until you will need the money to force all of your savings into safe investments right away. This would be the most conservative scenario, but it will also increase your savings requirements. Play around with the numbers to see how they change. That's what Guru is there for.

This analysis handles only one future need at a time. So if you want to save for 4 years of college, you will have to do four separate analyses and add the numbers together.

PLANNING FOR GENERAL NEEDS

You will use this part of Guru to plan and save for all your remaining needs. Here you will enter the amounts and timing for all of your future needs and the amounts you plan to save in various years. Guru will then do a year-by-year analysis to show you if you will have enough money to cover all the needs or if you will run out of money earlier. You can then adjust the amount and timings of your needs and savings to create a plan that will cover all your needs.

In addition to your planned savings and needs, the other key inputs for this analysis are your minimum holding period (MHP) and AH. If you set an MHP of 10 years, Guru will make sure that you invest in stocks only money that you will be able to keep invested in stocks for 10 years. And Guru will also advise you to sell the necessary amount of stocks AH years before you will need the money to cover a need. As before, you can control your risk by picking a longer MHP and AH. You should set the MHP and AH at 10 and 5 years, respectively, at the minimum.

UNDERSTANDING WHEN GURU SELLS STOCKS

To properly use the plans (output) Guru prepares for you, it is important for you to understand how Guru uses your assumed Anticipation Horizon (AH) to handle opportunistic selling. You know by now that to control risk, you will start selling stocks opportunistically once you reach your chosen AH. Because you cannot know now on exactly what schedule you will sell stocks during the AH, you or Guru cannot estimate what mix of stocks and safe investments you will hold and what return you will earn on your money during that period. And if you or Guru cannot estimate that, you cannot estimate how much money you will have to save over the years for a specific need or retirement.

To get around this problem, Guru assumes that you will sell the necessary amount of stocks in the year you reach your AH. This is generally a conservative assumption because Guru has to assume also that you will then put the money in safe investments and earn the lower safe-investment returns on the money in the later years. So in the plans (output) Guru prepares for you, you will generally see a large sale of stocks in the year you reach the AH. Recognize that you are not expected to sell this large chunk of stocks in that one year; you are supposed to opportunistically sell the stocks over the AH.

Similarly, exactly when you will sell stocks during retirement is uncertain. Under our strategy, in average or good years you will cover your annual expenses by selling stocks and in the years the market is doing poorly you will use money from your safe investments. Guru assumes that in the early years of your retirement you will sell stocks every year to cover your expenses, and once you run out of stocks—as you will see in Guru's outputs, this will happen SH years before your life expectancy—you will use money from safe investments to cover the expenses for the remaining years.

UNDERSTANDING HOW GURU HANDLES TAXES

Guru handles taxes differently for the retirement and in-retirement planning than it does for the specific needs and general needs planning.

For the retirement-related savings, Guru assumes that all of your investments are in tax-deferred accounts or are tax sheltered and does not deduct taxes anywhere along the line. So the withdrawals it shows are in pretax money, on which you will have to pay taxes at your average tax rate during retirement. (Remember that you can defer most of the taxes on your long-term money even in taxable accounts if they are in index funds you hold for the long run or in Series I Savings Bonds.)

On your investments for specific and general needs, Guru deducts taxes at the marginal and capital gains tax rates you specify. It deducts taxes annually (at your marginal tax rate) from your interest income and deducts capital gains taxes whenever stocks are sold. (To calculate the taxes correctly, you have to provide the tax basis for any investments you have in stocks at the time Guru's analysis starts.)

PART IV

FOR THE MORE ADVENTUROUS TRAVELER

This part has two chapters. Chapter 19, "The Most Dangerous Myth About Investing," is a detailed discussion of why active investing does not work and it also includes some supporting evidence. Because to achieve investment success you need to be absolutely convinced that you should not chase any active investment method, if there is any doubt in your mind in this regard, you should read this chapter now. But if you are already convinced, then you may read it at your leisure. Chapter 20 discusses a few additional investment options that are popular, but I do not think they are appropriate for most investors. I have provided this information on them in case you get curious. You can read it at your leisure.

◆

CHAPTER 19

THE MOST DANGEROUS MYTH ABOUT INVESTING

◆

The world of investing abounds with fantasies and myths that both individual investors and investment experts believe in and pursue with passion. The most dangerous of these is the myth that by diligently and cleverly analyzing the mountains of information and data available on individual stocks and the stock market, and suitably applying tea leaf reading, star gazing, and other investment techniques, investors, or at least experts, can predict what a particular stock or the market is going to do in the future.

Why am I calling this the most dangerous myth? Because all forms of active investing rely on this myth, and as long as you continue believing in it, you will keep chasing all kinds of active investment methods. Because no active investment method will work for too long, you will be constantly switching from one active investment method to another, one actively managed mutual fund to another, and one active investment expert to another wasting time, money, and opportunity. This is how millions of active investors miss out on making or actually lose hundreds of billions of dollars. Some even lose their entire savings in the process.

But how do we know this is a myth? What evidence is there that active investing does not work? Why doesn't it work? Those are the questions I will address in detail now because, as I have stressed throughout this book, to be a successful investor you have to stop believing this myth and embrace passive investing with conviction.

HOW TO JUDGE AN INVESTMENT EXPERT
OR AN INVESTMENT METHOD

How do we decide if an investment method works or an investment expert can produce superior returns for us? Answering this question rigorously is actually a lot more difficult than it looks on the surface. But we will adopt a simple answer that will work well in most situations.

We know that all of us can passively invest in "the market" (i.e., a little bit of all stocks) by just buying and holding a broad-based index fund. For that we do not have to do any work or make any judgments, we do not have to do any research, and we do not have to monitor various companies, the stock market, or the economy—and the costs are minimal. Unless an investment method or investment expert can convincingly do better than such an index fund, that is, beat the market, why should we consider following such an investment method or expert? So we will use the market, as measured by the Standard and Poor's (S&P) 500 Index or the Wilshire 5000 Total Market Index, as our benchmark for judging investment methods and experts.

To make sure that we do not get fooled by market-beating performance of investment methods or experts that may be just fortuitous, we should use a few more criteria for our evaluations. First, we should require that a method or expert have a record of beating the market for a long period, preferably 10 years or more. Why? Because over a period of just a few years any method or expert may do better than the market simply by luck, and some always will; but such performance will have little chance of continuing into the future.

Second, we should require that the method or the expert beat the market consistently. If an investment method or expert does very well relative to the market only every now and then and does poorly at other times, then chances are that those good years are attributable to just luck. Also, remember that the market goes through cycles where certain market segments, e.g., growth stocks or small cap stocks, do well for a few years, then certain other segments do well for the next few years, and so forth. So an investment expert who invests only in growth stocks, or an investment method that tends to pick only growth stocks, will probably do much better than the market during the period when growth stocks are in favor but will do much worse than the market when the spotlight moves on to another market segment. Over the long run, such methods or experts are not going to be able to beat the market.

Third, we should make sure that we are judging the performance of the same expert or same method over a long period of time. For example, if a mutual fund has done well over 10 years but it has been managed by four different money managers with different investment philosophies over the years, then the 10-year record is meaningless. We can base our conclusions only on the performance for the years the latest manager has been at the helm, and that may be too short a period for making any judgment. Similarly, most investment methods are almost continuously tweaked. When after a year or two an investment method does not work or stops working well, its proponents come up with new fixes that may work again for a year or two before needing more tweaking. In such a case you really have a 1- or 2-year record for the investment method instead of the 5- or 10-year records that you need to make judgments. The proponents of most investment methods try to tell you that a method has been used successfully for a long period of time. But most often the reality is that over the years the method has been changed so many times in so many different ways that there really is no long-term record you can use for reference.

Now you are probably starting to see why judging the performance of an investment expert or method can quickly become complex. And I have not even brought up all the issues. Nonetheless, even these simple criteria are sufficient to weed out almost all investment methods. Any time you want to judge a new investment method or expert you are considering following, you should also use these criteria to make your decision.

One thing you should keep in mind is that when you judge active investment methods, the burden of proof must be on the investment methods or the experts. Unless there is convincing evidence that they can do better than the market, you should invest in the market, that is, the low-cost, broad-based index fund. It is easy to check how you would have done investing in an index fund over the past 10, 20, 30, or even 50 years. There are no ifs or buts about that. Unless the track record of any alternate method is equally convincing and easy to check, you should err on the side of caution and follow the Only Proven Road to Investment Success.

HOW SOME INVESTMENT METHODS AND EXPERTS HAVE DONE IN THE PAST

Having established our simple criteria for judging investment methods and experts, we are now ready to look at how some of the prime candidates for our investment funds have done historically. For a number of reasons, I will primarily focus on the performance of mutual funds. First, most individual investors these days invest through mutual funds and, therefore, are interested in their performance. Second, it is much easier to find complete historical performance data for mutual funds than it is for private money managers, brokerage house analysts, and others. Third, most money managers and investment methods that show any promise are represented in mutual funds. So any conclusions we can reach about the performance of active mutual funds should be representative of active investing in general.

HOW WELL MUTUAL FUNDS HAVE DONE RELATIVE TO THE MARKET

Figure 19.1 shows the percentage of general equity mutual funds that were outperformed by the S&P 500 Index for every year between 1963 and 2000. Figure 19.2 shows the same comparison versus the Wilshire 5000 Total Market Index for the 1971 to 2000 period. If the mutual fund managers had the kind of investment expertise they claim to have, most funds should have outperformed the simple unmanaged indexes in most years. Instead, the indexes outperformed a vast majority of the mutual funds year in and year out. There were a few periods when more than 50% of the funds did better than the indexes, but most of the time the indexes outperformed more than 60%, 70%, or even 80% of the funds. Although averages may not be very meaningful here, it is interesting to note that on average the indexes outperformed about 60% of the funds every year during the period under consideration. (The data used in the figures and tables in this chapter were kindly provided by John C. Bogle.)

If you pay attention to what investment experts say day in and day out, under good and bad market conditions, the one mantra you will hear every month and every year is "this is a stock-picker's market." This means that they believe the market conditions are favorable for people like themselves, who have superior ability to pick winning stocks, to handily outperform the market. Since the experts have been saying this forever, they really cannot claim that they have been outperformed by the market so handily because market conditions have not been favorable to show off their skills. So what could be the reasons? Could it be that they have none of the skills they claim to have? That it is all a myth?

You may think that the data also show that every year there are at least some funds that do outperform the market, and as long as you invest in those winning funds, why should you care if the vast majority of the funds lag behind the market? Most investors keep investing in actively managed mutual funds with exactly that hope—that they will be able to pick out the funds that will outperform the indexes even if the vast majority won't.

FIGURE 19.1

Percentage of General Equity Funds Outperformed by the S&P 500 Index

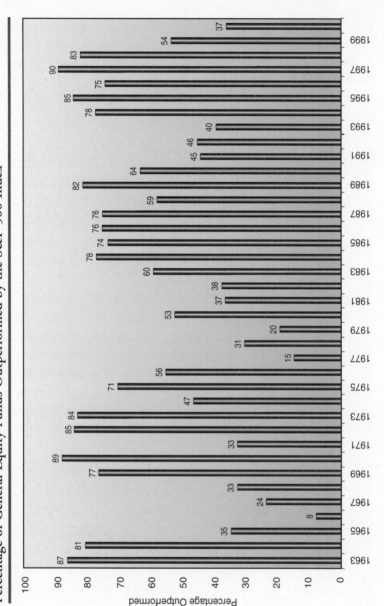

FIGURE 19.2

Percentage of General Equity Funds Outperformed by the Wilshire Total Market Index

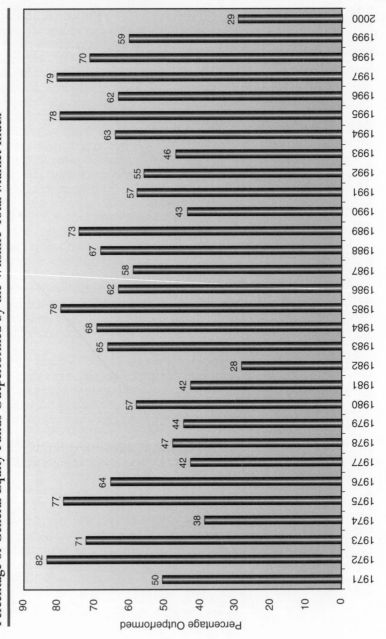

The major problem with that thinking is that no one knows how to pick the winning funds ahead of time. Most funds that outperform the market every now and then seem to do so at random. This year's winners rarely turn out to be the winners of the next year or the next few years. In fact, evidence shows that over time the performance of all funds moves toward the average. This means that if a fund has been doing better than the market for a year or two, it will probably lag behind the market in the future. So the most popular method of picking funds—investing in funds that have done well in the recent past—will not help you outperform the market. None of the other more sophisticated attempts to pick the winning funds of the future has been successful either. So you have to assume that you will end up with an average fund and if the average fund has not been able to outperform the market, then yours is not likely to do so either.

To get a clearer idea of what you are facing, let us look at how well the average equity mutual fund has done relative to the market over the years. Table 19.1 compares the performance of the average equity mutual fund with those of the S&P 500 Index and the Wilshire 5000 Total Market Index for various periods ending in the year 2000. The data show that both indexes provided about 1% per year higher return than the average fund for almost any length of time you consider. As we know, due to the Magic of Compounding, over long periods even a 1% higher annual return adds up to significantly higher accumulated wealth.

But the news is actually worse for mutual funds because the data for the

TABLE 19.1

Returns for Equity Indexes Versus Average Equity Mutual Funds

Periods (Years)	Average Equity Mutual Fund	S&P 500 Index	S&P 500 Advantage	Wilshire Total Market Index	Total Market Index Advantage
50	11.7%	12.8%	1.0%		
40	11.3%	11.9%	0.6%		
30	12.4%	13.2%	0.8%	13.1%	0.7%
25	14.5%	15.3%	0.8%	15.3%	0.8%
20	14.2%	15.7%	1.5%	14.8%	0.5%
15	14.0%	16.0%	2.0%	15.0%	1.0%
10	16.2%	17.5%	1.3%	17.0%	0.8%
5	17.2%	18.3%	1.2%	16.7%	−0.5%

average actively managed mutual fund are overstated for a number of reasons. First, the data do not reflect the effects of fund loads, which will definitely reduce the actual return you will earn if you invest in a load fund. Contrary to the hope that load funds will slowly disappear because they have no advantage over no-load funds, more and more funds are now starting to charge loads.

Second, the data exclude the results for many funds that had the poorest performance over the years. These funds were closed down or were merged into other funds and were dropped from the data. They had to be excluded because reliable data on them are not easily available. So the averages shown are like the average height of the students in a class, calculated excluding some of the shortest students. The true average returns for the funds are definitely lower than what we are considering here.

Third, if you own actively managed mutual funds in taxable accounts, your returns will be further reduced by taxes you will have to pay over the years because many of the fund managers buy and sell stocks frequently, creating tax liabilities.

Clearly, on average, the market (i.e., broad-based index funds) has handily beaten most mutual funds and their average returns. So to win with active investing, you have to be able to keep picking and switching to the funds that will come out on top next year. Can you or your expert advisors do that? Let us take a look at the record.

THE RECORD OF THE MORNINGSTAR RATING SYSTEM

We started off by looking at the performance of mutual funds in general because it is much easier to look at them as a group and arrive at some broad but convincing conclusions. Once it comes to picking winning individual stocks or mutual funds, checking out all the claims becomes impossible because you have to check them out one at a time. Anyone can claim that he has a method for picking winning funds, and that's what most investment advisors, investment newsletters, and other experts do. But unless you can collect sufficient data and have the time and expertise to properly test the claim, you cannot make any judgment.

Over the years researchers have tested thousands of such claims, and they have not found any method or expert whose claim really holds up under careful long-term testing. Because it is not possible to look at even a fraction of the tests that have been conducted on fund-picking methods, let us just look at how the most widely quoted fund rating system has fared under testing.

This rating is published by Morningstar, a mutual fund information service that collects and provides the most detailed information on almost 12,000 mutual funds. Morningstar puts so much time and resources into collecting and analyzing all possible information about mutual funds that if anyone can identify the funds that will outperform the rest in the future, it has to be Morningstar. Morningstar rates most funds on a scale of one to five stars, where a fund with five stars is supposed to have earned the highest return relative to the risk it took.

To its credit, Morningstar states that this is a rating of a fund's historical performance, and it does not necessarily predict how well the fund will do in the future. Nonetheless, almost everyone believes that if a fund earns a high rating for its past performance, the performance must be the result of the superior investment skills of the fund's manager, and therefore the fund should continue to do well in the future. In the mutual fund industry a Morningstar five-star rating is highly coveted. Mutual fund companies prominently advertise the high ratings of their funds, and the ratings are widely used by individual investors and investment advisors for picking funds.

How well has this fund rating system worked? Not well at all. If you buy a fund with a four- or five-star rating, you would expect that the fund will do well in the future, that is, will be able to maintain its high rating for the next few years. But in practice, few funds are able to maintain their high rating for long, meaning that if you buy a highly rated fund, there is no assurance that you will earn superior returns in the future. If Morningstar with all its resources and incentives cannot identify tomorrow's winning funds today, does it make sense for you to try to do it on your own in your spare time or believe that investment gurus or newsletters can do it for you?

(You can look up the results of many other similar tests in the books I have recommended in the Appendix under Miscellaneous Resources.)

WHY NO ONE CAN CONSISTENTLY BEAT THE MARKET

Now that you have seen that there is overwhelming evidence that no investment method or expert can beat the market, you may wonder, "Why is this so?" "How come professionals, with all their education, efforts, and resources, cannot beat the market?" Let's start off by looking at some of the reasons.

FREQUENT RANDOM CHANGES IN THE ENVIRONMENT

To successfully pick winning stocks or get into and out of the market on time, an expert or an investor has to correctly predict too many things too far into the future. He has to predict how a company, its industry, its markets, etc., will do for years to come. This is impossible to do because so many things around us keep changing unpredictably all the time. All of these random changes make stocks and the market fluctuate essentially at random, making it as unpredictable as the toss of a coin or the winning number on a roulette wheel.

If you are curious, for a while pay attention to one or two experts on TV who predict with confidence what a stock or the market is going to do in the next weeks or months. They invariably come back a few weeks or a few months later to explain why things did not work out the way they had predicted. And the explanation is always that something changed. But that is the point. Something that no one had considered always changes, and there are too many of those changeable things. That's what makes all of this so unpredictable.

HIGH INVESTMENT COSTS

The costs of active investing make it essentially impossible for active money managers or investors to beat the market, that is, to beat the performance of passive investing. As we have seen, the total investment costs for active mutual funds easily can be more than 2% per year, and for some of them the costs are even 3% or higher. This means that an active fund manager has to produce a 2% to 3% higher return than the market just to keep up with it. When you consider that the long-term return on stocks has been in the range of 10% per year, expecting a money manager to consistently earn another 2% to 3% return on top of that is just not realistic.

These days most investment advisors also invest your money through mutual funds. Their own fees then create an additional layer of costs that makes it even more difficult for them to beat the market. If instead of investing in mutual funds you invest directly in stocks and bonds through a broker, you will most likely rack up the same kind of investment costs and create an insurmountable hurdle for yourself or your broker. Also remember that every time your money manager or you trade stocks, you may make the wrong decision and sell future winners and buy future losers. You may even create more tax liabilities. All in all, for active investing to beat the market, too many things have to work out just right most of the time, which does not happen too often in real life.

DISAPPEARANCE OF BARGAINS BECAUSE OF COMPETITION

There is a major difference between predicting something like the weather and predicting something like the price of a stock. Even if we get very good at predicting the weather and even if an army of people gets into that business, the weather is not going be affected by their forecasts. But that's not true of stocks. Remember that to do better than the market an active investor has to identify and buy a stock when it is still selling at a bargain price because others have not recognized its potential yet. But as professional investors identify a bargain stock and start buying it, the stock's price goes up and very soon it does not remain a bargain any more. So if enough smart people get into the game with enough resources, pretty soon there will be no bargains left in the stock market. That is exactly what has happened. In a way, all the smart investors and money managers have been the victims of their own success. To make money, they have to find bargains, but their success has eliminated all the bargains. Ironic, isn't it?

RELYING ON SPURIOUS PATTERNS

All—yes all—active investment methods are based on finding patterns in historical data for stocks. For example, an investor may notice that in the past few years, most of the time when a stock went up for 3 months in a row it was up significantly over the following 12 months. So he may start looking at this as something that will continue to happen and make it into an investment method. The problem is that almost all such historical relationships are accidental. They do not hold for too long. Believing in them is similar to believing that because in a series of coin tosses, many times three heads were followed by a tail, then we can bet on that pattern continuing. And yet all active investors invest based on such patterns even though they do not recognize that that's what they are doing. Because all such patterns or historical relationships are temporary or accidental, the active investment methods based on them do not work for any length of time. Over time they lose more money for investors than they make for them.

WHY INVESTORS STILL FIND IT DIFFICULT TO BELIEVE THAT NO ONE CAN BEAT THE MARKET

Given the evidence I have cited and the logical reasons I have offered to demonstrate that active investing does not work, why do most investors still find it difficult to believe? Why—when more and more of the smartest fiduciaries, the sponsors of the huge pension funds, endowments, and foundations, whose job it is to seek out and use the best money managers, are shunning the active money managers—do individual investors keep chasing active investment methods? Let me offer some answers to these questions.

Most investors believe that active investing is the only choice they have, and that they have to find the best active money manager or active investment method. Intuitively, investors want to believe that just as in any other profession, investing must have its experts. They see these so-called experts on TV or read about them in newspapers and magazines all the time. So they keep searching for the best. What they almost never get to see are systematic evaluations of the performance of these experts, especially compared with passive investing, to realize that these experts do not have the claimed expertise.

Let me address two other things that confuse or mislead investors.

First, there is always news about funds that did spectacularly well in the past quarter or past year or even past 5 years. How do we explain that kind of performance? There is actually a simple explanation. Just by chance some funds will always do well over any period of time. Remember, what matters is consistency and predictability. If the same fund manager did well year after year or if you could somehow tell ahead of time who is going to do well next year, that would be great. But we have discussed that you just cannot bet on a fund manager based on his past record or any other criteria we know and expect to do better than the market in the future. What is happening here is the same thing that happens with lotteries. Some people win each time, just by luck. But that does not make them experts in winning lotteries, and you would not want to bet on them or ask for their advice on how to win lotteries. I know it is harsh to compare active investing with buying lottery tickets, but we cannot ignore the evidence.

Second, people wonder, if active investing does not work and passive investing is the Holy Grail, how come there are all these mutual funds, brokers, financial news channels on TV, financial advisors, newspapers, and financial magazines promoting one or another form of active investing all the time and we hardly ever hear about passive investing. It is a good question, but not a difficult one to answer.

What is at work here is the plain old profit motive. There is very little money to be made by promoting passive investing. If you are just going to buy a bunch of stocks or a passively managed mutual fund once and hold onto them forever, why would you buy the services of any of these other people? How are they going to make their living? They make money when you pay them big fees for actively managing your money in a fund, when you pay brokerage fees for buying and selling stocks, when you watch their programs and the advertisements, and so forth. They have to fill their air time and magazine pages, and sell advertising time and pages to make money. They cannot do any of that with passive investing. There is no excitement in it. There is nothing new in it from one day to another. If they told you active investing does not work or tried to convince you to become a passive investor, they would not just hurt their own pocketbooks, they would go out of business.

To be fair, I have to admit that many of these people genuinely believe that active investing works and they are providing you with a valuable service. But the evidence just does not support their belief.

THE CONCLUSION

The conclusion you have to draw from this fairly lengthy discussion is simple. Lots of active investment methods or investment experts are claimed to have the ability to beat the market. The evidence shows, beyond any reasonable doubt, that the vast majority of these claims are totally unfounded. There may be a few investment methods or investment experts on whom the jury is still out, and new claims are, of course, made every day. But your chances of being able to identify any method or expert that will be able to actually beat the market for you is miniscule. Remember, even if you succeed in your search, you will probably end up earning only a little higher return than you would have by simply putting your money in the right index fund. On the other hand, if you fail and pick the wrong method or expert—and given the odds you are very likely to do so—you will probably end up making a lot less money over the years than you could have without any effort at all.

Given that you will go through life only once and will never be given a chance to recoup any time you waste in any wild goose chase, which way would you want to bet?

CHAPTER 20

◆

A FEW OTHER INVESTMENT CHOICES

◆

Here I will cover four investment options that you are likely to encounter and may even want to consider for your portfolio under special circumstances. They are foreign stocks, real estate investment trusts (REITs), zero-coupon bonds, and exchange traded funds (ETFs). I did not recommend them as primary investment choices either because they do not meet all our investment criteria or because they are not likely to improve the long-term risk or return of your portfolio. Following Rule #1, we want to keep everything as simple as possible and do not want to add layers of complication unless they can be justified.

Because I do not think these are attractive choices for you, you do not have to read about them now. If for some reason you get interested in them in the future and want to consider investing in them, then you can read about them here before committing any money. As is often the case, you generally hear only a part of the story about most investments and can end up investing without full information. The detail about these investments is here to help ensure that you do not overlook anything important on either the plus or the minus side.

FOREIGN STOCKS

Of the four choices I cover here, you will hear about this one most often. To some extent it makes sense to consider investing some of your money in foreign stocks. The main argument in favor of doing so is one of diversification—the expectation that they may do well just when U.S. stocks do poorly, thus somewhat evening out the return on your portfolio. This has been true historically, but it seems that with rapid globalization much of this benefit is disappearing and the U.S. and foreign stock markets, especially those of the developed countries, now move more often together than separately. That reduces to a great degree, if not eliminates entirely, the benefits of investing in foreign stocks.

In talking about foreign stocks we need to make a distinction among stocks of companies in developed countries (e.g., Europe), developing countries (e.g., India), and emerging markets or countries where capital markets are in the early stages of development (e.g., Russia, Eastern Europe). As is the case with any classification system, there is dissent as to whether certain borderline countries should be put in one category versus another; but in general, this classification is helpful in discussing foreign stocks.

There are three major strikes against investing in foreign stocks. It is difficult to get good information on them. They are expensive to trade. And, they involve substantial currency risk, that is, if the foreign country's currency deteriorates relative to the U.S. dollar, you may end up losing money even if the stocks do well in their own currencies. You can get around at least parts of the first problem by investing through mutual funds that exclusively invest in foreign stocks. Managers of these funds travel extensively to the foreign countries where the companies are located, gather information from local sources, and so forth. In general they can do as good a job of investing in stocks of developed countries as they can with U.S. stocks.

But the stocks of companies in the countries of the other two categories are subject to so many political risks and uncertainties and go through such enormous roller coaster rides that most investors will not have the stomach to hold onto them for the long run. As usual, the investment management community will tell you that they have the expertise to get you out of these stocks just before a major disaster hits. But the reality is that they have shown no such ability. So chances are if you invest in stocks of these countries, you will invariably sell out at the bottom of one of these roller coaster rides and accomplish nothing other than losing some money.

In addition, the all-in investment costs of investing in foreign stocks, especially in stocks of developing countries and emerging markets, are so high that your chances of coming out ahead are pretty slim.

HOW TO INVEST IN FOREIGN STOCKS

If you insist on investing a part of your money in foreign stocks, you should do so through mutual funds. Here again, index funds are the best. You can either invest in a stock index fund of only developed countries (e.g., Vanguard Developed Markets Index Fund) or an index fund covering all foreign countries (e.g., the Vanguard Total International Stock Index Fund or the Vanguard Tax-Managed International Fund). Note that funds that have "global" in their names generally hold U.S. stocks as well, and you do not want that. So if you are investing in any fund other than the ones I have named, make sure it does not invest in U.S. stocks as well.

REAL ESTATE INVESTMENT TRUSTS

We all know that over the long run real estate has proved to be one of the best investments. It has also kept up with inflation fairly well, although there is so much variation within real estate by type, location, and so forth that it is difficult to come up with reliable data, as we can do with stocks and bonds, to judge exactly how well relative to inflation real estate has done. Even then, investing some of your money in real estate can be a good idea, especially because it will also reduce the overall risk of your portfolio to some extent by providing additional diversification.

Because the major real estate investment many of us already have, our homes, is not diversified at all, it is important that any additional real estate investment we make be well diversified both geographically and by real estate type (commercial, residential, etc.). Most of us cannot get that kind of diversification with the amount of money we can afford to invest in real estate. Fortunately, we can make diversified investments in real estate even with a small amount of money through a type of company called real estate investment trust (REIT) and we can diversify further by investing in mutual funds that invest exclusively in REITs. Let's now look at these options.

HOW REITS WORK AND THEIR ADVANTAGES AND DISADVANTAGES

In many ways REITs work just like corporations. They raise money from investors by selling shares and then invest the money either in various kinds of real estate properties or in real estate mortgages. The process actually most often works the other way around. A major real estate developer may buy or develop a number of properties, put them into a REIT, and sell the shares of the REIT to the public. Therein lies the major problem with REITs that we will discuss a little later.

We have already discussed the most important advantage of REITs—the opportunity to invest even a small amount of money in a diversified portfolio of real estate. A second advantage is that legally REITs are required to distribute 95% of their earnings to shareholders every year. As a result, REITs pay high dividends, which can be attractive to investors looking for current income. There is also a tax advantage. For tax purposes a good part of a REIT's dividend—maybe 25% or so—is treated as a return of capital, which reduces an investor's tax basis in his investment in the REIT. As a result, an investor has to pay current ordinary income tax on maybe 75% of the dividend. On the other 25% the tax is deferred and the investor ultimately pays it at the lower long-term capital gains tax rate when he sells his shares in the REIT.

What are the disadvantages? It all relates to fluctuation in the price of REIT stocks. They fluctuate with the general market. They also fluctuate as the value of real estate in general fluctuates. And then they fluctuate some more because the pros can take advantage of naïve investors. Because real estate developers and other knowledgeable players in the real estate market can pick the time when they will package and sell interest in their properties to the public through a REIT, they try to do so when real estate prices are unusually high or REIT prices are too high relative to the value of the properties they hold. It is their way of cashing out at the top and leaving the public holding the bag.

As a result, REITs have gone through their own boom and bust cycles, and that is why I do not recommend REITs as a primary investment choice. In a way, investing in REITs is like investing in one sector of the market, albeit a sector with excellent long-term potential. As happens with every sector, real estate and REITs will go through their own good and bad times, and it is difficult for the ordinary investor to take advantage of the price fluctuations instead of getting hurt by them. There is also the problem that even though REITs hold several properties, they tend to be similar in type or location and do not provide broad enough diversification. The alternative that has naturally developed to address these problems is REIT mutual funds.

HOW TO INVEST IN REITS

There are now many mutual funds that invest exclusively in the stocks of REITs, and for individual investors this is the preferred way to play the REIT game. As with other mutual funds, the expectations are that a fund will provide broader diversification, which they do, and that professional managers will do a better job of picking out the right REITs to invest in and taking advantage of the ups and downs of the market. As with investment in stocks in general, it is doubtful that the professional managers of the REIT funds are able to add enough value to the process to justify the high costs of the actively managed REIT funds. So here again index funds have come along and are the preferred choice.

The best way to invest in REITs is to put money into a REIT index fund like the Vanguard REIT Index Fund gradually over time and hold the investment for the long run. Be prepared to hold through several boom and bust cycles, because given the way the real estate and the REIT markets work, they are inevitable. Also keep in mind that despite the tax advantage, if you hold a REIT fund in a taxable account, you will pay a lot of taxes over the years on those high dividends. So consider holding REIT funds only in tax-advantaged accounts.

If you are interested, you may consider investing in a REIT fund up to 10% of the stock part of your portfolio. But do not get tempted by the higher dividends of REITs and invest a bigger chunk of your money during retirement in REITs with the plan of living on the dividends. Putting more than 10% or 15% of your money in REITs will amount to putting too many of your eggs in one basket: not a wise move.

ZERO-COUPON BONDS

When you invest in a regular bond, you get a fixed semi-annual interest payment (at the coupon rate) during the life of the bond and then the face amount when the bond matures. This makes it difficult to use ordinary bonds to save and invest for a specific amount of money that you will need at a specific time in the future, because how much money you will ultimately accumulate will depend on the interest rate at which you are able to reinvest all those future coupon payments. You cannot predict what those future interest rates, called the reinvestment rates, are going to be. This is called the reinvestment risk.

So what can you do if you want to be absolutely sure that you will have a certain amount of money in the future? You can invest in zero-coupon bonds.

As the name implies, these bonds have no coupons and they do not pay any cash interest over the years for you to worry about reinvesting. Instead, you buy a zero-coupon bond at a price less than—often much less than—its face value of $1,000. When the bond matures you get the face amount, and the difference between what you paid and the $1,000 represents your interest payment. So if you buy a zero coupon bond that will mature in 10 years, then you know that you will have exactly $1,000 in 10 years. No reinvestment risks here.

What determines how much you will have to pay for that bond today? It depends on the life of the bond and the interest rate today. Let us look at an example to understand how zero-coupon bonds are priced and how they work over the years. Let us say you want to buy a 10-year zero-coupon bond, and the 10-year interest rate is 4%. You will pay about $676 for the bond today. Table 20.1 (the second column) shows why this is the right price and how it will change over the years if you assume that the interest rate will remain unchanged during the entire 10-year period.

One year from today you will be entitled to 4% interest or about $27 on that original $676 investment you made. But because the interest is not paid out in cash, it will be effectively added to the price of the bond and the value

TABLE 20.1

How the Value of a 10-Year Zero-Coupon Bond Bought Today Will Change Over the Years if Interest Rates Remain Unchanged

	Value of Bond	
Year	4% Interest Rate	8% Interest Rate
Today	$676	$463
1	$703	$500
2	$731	$540
3	$760	$583
4	$790	$630
5	$822	$681
6	$855	$735
7	$889	$794
8	$925	$857
9	$962	$926
10	$1,000	$1,000

of the bond will go up to $703. At the end of the next year you will be entitled to 4% interest on the new $703 value of the bond—not the original $676 value any more—and this larger interest amount will again increase the value of the bond, which will now go up to $731. As shown in Table 20.1, the value of the bond will keep going up over the years, and at the end of the 10 years its value will be exactly $1,000, same as the face amount you will get. This shows that $676 is the right price of the bond today, and if you buy the bond at that price, at the end of 10 years you will end up earning exactly a 4% annual return.

If at any time during the life of the bond you want to sell the bond, then, as with any other bond, you will have to sell it in the market at a price a willing buyer will pay. If interest rates remain the same over the years, the price you will get will be close to the value of the bond shown in Table 20.1 at the different points in time. Note that if you get the right price, then you will have earned your 4% interest for the time you held the bond.

What price you pay for the bond today depends on interest rates today for debt of that maturity. The third column of Table 20.1 shows that if the 10-year interest rate is 8%, you will pay only $463 instead of $676 for the bond and its value will go up differently over the years. The price you pay will also depend on the maturity of the bond. If you want to buy a 30-year zero-coupon bond and the 30-year interest rate is also 8%, then the price of the bond today will be just under $100. Make sure you understand that the 10-year zero-coupon bond you buy at $463 and the 30-year zero-coupon bond you buy at $100 effectively pay you the same 8% interest per year. The price of the longer maturity bond is lower because the total amount of interest you will earn (including reinvestment of interest)—which is the difference between the $1,000 face amount and your purchase price—has to be much higher for the longer maturity bond.

ADVANTAGES AND DISADVANTAGES OF ZERO-COUPON BONDS

The primary advantage of the zero-coupon bond is that you can be sure that you will have a specific amount of money at maturity: it will not depend on what happens to interest rates or the stock market over the years. You also save yourself the work of collecting and reinvesting interest payments over the years, although, if you invest in regular bonds through a bond fund, the fund can automatically do the reinvesting for you.

There are four factors you should take into consideration in deciding if you want to invest in zero-coupon bonds. Whether they are disadvantages or just some things to keep in mind depends on your situation:

1. A zero-coupon bond provides you with a fixed rate of return over its life and therefore provides no protection against any rise in inflation rate.

2. The prices of zero-coupon bonds are very sensitive to changes in the interest rate. Therefore, if you have to sell your bonds before maturity and the interest rate at that time is higher than what it was when you bought the bond, you will lose a lot more money than you would have if you were holding regular coupon bonds.

3. Because zero-coupon bonds pay off only at maturity, you have to be careful with the credit quality of the bond's issuer and buy only highly rated bonds.

4. If you hold zero-coupon bonds in a taxable account, you will have to pay taxes annually on the interest that you are presumably earning even though you are getting nothing in cash.

HOW TO INVEST IN ZERO-COUPON BONDS

As with regular bonds, you have the choice of buying zero-coupon bonds from various issuers, including the U.S. Treasury. Investing through mutual funds is not a viable option because there are only a handful of zero-coupon bond mutual funds and their investment costs are quite high. So you will have to go through your broker, and if you tell him what approximate maturity and credit quality you are seeking, he will be able to tell you what choices you have. Unfortunately, for a small-quantity purchase you probably will get poor pricing. As I already mentioned, be very conscious of the credit quality, and for anything longer than 10-year maturity, go with U.S. Treasury zero-coupons only.

One last issue. If you want to save for a $10,000 future need, you need to buy only $10,000 face amount of zero-coupon bonds that will mature in the year you will need the money. That should cost you much less than $10,000 today. Do not buy a quantity of bonds that costs you $10,000 today. That will be buying too much, most often way too much.

SHOULD YOU INVEST IN ZERO-COUPON BONDS?

I think the only time you should consider investing in zero-coupon bonds is if you have a future need that will require a fixed number of dollars instead of a certain amount of buying power. We rarely have such needs. For this and other reasons I have discussed, I did not recommend zero-coupon bonds as one of your primary investment options. I covered them here in some detail because people are likely to recommend them to you, and what you have now learned will help you decide if zero-coupons are right for a specific need you have.

EXCHANGE TRADED FUNDS

Exchange traded funds (ETFs) may be considered the newest form of mutual funds, although a few of them have been around for a number of years. Basically they allow you to buy and sell a mutual fund like a stock, that is, at any time during the day by placing an order through your broker as opposed to only once a day at the end-of-day price as you are allowed to do with a regular open-end mutual fund. Legally their structures—and there are several different legal structures for ETFs—are quite different from that of an open-end mutual fund, and this has certain ramifications that I will discuss. But on the surface, you would not see much of a difference other than this opportunity to trade them all day long. All ETFs are passively managed, and many of them mimic popular stock indexes like the Standard & Poor's (S&P) 500 and the Nasdaq (NSD) 100.

Are there some real advantage to ETFs? Should you buy your index fund this way? Let us review the advantages claimed for them.

First, of course, there is that flexibility to be able to buy and sell shares any time during the day. Because you should be thinking more in terms of buying about once a month to make new investments and selling about once every 5 or 10 years, this should not excite you. Actually this worries me a lot because if you invest through one of these on a day when the market is in its panic mode, you may also panic and sell your fund just when you should not.

Second, when you buy and sell stocks of an open-end mutual fund, you deal directly with the fund and you get a price based on the value of the fund's holdings. When you buy and sell shares of an ETF, you will be dealing with other willing buyers and sellers and not the fund itself, and you will get a supply-demand determined price. There are mechanisms in place to try to make sure that the price you get will not be much different from the value of the assets in the fund. Still, you cannot be sure that if you try to buy or sell an ETF in the middle of a 1987-type market crash, you will not get a price far different from the value of the assets in the underlying portfolio.

Third, at least at the moment, ETFs have slightly lower investment costs— expense ratio of 0.09% for the lowest cost ETF versus 0.2% for the lowest cost open-end index fund. But because you have to buy and sell them like stocks through a broker, you will incur brokerage fees. If you are going to invest small amounts of money every month, the brokerage fee will most likely more than offset the lower expense ratio of the ETFs and make this an expensive proposition in the long run.

Fourth, there is a claimed tax advantage, which could be attractive, but it is not certain that the advantage will be there when the time comes. The tax implications are too complicated to review here, but you should be skeptical of the claimed advantages.

Fifth, you can buy ETFs on margin and you can even sell them short; you cannot do that with regular mutual funds. One can dream up convoluted examples of how these could be advantages in certain circumstances for about three or maybe four investors. For the rest of us, that's an invitation to disaster. You do not need that kind of advantage.

A FINAL WORD OF CAUTION

One of the most popular ETFs is based on the NSD 100 index and trades under the symbol QQQ. It invests in the largest 100 Nasdaq stocks and is heavily concentrated in technology stocks. There are and I am sure there will be more such concentrated ETFs. Do not invest in any of them no matter how strongly people recommend them to you or how attractive their recent performance. None of them is the kind of broad-based index fund you should invest in.

Overall, ETFs seem like another innovation made more for the benefit of the companies offering them than their customers, and, at least for now, you should just stick to the old-fashioned open-end mutual fund.

◆

RECOMMENDED FUND COMPANIES AND FUNDS

◆

RECOMMENDED FUND COMPANIES

As I mentioned at the end of Rule #6, over the years the Vanguard Group has stood head and shoulders above other fund companies in giving the interest of the investors the highest priority. The Vanguard Group itself is financially structured to benefit the investors. It is the only fund company that is actually owned by the funds it offers, and therefore indirectly by investors who invest in those funds. All profits of the Group's operations are paid back to the investors. Although this is not the only reason, this is one of the reasons why Vanguard's funds in almost every category have just about the lowest investment costs. All other fund companies are owned by external shareholders, and in recent years many fund companies have changed hands for hundreds of millions of dollars because fund companies offer their shareholders the opportunity to make huge amounts of money by charging high fees. And almost all fund companies have taken as much advantage of that opportunity as possible.

Vanguard was also the pioneer in offering index funds, and it offers a complete array of outstanding index funds that can meet all your needs. So I highly recommend that you make all your investments through Vanguard's funds and deal with them directly without even bothering to open a brokerage account anywhere. As far as keeping things simple, you could not do better.

I will also not hesitate to recommend T. Rowe Price and Fidelity funds, although the investment costs of their funds tend to be higher than those for Vanguard's funds. If you are already with them, you have to make your own judgment based on taxes and other considerations if you want to make a move. All three companies have very informative web sites, offer excellent free literature on many aspects of investing, and have well-informed and helpful customer service representatives.

TELEPHONE NUMBERS AND WEB SITE ADDRESSES

The Vanguard Group: (800) 831-9996. www.vanguard.com
Fidelity Investments: (800) 544-1775. www.fidelity.com
T. Rowe Price: (800) 638-5660. www.troweprice.com

RECOMMENDED FUNDS

I am only recommending Vanguard funds here. Fidelity, T. Rowe Price, and many other companies offer similar funds.

MONEY MARKET FUNDS

Prime Money Market Fund

This is a regular money market fund that invests in commercial papers, bank certificates of deposit (CDs), and so forth. In a taxable account you will pay both federal and state income taxes on the returns on this fund.

Treasury Money Market Fund

This fund invests only in direct obligations of the U.S. Government, primarily Treasury bills. The returns on this fund will be exempt from state income taxes but not from federal income taxes.

Tax-Exempt Money Market Funds

There are several state-specific money market funds for the large states (New York, New Jersey, California, etc.). If you invest in one that is specific to the state in which you live, the returns will be exempt from both federal and state income taxes.

SHORT-TERM BOND FUNDS

Inflation-Protected Securities Fund

This fund invests in the Treasury Inflation-Protected Securities (TIPS) that I have been highly recommending and similar inflation-protected bonds of corporations and government agencies. (Note that the quoted yield on this fund may look very low because it does not include the inflation adjustment. Don't let that bother you. You effectively earn the quoted yield plus the rate of inflation.)

Short-Term Corporate Fund

This fund invests in high-quality corporate bonds with an average maturity of 1 to 3 years.

Short-Term Bond Index Fund

This fund invests in U.S. government and high-quality corporate bonds with an average maturity of 1 to 5 years. This is an index fund, meaning it is passively managed.

Short-Term Tax-Exempt Fund

This fund invests in tax-exempt bonds with an average maturity of 1 to 2 years.

STOCK INDEX FUNDS

Total Stock Market Index Fund

This fund mimics the Wilshire 5000 Total Market Index and effectively invests in every stock traded in the United States. How much more diversified can you get? This is the one I recommend you use for investing in stocks. The only hesitation I have is that because the fund has been around for some time, it has substantial unrealized capital gains. If there is a lot of net withdrawal from the fund in a bear market and you are holding it in a taxable account, you may get stuck with some tax bills. (See the discussion of this issue under Rule #7.) It is fine for your tax-deferred accounts, but for your taxable accounts make a careful choice between this one and the two tax-managed funds I recommend below.

500 Index Fund

This is a Standard & Poor's (S&P) 500 Index fund, but it is also more suitable for your tax-deferred account. It has huge unrealized capital gains and the same potential tax problems as the Total Stock Market Index Fund. Like all other S&P 500 Index funds, it will have higher distributions over the years on which, in a taxable account, you will have to pay current taxes. So for your taxable accounts, consider one of the tax-managed funds as well before making your decision. One last thing to keep in mind is that all S&P 500 funds leave out small stocks. They have done very well in the recent bull market when the large stocks did much better, but over the long run the Total Stock Market Index Fund may do better.

Tax-Managed Growth and Income Fund

This is a tax-managed version of the S&P 500 Index fund. Vanguard uses several techniques to minimize potential distributions from this fund so that in a taxable account you will not end up paying a lot of taxes when you are just holding onto this fund. One of the ways Vanguard minimizes distributions is by trying to filter out short-term investors. The fund has a $10,000 minimum and charges a redemption fee of 2% if you sell within 1 year and 1% if you sell in the second to the fifth years. If you are reasonably sure that you will hold the fund for a while and can meet the minimum requirement, this is a good choice for your taxable accounts. One other advantage is that this is a relatively new fund and has much less unrealized capital gains. On the negative side, being an S&P 500 fund, it basically holds stocks of only large companies. (Remember that the redemption fee goes back to the fund. So if you are going to hold the fund for a long time, the redemptions fee works in your favor.)

Tax-Managed Capital Appreciation Fund

This fund is very similar to the Tax-Managed Growth and Income Fund (including the redemption fees) except that it is based on the Russell 1000 Index. It holds the 1,000 largest stocks, including most of the 500 that are in the S&P 500 and another 500 stocks of smaller companies. Even then, all the companies included here are pretty big companies. If you are comfortable with its constraints, this is another excellent choice for your taxable accounts.

Small-Cap Index Fund

This fund mimics the Russell 2000 Index and therefore invests only in smaller stocks—the 2,000 stocks just below the largest 1,000. You would never want to own it by itself, but you may want to use it to supplement a large-cap index fund such as the S&P 500 or even a Russell 1000 fund that you may already hold or are forced to hold in your 401(k)–type account. But remember that you should invest in it only 30% to 40% of the amount of money you have in one of the large-cap index funds. Otherwise you will have too much small-cap investment. (There is also a Tax-Managed Small-Cap Index Fund, which holds a slightly different group of small company stocks and has the same tax-managed features.)

Extended Market Index Fund

This is also a small-cap index fund and invests in the smaller stocks in the Wilshire 5000 Total Market Index that are not part of the S&P 500 Index. You would never want to own it by itself, but you may want to use it to supplement an S&P 500 fund that you may already hold or are forced to hold in your 401(k)–type account. But remember that you should invest in it only 30% to 40% of the amount of money you have in one of the large-cap index funds. Otherwise you will have too much small-cap investment.

Developed Market Index Fund, Total International Stock Index Fund, and Tax-Managed International Fund

If you decide to invest some money in foreign stocks, these are good choices. Do not invest in index funds of specific groups of countries that Vanguard and others also offer. That would be trying to choose long-term winners and losers that none of us is capable of doing. And do not invest in index funds of emerging markets.

REIT Index Fund

If you decide to invest some money in Real Estate Investment Trusts (REITs), this is a good choice.

COMPARISON OF SAFE INVESTMENT OPTIONS

♦

	Advantage	*Disadvantage*
Money market funds Best for money you want to keep readily accessible	Money accessible at any time Essentially no principal risk Inflation protected	Relatively low return
Bank CDs (less than 2-year maturity) Use whenever you can get a higher return and can tie up the money	Sometimes provides high returns No principal risk No investment cost	Money tied up until maturity A little higher inflation risk
Short-term bond funds (less than 5-year maturity) Good alternative to money market fund or CDs for short-term investment	Generally higher return than money market funds	A little higher inflation risk Some principal risk
Inflation-protected bond funds (primarily hold TIPS) Excellent choice for long-term money you want to invest safely	Long-term inflation protection Over time likely to earn highest return	Some principal risk Unusual tax treatment

	Advantage	*Disadvantage*
Series I Bonds Best choice for long-term money you want to invest safely	Long-term inflation protection Over time likely to earn highest return Opportunity to defer taxes for up to 30 years No principal risk No investment cost	Limited to $30,000 investment per year per person Penalty for cashing in within first 5 years

APPENDIX C

♦

MISCELLANEOUS RESOURCES

♦

This list of resources is meant to help you find any additional information you may need on investing, especially information on matters that change over time, such as tax laws. I am providing this list with a certain amount of trepidation. On the one hand, I think you will enjoy and benefit from learning more about investing and staying abreast of the world of business and finance. On the other hand, so much superfluous, contradictory, and often even dangerous information about investing is hurled at you from all directions all the time that unless you are very selective and careful, your attempts to become better informed can actually backfire. You may slowly go back to being an active investor who tries to follow investment advice from many different sources, keeps changing his investment approach every so often instead of following a long-term comprehensive investment plan, and ends up with poor results over the years.

In this book I have provided for you in one place all the information you need to be a successful investor. Some of the information I have provided will need updating from time to time, but most of it, I believe, is timeless. So it is my hope that over the years you will use these and other resources to become a better informed investor, but you will steadfastly stay on the Only Proven Road to Investment Success.

BOOKS

You can definitely benefit from learning more about all aspects of investing, and for that here are four classics in the field that I can recommend without any reservation. Because all of these authors advocate essentially the same investment approach as the one I have in this book, you do not have to worry about encountering a lot of conflicting advice.

A Random Walk Down Wall Street, by Burton G. Malkiel. Professor Malkiel does an outstanding job of discussing in plain English some of the extensive scientific research into investing that I mentioned and have based this book's recommendations on. If you need more convincing that you should not listen to the so-called investment experts because they have no superior knowledge and cannot beat the market (the simple index fund), then this is a good book for you. Professor Malkiel also provides an excellent history of the stock market and sound investment advice. All in all, this is a highly entertaining, readable, and informative book.

Common Sense on Mutual Funds and *Bogle on Mutual Funds,* by John C. Bogle. As I mentioned at a number of places in this book, Mr. Bogle is not just the founder and former Chairman of the Vanguard Group, he has also been and still is the most ardent advocate of the interests of the mutual fund investors. Both of his books (*Common Sense* is the more recent one) provide excellent detailed advice on all aspects of investing through mutual funds. In addition, *Common Sense* provides a perspective on the mutual fund industry itself from which all mutual fund investors will benefit.

John Bogle on Investing: The First 50 Years, by John C. Bogle. This is a collection of John Bogle's speeches and writings, and it is a gem. Mr. Bogle presents the most devastating case against active investing and the myth that there are investment experts with superior investment skills. If you need further convincing on this matter, this is the best source you can consult. He covers many other aspects of investing in mutual funds and the mutual fund industry. On top of everything else, the writing is superb. Incidentally, if you get fascinated by Mr. Bogle's speeches and writings, as you are likely to be, you can keep up with them by checking the Bogle Center on Vanguard's web site (www.vanguard.com), where these are posted regularly.

Stocks for the Long Run, by Jeremy J. Siegel. With extensive data, this book makes a very strong case for investing in stocks for the long run. It also provides sound investment advice.

NEWSPAPERS AND MAGAZINES

Strictly from an investment point of view, you do not need to stay up to date with daily, weekly, or even monthly business news. But if you want to, the *Wall Street Journal* is, of course, the one newspaper that almost every business and finance professional reads every day. Most major general newspapers, like the *New York Times* and the *Washington Post*, also provide excellent coverage of daily business news. Incidentally, you can access the complete *Wall Street Journal* on the Internet (www.wsj.com) for a modest annual fee and the *New York Times* (www.nyt.com) for free.

The two major personal finance magazines are *Money* (www.money.com) and *Smart Money* (www.smartmoney.com). The print versions of both are published monthly, and the print versions as well as the Internet sites of both carry a lot of useful and interesting information. The only caveat is that both frequently, if not every month, publish lists of recommended mutual funds, stocks, and so forth, and their track records in this matter are as embarrassing as those of all other experts. So ignore those articles, but read the magazines for information on changes in tax laws, where to find the best mortgage rate or credit card, and things of that nature. The annual subscription rates for both are modest.

The three major business magazines are *Business Week*, *Fortune*, and *Forbes*. Of these I think *Fortune* has the most interesting coverage. But the three are quite different from one another, and you may like one or the other more. All three have Internet sites under their names, and you can find a variety of information, including subscription information, there.

DETAILED INFORMATION ON FUNDS AND STOCKS

The most convenient one-stop source for almost any information you may want on mutual funds and individual stock is Morningstar (www.morningstar.com). You can get a lot of the information for free at their site and for a small monthly fee (for the subscribers-only part of the site), you can find essentially every detail on a mutual fund or stock you may need. There are lots of tools for selecting mutual funds based on many different criteria, comparing one fund to another, and so forth. If you want to invest in funds (including index funds), other than those I have recommended, this is the best place to go to for information. But be prepared to spend some time learning how to interpret all the statistics and other information they provide.

Be very wary of the five-star system they use for rating funds. This is supposed to be a historical measure of how well a fund has done in the past relative to its risk. Whether it is even a good measure of a fund's historical performance is debatable, but there is no question that it tells you little about how a fund is going to perform in the future. Even Morningstar does not claim any forecasting ability for its star ratings. Yet, fund companies extensively advertise the star ratings of their funds, implying that a fund highly rated under this system will do better than the others in the future.

Morningstar offers a number of print publications as well, including one called *Morningstar Mutual Funds* ($495 per year), which is a comprehensive coverage of mutual funds. It is available at many libraries for reference. But you can get all the information it includes and much more at a lower cost by subscribing to the full Morningstar web site.

INVESTMENT NEWSLETTER

I can recommend only one investment newsletter, the *Hulbert Financial Digest* (www.hulbertdigest.com), in good conscience, and it is actually a newsletter that rates all major investment newsletters. The *Hulbert Financial Digest* (*HFD*) keeps track of how an investor would have done if he had followed the advice of specific investment newsletters over a long period of time. As *HFD* shows and I have told you, you should stay away from all these investment newsletters—their advice is pretty much useless and sometimes even dangerous. You actually don't need to subscribe to *HFD* either, but if you ever feel tempted to subscribe to or follow the advice of any newsletter, look up its historical performance in *HFD* first before making your decision.

USEFUL INTERNET SITES

There are hundreds of sites related to business, finance, and investment on the Internet, most of them geared toward active investors. I will mention here only the few that you, as a passive investor, may find useful:

www.cbsmarketwatch.com: provides comprehensive financial news.
www.quicken.com: provides a variety of financial information and tools.

www.bigcharts.com: provides lots of data and information on stocks, but not of much use to passive investors.

www.indexfunds.com: provides comprehensive listing of index funds and links to other sites for more information on them.

www.publicdebt.treas.gov: has almost everything you may want to find out about the debt of the U.S. Treasury, that is, the federal government, including how to buy government bonds directly.

In addition, most major mutual fund companies have good sites with lots of good information and tools.

INDEX

◆